**"DICK SCHAAP IS A MASTER STORYTELLER . . .
You will be committing a grave error
if you don't read this one—it is
entertaining, instructive and great fun."**

"THOROUGHLY ENTERTAINING."

**"CONSISTENTLY FUNNY . . .
If you like Schaap you will like this book."**

**"A delightful read. If you don't enjoy this
one, find another planet."**

Flashing Before My Eyes

He has played golf with Bill Clinton, tennis with
Bobby Fischer, cards with Wilt Chamberlain.

He has written books with Joe Namath
and Joe Montana.

He has taken Brigitte Bardot to dinner and Lenny
Bruce to a World Series.

He saw the Baltimore Colts beat the New York Giants
in sudden-death overtime, and the Green Bay Packers
beat the Dallas Cowboys in the Ice Bowl.

He saw Bill Mazeroski end a World Series
with a home run, and Willis Reed lift the
New York Knicks to an NBA title.

He has covered murders and riots, presidential
campaigns and Broadway openings.

He introduced Muhammad Ali to Billy Crystal,
and Billy Crystal to Joe DiMaggio.

He is Dick Schaap and this is his story.

*Turn the page to hear what everyone
is saying about Dick Schaap . . .*

"Of all the stories Schaap has covered, the best one turns out to be his own. In a brilliant flash of fifty years, whether the game is played with a ball, a stick, or the human spirit, stay near Schaap for the best seat in the house."
Herb Gardner

"The ultimate 'As told to Dick Schaap' book . . . weaving together the plentiful laugh-out-loud and tears-in-your-eyes moments of his own life, making it feel like a conversation in his den (or, more likely, in a bar where he's picking up the tab). We are richer for it . . . Dick Schaap seems to know everybody worth knowing. *Flashing Before My Eyes* gives us the pleasure of knowing Dick Schaap."
St. Petersburg Times

"I've always thought I had the best seat in television, to Dick Schaap's left, every Sunday on *The Sports Reporters*. Schaap always acts as if it's a privilege to know the people he's known. The privilege, as you will discover in this book, is all yours."
Mike Lupica

"Hard to put down . . . Schaap has written 33 books in 39 years, most of them about sports figures. Most of them cannot be as good as this book, because none of them is about Dick Schaap's adventures."
Milwaukee Journal-Sentinel

"When I was a kid delivering the *Bronx Home News* door to door, I would begin the route every day by sitting on the curb and reading Jimmy Cannon's column. He was a sportswriter but he covered it all and I sat there loving every word. Now fifty years later here's this book by Dick Schaap and it's the same magic all over again. I can't stop reading it. I'm a kid again in the Bronx and I'm loving every word. Thanks, Dick."

Regis Philbin

"A breezy and delightful work of staggering anecdotage featuring a cast of just about everybody he has ever met . . . Had the long-distance runner Pheidippides not dropped dead in 490 B.C. after running 25 miles from Marathon to Athens to tell the Greeks they had beaten the Persians, he might have hired Dick Schaap to write his life story." *New York Times*

"Dick Schaap's life sounds highly improbable to me, but I'll take his word for it." Gene Shalit

"Schaap loves people and his profession. That passion is evident on every page as he relates self-deprecating anecdotes with leading characters such as Ali, Billy Crystal, chef Paul Prudhomme, Bobby Knight, former New York mayors John Lindsay and Abe Beam, George Plimpton, William Buckley, and Rocky Graziano."

Booklist

"To not be among the luminaries mentioned in this fine book cuts me to the quick. In fact, the only way to finagle my way in was to provide this blurb. Shameless but clearly effective."   Bob Costas

"Dick Schaap is an eloquent writer who employs with consummate skill the highly individual touches of wit and irony and style. He is a master storyteller . . . You will be committing a grave error if you don't read this one—it is entertaining, instructive and great fun. It is pure Schaap, which means it is a book that I'm betting you will cherish."   *San Diego Union-Tribune*

"Leave it to my (and half of western civilization's) good and dear friend Dick Schaap to write a memoir without an index, so I couldn't just skip to the parts about me. Okay, so I'm not in there as much as Ali but at least I got more ink than Costas."   Tony Kornheiser

"Artful storytelling . . . Schaap's combination of intelligence, quick wit, and discerning eye allows him to look back with wonderful insight."   *Palm Beach Post*

DICK SCHAAP

{ AS TOLD TO DICK SCHAAP }

FLASHING BEFORE MY EYES

50 YEARS OF HEADLINES, DEADLINES & PUNCHLINES

INTRODUCTION BY MITCH ALBOM

HarperEntertainment
An Imprint of HarperCollinsPublishers

HARPERENTERTAINMENT
An Imprint of HarperCollins*Publishers*
10 East 53rd Street
New York, NY 10022-5299

Copyright © 2001 by Dick Schaap
Cover photograph by Neil Leifer
ISBN: 0-380-82015-3

Most HarperEntertainment paperbacks are available at special quantity discounts for bulk purchases for sales promotions, premiums, or fund-raising. For information, Please call or write:
Special Markets Department, HarperCollins Publishers Inc.
10 East 53rd Street, New York, New York 10022-5299.
Telephone: (212) 207-7528.   Fax: (212) 207-7222.

HarperCollins®, 🖥®, and HarperEntertainment™ are trademarks of HarperCollins Publishers Inc.

First HarperEntertainment paperback printing: November 2001
First William Morrow hardcover printing: January 2001

Printed in the United States of America

Visit HarperEntertainment on the World Wide Web at
www.harpercollins.com.

10 9 8 7 6 5 4 3 2 1

For Trish McLeod, a beautiful Scottish Highlander, my third and final wife, of whom Mickey Mantle once said to me, "You're overmarried." If I were not already in love with her, I would have fallen for her the day she met Reggie Jackson for the sixth or seventh time, and he said to her, "What's your name again?" and she said, "Trish. And yours?" Reggie did not laugh.

I was equally proud of her the evening we had dinner with another formidable athlete, Wilt Chamberlain, who had just written a book in which he casually mentioned, as casually as you can mention such things, that he had enjoyed twenty thousand sexual experiences. Trish reached out and touched Wilt's elbow and said, "Does that count?" Wilt did laugh.

Darling, this one counts.

Contents

Introduction

Let's be honest. Pretty much everyone's favorite subject these days is themselves. Rap songs celebrate the rappers who rap them. Athletes refer to themselves in the third person. Radio hosts declare, "This is *my* show," and callers begin by saying, "*I* think . . ." The Internet is rife with sites dedicated to their creators (www.MyHomePage.com). Therapists' offices are filled with patients prattling about their "issues." Bookshelves are stuffed with bestseller after bestseller, all about your favorite home improvement subject: yourself.

And then there's Dick Schaap, who has walked with kings, ridden shotgun with legends, dined with the power elite, and gotten drunk with some of the biggest sports stars of our time. And what he comes away with is not a swelled head, an inflated sense of his own importance, or a need to lecture the world with an opinion much richer than ours.

What he comes away with is stories.

People stories. Dick Schaap collects people stories the way nets collect fish. According to the Jewish religion—Dick's religion—once a year, God opens the Book of Life, and in that book is every person on earth, everything they have said, everything they have done.

Does God really have a Book of Life? I have no idea. I do know this: If He ever misplaces it, He'll come to Schaap and ask to borrow his.

I *thought* I knew a lot of people. That was before I met Dick Schaap. Compared with Dick, the rest of us might as well live in caves. Dick not only knows, intimately, Muhammad Ali, Joe Namath, Jimmy Breslin, Yogi Berra, Herb Gardner—I'm stopping at five, because I don't have room for five thousand—but he also knows your mother, your second-grade teacher, your agent, your congressman, and your priest. And if he doesn't, he knows someone who does. Or he went to the World Series with that guy's cousin.

Dick, I firmly believe, knows the world. The reason is simple: He doesn't just meet people; he absorbs them. He is like those Japanese businessmen who are always asking for your card, then slipping it into their front pockets. Dick does his own version of that, only without the cards, and with no need for the front pocket. The people he meets go straight through to his heart. "How do you do it?" I asked him not long ago on the set of *The Sports Reporters,* the ESPN TV show we do together on Sunday mornings. "How do you keep everybody straight?"

"It's not that big a deal," he answered with characteristic modesty.

"Everybody has one thing they can remember well. Some people remember every Broadway show. Some people remember every Super Bowl. I just happen to remember people."

And Wilt Chamberlain happened to like women.

Now, as a journalist, I can attribute Dick's talent to a quality that is increasingly rare in our business: an ability to listen. Unlike many reporters, who are writing the story before the subject opens his or her mouth, Dick is legitimately fascinated by what people have to say. He is willing to float downstream on their interpretations and confessions. He also knows that being there, the fly on the wall, the eyes in the rearview mirror, is what turns reportage into storytelling.

And so, over the years, Dick has put himself in position to witness wonderfully memorable moments, like the time he took a young Cassius Clay to Harlem to meet Sugar Ray Robinson, or the time he took Lenny Bruce to his first baseball game, or the time he brought the actor Peter Falk along with him to interview drug addicts, and one of the addicts asked the future "Columbo" if he would be his lawyer.

It is because of experiences like that, that those of us who know Dick have been pressing him for years to write this book, his book, his story, which, Dick being Dick, is the story of so many others. To be with Dick is to be with a buzzing hive of voices, a cast of thousands. In a single commercial break of *The Sports Reporters,* he'll tell several stories that are more interesting than anything you'll hear all month. His cross-referencing would put Microsoft Access to shame. You can say to Dick, "Pass the ketchup," and he will reply, "Did I ever tell you about Bobby 'Catch-up' Johnson, the one-legged soccer player I met in Belgium?"

Dick doesn't forget. (Honest to goodness, there is a reference in this book to the fact that during Dick's visit to the island of Ibiza in 1967, Clifford Irving, the novelist, "had one of the few working toilets on the island." Who *remembers* stuff like that?) But because of that, this book is rich in anecdotes, and there is not a page that doesn't make you wish you were there with Dick, walking alongside Joe DiMaggio; meeting deadlines for *Newsweek;* sharing a house with Chuck Barris, creator of *The Gong Show;* talking baseball with Jackie Robinson; traveling with Richard Nixon during the 1968 campaign; or sipping drinks at a party in Norman Mailer's house. And yet it would be unfair to characterize Dick as a gadfly, a party lover, or even a collaborator with the rich and famous (although, with thirty-four books to his credit, he has done more duets than Willie Nelson and Celine Dion combined). What he downplays, and what too many ESPN watchers forget, is that Dick is first and foremost a reporter, a damn fine one, and a wonderful writer to boot.

So, in a twist, the Cracker Jack in this box turns out to be the famous athletes, the well-known actors, the bloated politicians, and the recognizable newsmakers, while the hidden prize is the unveiling of Dick himself, how he came to be a writer, how his Brooklyn and Long Island childhood forged so much of his later life, how his college experiences transformed him, how he wrote books about the drug culture and about Robert Kennedy, how he made mistakes along the way, lost some dear friends to tragedy, and even encountered a few people whom he didn't like.

That last part is, of course, the hardest to believe, because Schaap is the very definition of "hail fellow well-met." In fact, Dick can be the calling card that turns strangers into friends.

Not long ago, I sat down to do a radio interview with a very busy Billy Crystal. He was harried. His people were rushing him. I did not know the man. But I opened this way: "We're joined now by Billy Crystal, who has something in common with me. We are both members of the Dick Schaap fan club. . . ."

Crystal smiled broadly.

And I had him.

In your hands is a book that grants admission to the same club, free of charge, without obligation, yet unavoidable by the final page. You will, like the rest of us, like Dick Schaap. It is not everyone, after all, who grew up loving Ralph Branca, hating Bobby Thomson, and eating dinner with both of them years later.

I know that, as a lover of other people, an autobiography may be Dick's least favorite subject. But readers will not suffer the same prejudice. On the contrary, they will be inspired by a writer who admits he likes most of his subjects and proves that compassion and journalism are not mutually exclusive.

Dick often quotes one of the zillions of people he's met, and, ever the responsible journalist, he dutifully adds, "His words, not mine."

Here now, finally, Dick's words, long anticipated and worth the wait.

Mitch Albom
Franklin, Michigan
July 2000

1

My Favorite Sport

This is the story of my life, but it's not about me. It's about the people I have met during half a century in sports and journalism. It's about athletes and actresses, cops and comedians, politicians and playwrights, the eclectic mix that has made almost every day of my life seem like a fantasy to me.

Often I am asked what my favorite sport is, and always I say, "People." I collect people.

I once asked Paul Prudhomme, the Cajun chef, his idea of a great taste, and he said, "Chocolate ice cream—with curry sauce—because they're so different." I feel exactly the same way—about people.

2

Collector's Items

When Muhammad Ali was eighteen years old and still Cassius Clay, before he fought his first professional fight, I visited him in his hometown of Louisville. One afternoon, as we drove down a main street, I stopped at a traffic light and noticed a lovely young woman who happened to be white standing on the corner. "Boy, she's pretty!" I said to Clay, and he grabbed my shoulder and said, "You crazy, man? You can get electrocuted for that! A Jew looking at a white girl in Kentucky."

Not long after the New York Jets won Super Bowl III, in the rebel days at the height of his career, Joe Namath came to my house for dinner one night, lay down on the floor of my living room, cadged a joint, puffed, and blew the smoke into the mouth of my dog, a collie named Max. As far as I know, neither the quarterback nor the collie inhaled.

* * *

In the 1970s, when Norman Mailer assembled a book called *Genius and Lust,* an annotated collection of the works of Henry Miller, I went with Mailer to Miller's home in Pacific Palisades, California, to interview the two of them for the *Today* show. "Norman," I began, "when did you first read Henry Miller?"

"I was a freshman at Harvard," Mailer said, "and someone smuggled in a copy of *Tropic of Cancer* and I read it and Henry Miller immediately became one of my heroes."

"Mr. Miller," I said, "when did you first read Norman Mailer?"

Miller looked at me, at Mailer, then at the camera. "To tell you the truth," he said, "I've tried."

Mailer winced, and Miller turned and said, "Norman, can't you write a simple English sentence?"

Mailer recovered quickly. "Have you read *The Naked and the Dead*?" he said. "The first sentence is, 'Nobody could sleep.' You'll like that one."

After several drinks one night, John Chancellor and Paddy Chayevsky and I decided to visit Plato's Retreat, a notorious establishment of the 1970s that catered to the sexually uninhibited, especially so-called swingers, people who enjoyed multiple or successive partners. None of us had ever been there.

When we entered Plato's, we found ourselves surrounded by revelers, some bobbing in a swimming pool, most in various states of undress and entanglement, neither of which was compulsory. Plato's did not serve alcoholic beverages, but Chancellor offered to get soft drinks for Chayevsky and me.

Paddy and I sat down, and as Chancellor stepped up to the bar, a naked couple engaged him in conversation. When John finally returned with our drinks, he was beaming. "They wanted to talk about the Middle East," Chancellor said, "and all I could think was, 'Tits, tits, tits.'"

When Hank Greenberg, the Hall of Fame baseball player, was in his sixties, he and I were partners in a tennis doubles match against Johnny Carson and Johnny's lawyer. The lawyer was a very good player, which meant each team had one very good player, and one very mediocre player. Greenberg, a slugger on the baseball field, was a genius of junk on the tennis court—lobs and dink shots. During our match, he hit a drop shot delicately over the net, too soft for Carson to reach it. Johnny looked at Hank and said, "Oh, and does *Mr.* Greenberg also play tennis?"

Late in Julius Erving's career, he and Larry Bird got into a fight during a game in Boston Garden. It wasn't much of a battle—no damaging blows were struck—but it was noteworthy because it involved two of the greatest players in basketball history. I was dispatched to interview the combatants.

First I went to Boston to get Bird's version, and Larry was in his customary monosyllabic mode. "Yep" and "Nope" were his favorite answers, and when I asked him if he had any message for Julius, he stuck out his tongue at the camera. It was his most eloquent moment.

Then I went to Philadelphia to hear Dr. J's account. Julius sat by his locker, and the camera rolled. "You must understand," Erving began, "that Larry and I are not only friends, we are also business associates. We work together for Converse. We have tremendous respect for each other as basketball players and as human beings, and what happened, in the heat of an intense game, was that we lost our tempers and swung at each other. It was something that would never happen again, because we have far too much respect and admiration for each other."

I said, "Thank you, Doc," the camera clicked off, and Julius Erving said, "He's *such* an asshole."

When Billy Crystal and I completed *Absolutely Mahvelous,* his miniautobiography, we celebrated with dinner at a favorite restaurant, an Italian oasis in East Harlem called Rao's. When we sat down, we saw that Claus von Bülow was sitting at a table on one side of us, and Roy Cohn at a table on the other. We thought we had died and gone to hell.

Billy jumped up and went to the jukebox. He wanted to play "Sonny" for von Bülow.

In 1992, when Madison Square Garden unveiled its Walk of Fame and hosted a reception for the honorees, I was fortunate enough to pose for a photograph with Wilt Chamberlain, Bob Cousy, and George Mikan, arguably the best basketball player of the 1960s, the best of the '50s, and the best of the '40s. Wilt and Mikan, the seven-footers, were the bookends. Cousy and I, the six-footers, stood in the middle. A crowd gathered, drawn by the three stars, and I couldn't resist turning to our audience and saying, "Do you realize that among the four of us, we've had twenty thousand and ten women?"

Everyone laughed, except the three guys I was standing with.

Mikan and Cousy informed me that they had had

only one each. But Wilt was more upset. "Hey, Dick," he said, "that book is two years old."

When Peter Falk, a good golfer, played the pro-celebrity round of the 1993 Los Angeles Open with a teenager who was competing in his first professional tournament, I walked the Riviera Golf Course with them. "What do you think of the kid?" I asked Falk after the round.

"I like his chances," Peter said.

The kid was Tiger Woods.

The season before the Packers won Super Bowl XXXI, I was in Green Bay and mentioned to Reggie White, the team's defensive captain and an ordained minister, that I was feeling terrible pain in my right knee. "I'll pray for you," he said. I assumed he meant on Sunday, in church. But he went to the team's locker room and came back with his teammate, Keith Jackson, and with a jar of ointment. Reggie dabbed a little cream on my forehead.

Then White and Jackson, 558 pounds of football players, kneeled in front of me, bowed their heads, and began praying aloud for my knee. Their sincerity was obvious, and I was so moved that, perhaps in a rush of adrenaline, the pain in my knee subsided. I thanked Reggie and Keith for their kindness, and they went off to practice.

Fifteen minutes later, my knee remembered it was Jewish and began to throb again.

Have I broken the world record for name-dropping yet?

3

A Kid Grows in Brooklyn

I was born on September 27, 1934, in the Flatbush section of Brooklyn. Sophia Loren, Brigitte Bardot, and Roberto Clemente were born the same week. My theory is that He gave them all the good parts, and I got what was left over.

My paternal grandparents were born of Dutch descent in New York City. My paternal grandfather, who practiced law, used to sit me on his knee and sing Gilbert and Sullivan to me. He died when I was very young, but I still hear him singing, "My object all sublime . . ." and "Dear little Buttercup . . ." and "Now he is an admiral in the Queen's *nivy.*"

My paternal grandmother was a teacher by trade and inclination. She introduced me to spelling and arithmetic before I entered kindergarten. She graduated from Female Normal School, which became Hunter College, in the Class of 1901—the naught-y ones, they called themselves.

My maternal grandparents graduated from czarist

Russia. He was in the plumbing supply business. She introduced me to chocolate cake with green icing from Ebinger's Bakery. He used to take great time and care chopping tomatoes and onions. She taught me to shuck peas and let me eat one from each pod.

Both of my grandmothers were named Rose, and I am pleased that one of my four daughters, who was given Rose as her middle name, chose to promote it to her first.

My grandparents lived in Brooklyn, and both of my parents graduated from Erasmus Hall High School, the alma mater of Sid Luckman, the football star, and Barbra Streisand, the star.

My mother, Leah, was a vivacious woman, considerably more outgoing than my father, Maury. The family joke was that I was ten years old before I discovered my father was not mute. In her late forties, my mother went back to college, earned a master's degree, and taught French in grammar schools. Years later, strangers came up to me on the street and said, "Madame Schaap was my French teacher."

My father was a good man, honorable and unassuming, who took great pride in his family. He graduated from Cornell University the year the Depression began and went to work by day and law school by night. One of his law professors was Judge Joseph Force Crater, who one day in 1931, not long after my father's final class with him, famously disappeared.

My father, too, dropped out, but only from law school. I think he would have made a good lawyer, not in a courtroom, not in a setting that would reward showmanship and ego, but in a library, a back room, meticulously researching cases, collecting the information that would make more flamboyant attorneys look smart.

Instead, my father became a salesman, first at Bloomingdale's, where his uncle, Michael Schaap, a former judge and state legislator and Bull Moose Party colleague of Teddy Roosevelt, was the president. Later, my father worked in the silverware business, but he never seemed fulfilled as a salesman. I never met anyone who disliked my father, but unlike a more famous salesman, he did not lust to be well-liked. His pleasure came from competing at golf and softball, swimming strongly in the ocean, and attending sporting events.

One of the few times I saw my father truly angry was when he came home from the 1941 World Series game in which the Dodgers' catcher, Mickey Owen, dropped a third strike, allowing the Yankees to rally for a critical victory. My father bled Brooklyn blue.

One of the many times I saw him truly happy was when he played a round of golf with Joe Namath and me. My father would have been an even more contented man if he had preceded me into sportswriting.

My parents' marriage lasted more than fifty years. Not until my father's death did my mother, or I, realize how dependent she was on his quiet support. She died a lonely decade later.

My brother Bill was born when I was five, and a year later our parents took us out of Brooklyn, to Freeport on the South Shore of Long Island, a clam diggers' town. My memories of Freeport are good, even though the town certainly had its shortcomings. The archconservative John Birch Society's first chapter on Long Island sprang up in Freeport, and racial tension divided the white majority and a sizable black minority concentrated in a suburban ghetto. Almost all of the black kids went to the Cleveland Avenue School. We had only one African-American in my school, the Columbus Avenue School.

I must have been a reasonably good student because in the middle of the third grade I was "skipped"—not that uncommon a practice in those days—to the middle of the fourth grade. I became the youngest member of my class, an uncomfortable distinction I would retain until college that would set me back educationally and socially.

In the summer of 1944, when I was nine, the Brooklyn Dodgers played an exhibition game against my hometown's semipro team, the Freeport Gulls. I went out early to Freeport Stadium, hoping to get a glimpse of the Dodgers. When they arrived, one of their players saw me and said, "C'mon, kid," and took me into the ballpark.

The player was an eighteen-year-old from Oklahoma—Calvin Coolidge Julius Caesar Tuskahoma McLish. He was named after a president, an emperor, and an Indian chief. His teammates called him Buster. He was the first professional athlete who ever spoke to me, and thirty years later, when he was a pitching coach for the Montreal Expos, I remembered to thank Buster for his kindness.

I turned ten soon after my sister Nancy was born, and the following month, my father took a job in Miami. We moved south and I entered the Florida school system. Suddenly, I was a genius. I won the sixth-grade spelling bee almost every week at Citrus Grove grammar school. I lost once when I misspelled "acquaint." I left out the "c."

Then we moved back to Freeport, and from seventh grade through twelfth, my marks were not spectacularly above average, and my social life was considerably below. Only my passion for sports was consummated.

4

Joe DiMaggio as Muse

Joe DiMaggio sat on the Yankee bench, his young son, Joe Jr., perched beside him, clutching an oversized glove and wearing a Yankee cap. Both of them were smiling as the father pointed his forefinger toward the field he roamed each day with matchless grace. Joe DiMaggio was thirty-one at the time, Joe Jr. was four, and I was about to turn twelve. It was September 1946, and not long after I looked at the posed portrait of the DiMaggios side by side on the cover of my copy of the first issue of *SPORT* magazine, I realized I wanted to be a sportswriter.

I probably couldn't have put it in words then—very few twelve-year-old Jews knew what an epiphany was—but, somehow, I perceived that *SPORT* was different from the half-dozen daily newspaper sports sections I read so religiously, that it emphasized people, not games, and valued writing style over statistics. *SPORT* convinced me that even if I had trouble standing up to a fast ball, let alone a curve, even if I did not have the speed, strength, or hand-and-eye coordination to be a great athlete, or a good one, I still might be able to find a place in a world that clearly preoccupied me, the world of sports.

If anyone had told me when I read the first issue of *SPORT* that eventually I would be editor of the magazine, that someday I would interview both Joe DiMaggio and Joe Jr., that I would come to know and admire the senior DiMaggio, that I would write and narrate a profile of him that appeared on ABC when he won the Jim Thorpe Award in 1993 and then half a dozen years later write and narrate his obituary for ABC News, I would have been incredulous. As a teenager, I hated DiMaggio. He represented the New York Yankees, the perennial world champions. I grew up rooting for the Dodgers, dreaming of beating the Yankees and winning a world championship next year, or next year, or next year.

But thirteen years after that first *SPORT* cover, when I was twenty-five and the assistant sports editor of *Newsweek,* I went to Lawrenceville Academy in New Jersey to interview the place kicker on its football team, primarily because his name was Joe DiMaggio Jr. "The face, the nose, the smile—everything but the uniform was familiar," I wrote. His coach told me, "DiMaggio can be as good as any college kicker." From Lawrenceville, the youngster went to Yale and kicked for the freshman football team.

Years later, I heard through an intermediary that Joe Jr., who had dropped out of Yale and joined the Marines, wanted to talk to me about the possibility of writing a book about his father. I was told he did not intend to paint a flattering portrait. I never heard from him directly, and did not hear of him again until 1999 when, after years of estrangement, he was one of the pallbearers at Joe's funeral. By then, Joe Jr. was living in a battered trailer in Northern California and working in a junkyard. A few months after his father's death, Joe Jr. also passed away. He was only fifty-seven.

I did not know Joe DiMaggio during his playing days, but over the long years of his retirement—he remained a recognizable national figure for an astonishing sixty-plus years, from the mid-1930s until his death, a span challenged only by Katharine Hepburn, Frank Sinatra, and maybe Mickey Rooney—our paths frequently crossed. In the 1970s, a friend of mine named Isadore Becker, who was chairman of the board of Schenley Industries, a liquor company, and president and part-owner of the Riviera Hotel in Las Vegas, staged an annual tennis tournament at the Riviera called the Dewars Cup, which attracted athletes from a variety of sports. DiMaggio served as an umpire for the matches, and his fellow Hall of Famer Hank Greenberg habitually won the event. Greenberg took understandable pleasure in beating professional athletes who were thirty or more years his junior, including Rick Barry, Earl Monroe, Lynn Swann, Julius Erving, and John Havlicek. I attended the tournament two or three times and exchanged a few words with DiMaggio.

Each year, on the last day of the tournament, the athletes would stage a talent show. Lynn Swann would sing; his big number was "Bojangles." John Havlicek would try to sing; he didn't have a big number. Walter Payton, who played the drums, and Calvin Murphy, who twirled a baton, were probably the most accomplished entertainers among the athletes. In 1979, as the

closing act of the talent show, DiMaggio and Greenberg were, literally, the end men for a chorus line of
prominent female athletes: Suzy Chafee, the glamorous
former Olympic skier, was among them; so was the
diminutive skater Judy Sladky, who has made a career
of portraying Peanuts' Snoopy on ice and off and portraying Baby Snuffleupagus on *Sesame Street*. A pair of
All-American basketball players—Ann Meyers, who
married the pitcher Don Drysdale, and Nancy Lieberman, who lived for a time with Martina Navratilova—
were also on the Dewars Cup chorus line.

DiMaggio and Greenberg and the young women
sang "Take Me Out to the Ball Game." I still have the
videotape of the two men leaning on baseball bats and
singing. Unfortunately, the photographer who was
shooting for me switched off his camera just before six
of the female athletes spun around, bent over, and
mooned the audience. Letters printed on their muscular *glutei maximi* spelled out "D-E-W-A-R-S."

Sladky admits she was one of the letters. "We were
always responsive to corporate sponsorship," she explains. Chafee says she cannot remember whether she
mooned or not. "But if I didn't," she says, "I should
have." Ann Meyers and Nancy Lieberman flatly deny
they bared anything beyond their enthusiasm.

Once, when Ann and Nancy and Suzy and Judy
were playing softball, Hank Greenberg looked at them
and turned to me and said, "The girls who played
sports when I was young never looked that good." (The
trend accelerated over the last twenty years of the
twentieth century; by 2000, many female athletes
looked like models, and vice versa.)

The following year, Iz Becker invited me to stay at

the Riviera while I covered the heavyweight championship fight between Muhammad Ali and Larry Holmes. Iz also invited DiMaggio and Julius Erving. I invited Billy Crystal. In the late 1970s, Billy was one of the stars of the television series *Soap* on which he portrayed Jodie, a homosexual. We got very strange looks when we went up to the room we were sharing.

The night of the fight, Iz hosted a dinner for his guests. Crystal, who grew up a Yankee fan and a basketball player, sat near DiMaggio and Erving, two of his heroes. He sat close enough to overhear DiMaggio's two remarks during dinner. Once, Joe called over the waiter and offered culinary advice: "Too much cheese in the antipasto." Later, he offered career advice to Erving. "Don't stay too long," DiMaggio said, an allusion to Ali, who, instead of quitting at or near the peak of his career, risked declining skills against the younger, stronger Holmes. Joe himself had worn Yankee pinstripes no more than one season too long. In 1951, as his gifts faded, Mickey Mantle's began to emerge.

As we left the private dining room to go to the fight, a woman spotted DiMaggio and, conditioned by his television commercials, said, "Oh, look, there's Mister Coffee."

In later years, as I got to know him better, I tried to persuade DiMaggio to allow me to collaborate with him, as I had with other athletes, on an autobiography. He declined, of course, fiercely guarding his privacy, but once, when we both happened to be eating breakfast in a Marriott hotel near Fisherman's Wharf in his hometown of San Francisco, he teased me, saying, "I'm almost ready." And then he smiled, and I smiled, both of us knowing he would never be ready to share the intimate details of his baseball career or his equally sensational marriage—to Marilyn Monroe. From then on, whenever I saw him, once or twice a year, I'd ask, "Are you ready now?" and we'd both smile.

Once, in 1991, the day he was inducted into the Italian-American Hall of Fame near Chicago, I interviewed DiMaggio, and he told me a lovely story about his father, an immigrant fisherman, and his mother, neither of whom could read or write English. When he was playing for the San Francisco Seals in the Pacific Coast League, Joe said, his father used to wake up at four each morning when the early edition of the *San Francisco Chronicle* arrived at their door. He would pick up the *Chronicle,* turn to the front page of the sports section, which was printed on green paper, and study the box score of the Seals' latest game. He would look at the Seals' lineup, count down three names, find the name "DiMaggio," then check the numbers next to the name. He could read the numbers, read how many at bats, runs, and hits his son had recorded. "If I had three hits or more," Joe told me, "he would go back to their room and wake up my mother and tell her. If I had less than three hits, he would let her sleep."

The story told so much about what sports once meant in America, and sometimes still means. Immigrant families were Americanized by their appreciation of sports, and were lifted through the achievements of their sons and daughters, or through the achievements of the sons and daughters of people of similar backgrounds. The athletes were people to look up to then. They weren't threatening to walk out on their jobs, not whining for more millions, not abusing drugs and their own celebrity. They had their faults, certainly, but, partly because reporters were less zealous, they were not defined by those faults.

A painting of DiMaggio hangs on the wall of my office. One of the last times I saw him, he inscribed it to me, "From one Old Timer to another."

I was in good company.

5

I Was a Teenage Big Shot

At the start of my freshman year in high school, before I turned thirteen, I took a beautiful girl to the movies. She was a month older than I. With embarrassing honesty, I bought a full-price ticket for her, and a half-price under-thirteen ticket for me. I believe that was our first and only date.

Half a century later, déjà vu: I took my wife to the movies in Manhattan, bought a full-price ticket for her and a reduced-rate senior-citizen ticket for myself.

I did not play on any of my high school's teams for only one reason: I was not good enough. I did, however, play on a summer baseball team called the Freeport Barons. We won the New York State Kiwanis League championship in 1949 and again in 1950. In 1949, we won in the Polo Grounds, the home of the New York Giants, and the next year we won in Ebbets

Field, the home of the Dodgers. I played one inning in
the Polo Grounds, six in Ebbets Field.

I was captain of the Barons, mostly because I organized the team. The first year, the key was persuading
my friend Jay Schmidt, who was fifteen and six-foot-
five, to pitch for us. Jay pitched four shutouts in a row.
He intimidated our opponents in the championship
game by hitting a ball over the Polo Grounds' left-field
fence during batting practice. I predicted Jay would
play in the major leagues, but despite his size—he
grew to six-seven—and skill, and a brief fling in the
Philadelphia Phillies' organization, he did not make it.
I have since made many similarly astute assessments.

The next year, eager to reprise our championship
season, I went out and recruited players for the Barons.
I was a master, a teenage Tarkanian. I may not have
broken the rules, but I stretched them. I went beyond
our town limits, to Merrick, Seaford, and East
Meadow, to find players. I didn't find a Jay Schmidt
the second year, but we had a better lineup, even when
I was in it. At one point during the season, I was batting .480, twelve for twenty-five. More than half of my
hits were bunts.

One of my responsibilities as the Barons' captain
was to let our players know before each game where
we would meet and when. Our first baseman the first
season was a lanky kid named George Kandiloros.
George's mother was born in Italy, his father in
Greece. Every week, when I called George's home, his
mother would answer the phone and ask who was calling. "Dick Schaap," I would say, and she would say,
"Big shot?" I would say no and repeat, "Dick Schaap,"
and she would again say, "Big shot?" I thought of

changing my name to "Big Shot," but then, of course, she would have said, "Dick Schaap?"

In those days, George was not much more comfortable with English than his mother was. He was also uncomfortable with traveling beyond the boundaries of Freeport. When we played at the Polo Grounds, George wondered if we were going to take the Triborough Bridge from Long Island to Manhattan or the Midtown Tunnel. He was afraid the bridge would collapse, and equally afraid the tunnel would cave in.

George survived, went to college at Hofstra, starred in lacrosse and football, and, as a running back, tried out for the great New York Giants team of the late 1950s. With Frank Gifford in the lineup, the Giants decided they could win without Kandiloros. A decade later, I heard that George had changed his last name to Loros and had become an actor. He was playing Shakespeare in Kentucky.

Later, George appeared in the film *Serpico,* on Broadway in Herb Gardner's *Thieves,* and, more recently, in the HBO television series *The Sopranos.* Obviously, George has grasped the English language. He is a serious actor and a dedicated teacher at the Actors Studio.

I also organized a summer basketball team in an outdoor league in Freeport. Again, my forte was recruiting. I lined up a former Baltimore Bullet named George Feigenbaum to play for our team under an assumed name. Feigenbaum, who had lasted only twelve games in the NBA, was delighted to play under any name other than his own.

A man named Paul Lynner, who had set scoring records at Rutgers, was our leading scorer. We played outdoors. Occasionally, during practice and even during games, Lynner played with a cigarette dangling from his mouth. I figured if Paul was that good, maybe it would help me. So at the age of sixteen, I took up smoking. It didn't help.

I didn't stop smoking until twenty-four years later. By then, I was smoking three, sometimes four packs a day. I stopped cold one night when the gambler and television commentator Jimmy Snyder, "Jimmy the Greek," bet me a thousand dollars I couldn't stop for three years. I have not smoked a conventional cigarette since.

I suffered during the early stages, snapped at coworkers, and believed that without a cigarette staining my fingers and eroding my lungs, I would never be able to write a coherent sentence again. The urge to smoke, however, wore off completely in a decade or two.

A week before the three years were up, I saw the Greek at a ball game and said, "Jimmy, in a week you're going to owe me a thousand bucks," and he said, "I should send you a bill, I saved your life," and I knew right then he was going to welsh on the bet. He was right, of course—he had saved my life—but if I had slipped and smoked even one cigarette, I would have paid him the thousand.

Jimmy had paid off an earlier wager. In 1973, when the New York Mets were in last place with two months to go in the baseball season, he gave me 100-1 that the Mets would not finish first. I put up a dollar, and when the Mets won the pennant in the final week of the season, Jimmy sent me a check for one hundred dollars. I thought of framing the check, not cashing it, but cooler heads prevailed. I framed a photostat.

* * *

Another player in our summer basketball league was a precocious high-school sophomore named Jim Brown. He was one of the three best athletes I've ever seen. The others were Wilt Chamberlain and Bo Jackson. I played basketball against Brown in the summer league and lacrosse against him in college. I also played against Wilt—in tonk, a five-card rummy game that few white people comprehend. I beat Wilt—and the heavyweight boxing champion Floyd Patterson—in tonk. I never beat Jim Brown in anything.

In my junior year in high school, I began writing a sports column for the town weekly, the *Freeport Leader.* I think I was paid five dollars a column. I've reread some of them. I was overpaid. My column was called "Scanning the Sports Scene"—alliteration was my strong suit—and I began one, typically, I'm afraid, "The local football season is about to open with a bang! Two of the local titans, Freeport and Hempstead, clash in what should be the top game of the week." In subsequent columns, the prose did not noticeably improve.

Then I stepped up to a daily newspaper.

6

"You Oughta Know Better Than to Tell Me Things"

When Jimmy Breslin, the Pulitzer Prize–winning columnist, became my first boss, he was twenty, and I was fifteen. He was the night sports editor of a newspaper on Sunrise Highway in Rockville Centre, New York, called the *Nassau Daily Review-Star*. He was in college, theoretically, at Long Island University. I was in my junior year at Freeport High School, and I was one of his ace reporters. I worked four hours a night, four nights a week, for a dollar an hour. You can imagine how good a newspaper it was. Understandably, the *Review-Star* folded a few years later, after Breslin and I had both left it. In time, we worked together on three more newspapers—the *Long Island Press,* the *New York Herald Tribune,* and the *World Journal Tribune*—that died despite our brilliance.

Breslin and I have been friends now for more than half a century. The only people I have known longer are my brother Bill, my sister Nancy, and our Uncle

Walter. I have other relatives, but we have not stayed in touch. Breslin has. Constantly. He does not call quite so often as he used to, or at such strange hours, but his calls still start the same way. "Waddaya doin'?" he says.

It is a magnificent journalistic opening. You must come up with an interesting answer, or he will demand, "What else? What else?" Sometimes he will vary his approach and ask, "What's goin' on?" He has used this technique his entire reportorial life, and it has always worked. People tell him things.

Steve Smith, the brother-in-law and confidant of John F. Kennedy, once told Breslin things. Things Smith did not want repeated. Breslin promptly put them in his column in the *Herald Tribune*. That morning, I answered the phone in the office Breslin and I shared at the newspaper. Smith was calling, and he was furious. He swore at Breslin, and at me, too, guilt by association. When Breslin showed up, he returned Smith's call and yelled at him. "You oughta know better than to tell me things," Breslin said.

I certainly should have known better. But, in 1968, when I was finishing a book called *Instant Replay,* Jerry Kramer's diary of a championship season with Vince Lombardi's Green Bay Packers, Breslin called me one day and began asking me about the book. "Tell me something about Lombardi," he said.

"C'mon, Jimmy," I said. "This stuff is for the book."

"Just tell me one story," he said. "Not to write about. Just to tell me."

He was not going to leave me alone until I told him one story. I told him about a team meeting to determine who would get shares, or partial shares, of the Packers' playoff money. The players were selfish. They awarded only token shares to management people and groundskeepers and players on the inactive list. When Lombardi saw the miserly way the money had been divided, he exploded. "I'm ashamed of you," he told his team. "Just take my share off that list. Just take it off and split it up. Split it up, if that's the way it's gonna be. Just split it up."

Lombardi's displeasure prompted the players to vote again and to be slightly more generous. Lombardi even got his share back. I told this story to Breslin, and I said, "It's a great story for the book, so please don't repeat it."

"On my life," Breslin said. "What do you think I am?"

A few days later, I was at a cocktail party and someone came up to me and started telling me my story about Lombardi and the Packers and the playoff shares. "Where did you hear that?" I asked.

"Oh, some fat guy was telling it on television last night," I was told.

Breslin was heavier in those days than he is now. He drank then, although never as much as he pretended to. He also pretended he never went to college. And he hated to admit that his mother taught English. He didn't want to tarnish his image.

Jimmy was my mentor from the day I went to work at the *Review-Star*. I got a chance to work there because my father served in the National Guard with a man named Bob Stirrat, who was sports editor of the *Review-Star* and later became publicity director of Little League baseball. My father asked Stirrat if I could phone in the results of the Freeport High School football and basketball games. Every school had a kid, a "stringer," who phoned in results. I suppose we got paid, but the amount was negligible. After I had been phoning in results for a few weeks in the fall of 1949, I asked if I could come to the office and write up the games myself. Stirrat said sure. The paper was not overstaffed.

My drawbacks included inexperience and an inability to type. I hunted and pecked with one finger and took hours to write a story two or three paragraphs long.

One night in the infancy of my journalistic career, Breslin wrote a script for me. He told me I was to call Fred McMorrow at the *Long Island Press,* our sister paper, and I was to repeat his words to McMorrow with feeling and exactly as he had written them.

I did as I was told. "Mr. McMorrow," I said, when I reached him on the phone, "my name is Dick Schaap and I am fifteen years old and I am working in the sports department of the *Nassau Daily Review-Star,* and when Mr. Breslin came in to work tonight, he took one look at the layouts Mr. Stirrat had left for him and said it was a bunch of shit and threw them in the wastepaper basket and walked out, and I am here all alone, trying to put out the sports section."

"Oh, you poor kid," McMorrow said, and then cursed Breslin for his character flaws.

"Mr. McMorrow, I've written a headline that says, 'Brooklyn Baseball Club Defeats Pittsburgh Baseball Club by Score of Three to One,' " I said, continuing Breslin's script. "And I have another one that says, 'Giants One Helluva Ball Club.' Is that okay, Mr. McMorrow?"

"Oh, you poor kid," McMorrow said again. "I'm gonna get you some help."

McMorrow then called the city desk of the *Review-Star* and asked them to assign someone to rescue me.

Breslin, possessor of a very good if warped mind, had thought ahead and informed the city desk of what he was doing to McMorrow. "We can't spare anyone," the desk told McMorrow.

He called me back and told me to do my best. "You poor kid," he said.

Meanwhile, of course, Breslin was putting out the sports section as well as could be expected on a paper with a twenty-year-old deputy sports editor and a fifteen-year-old reporter.

McMorrow phoned me again. "I've called every bar in Queens and Nassau," he said, citing the neighboring counties on Long Island that were home to the *Press* and the *Review-Star,* "and I can't find the bastard anywhere."

"I will do my best," I promised.

Finally, after the section closed, McMorrow called once more, and this time Breslin himself answered the phone. Breslin was sober, but his voice did not give it away.

"Where the hell have you been?" McMorrow shouted. "I've called every joint I know."

Breslin mumbled an expletive, hung up the phone, and congratulated me on a job well-done. Mr. McMorrow did not speak to me for many years.

Gradually, as my typing improved, climbing toward its cruising speed of sixty words a minute with two fingers (the forefingers, both of which are now short and bent), I was given more responsibility. I covered high schools besides my own, and for a while, even though I wasn't old enough to attend horseraces, I was the paper's resident handicapper. I was no worse than the experts who knew a paddock from a fetlock. I picked five winners one day, which salved my guilt about the people who trusted my earnest, but ill-informed selections.

As little as I knew at the time, I knew Breslin was good. I knew I wanted to be like him.

In the early 1960s, when I was a senior editor at *Newsweek,* I wrote a story for our press section about my former boss. "Jimmy Breslin looks like a fighter who got lucky—square at the shoulders, round at the belly, no marks on his baby face," my story began.

"He works out of gin mills," I went on, "elbow on the bar, foot on the rail, a cigarette in his mouth, a beer in his hand, and a twinkle in his brown, half-closed, bloodshot eyes. 'I ain't very reliable,' he says. 'I ain't very smart.'

"Breslin is a liar. He is smart enough to be one of the two or three best and busiest freelance sportswriters in the U.S. today. . . . His secret is a personalized staccato style, gruff and intimate like himself. He writes as if he's talking out of the side of his mouth."

Partly as a result of the *Newsweek* story, and mostly because of his enormous talent—he had just written a wildly funny book about the woeful first season of the New York Mets called *Can't Anybody Here Play This Game?*—Breslin was offered a job on the *Herald Tribune.* He started as a sports columnist, and his sports column quickly evolved into a general column, and soon he was the most readable, most entertaining writer in the city.

Later the same year, Breslin reciprocated. He persuaded the *Trib* to offer me a job. But first he sounded me out. I had been at *Newsweek* for more than seven years, since I'd finished graduate school. We met at Bleeck's, a saloon connected by a back staircase to the

Tribune, and he said to me, "What's goin' on at *Newsweek?*"

"Jimmy," I said, "I hate it. It's a jungle. Everybody's out to get everybody else. Everybody's got a knife in somebody's back."

Breslin looked at me, my friend and mentor, and said, "If that's what's goin' on there, you're gonna come out all right."

A few weeks later, at lunch on November 22, 1963, Jim Bellows, the editor of the *Herald Tribune,* offered me the job of city editor of the storied paper. (Mark Twain, Karl Marx, Stephen Crane, and Henry James, among others, wrote for the *Herald* or the *Tribune* before the papers merged in 1924.)

Bellows also offered me a cut in pay, from $21,000 annually at the magazine to $20,000 at the paper. Of course I accepted. I have never been good in financial matters. Within minutes after I said yes, the owner of the French restaurant in which we were dining, a former international auto-racing star named Rene Dreyfus, came to our table and said, "Excuse me, gentlemen, but your president has been shot."

We were journalists. While the country mourned, we rushed back to work.

When I was in my late twenties, and Breslin in his early thirties, before we both gave up smoking and cut down on our drinking, Jimmy and I used to call each other late at night and describe the symptoms of false heart attacks we were experiencing. Once I actually had a spastic esophagus; I don't know what he had. By the time we reached our sixties, and Breslin had endured brain surgery to remove an aneurysm, and I was a veteran of atrial fibrillation, we would call each other and brag about what great shape we were in.

Over the years, Breslin has often turned on friends and acquaintances—"people I'm not talking to anymore," he calls them—but he has always had kind words for me. When I published *Sport,* a collection of my work in newspapers, magazines, and books, Breslin wrote the introduction. "The sport Dick Schaap always has covered is the contest called living," he said. "And as he describes how people live their lives, he covers an astonishing range . . . in a variety of styles. He can play so many notes, and has so many ways of making you listen to those notes."

I still owe Breslin for that. I also owe him for the justification for immodestly repeating his praise. "If you do not blow your own horn," Breslin wrote in *I Want to Thank My Brain for Remembering Me,* his magnificent account of his brain surgery and his life, "there is no music."

Jimmy is a symphony orchestra.

I am merely a jazz quartet.

7

"C'mon, Ralph, We're Witcha!"

My childhood ended on October 3, 1951, when I had just turned seventeen and was starting my freshman year at Cornell University. I was in my room in my dorm, which was a World War II Quonset hut, sitting on the upper deck of a double-decker bed listening to the radio broadcast of the third and final National League playoff game between the Brooklyn Dodgers and the New York Giants. The winner would go on to the World Series to face the Yankees in the final season of DiMaggio and the first of Mickey Mantle.

The Dodgers led, 4–2, in the bottom of the ninth inning at the Polo Grounds. Ralph Branca relieved Don Newcombe just before Bobby Thomson came to bat, Giant runners on second and third, the potential tying runs, one man out. "C'mon, Ralph, we're witcha!" I cheered in chorus with a million other Brooklynites. Branca delivered, Thomson swung and connected, and the ball sailed toward left field, where, only two years earlier, I had spent one uneventful inning.

Thomson's drive cleared the fence—a three-run home run that beat the Dodgers. As the Giants' announcer Russ Hodges cheered, "The Giants win the pennant! The Giants win the pennant! The Giants win the pennant!" I fell off the upper deck of the bunk bed.

I hated Bobby Thomson for hitting the home run. I hated Ralph Branca for throwing the pitch that Thomson hit for the home run. If Branca and Thomson had appeared in front of me that night, and someone had handed me a gun, I would gladly have shot both of them. Most of the citizens of the borough of churches felt as murderous as I did.

If anyone had suggested then that someday I would share meals and golf courses with Branca and Thomson and, as the master of ceremonies at charitable fund-raising events, introduce "my friends, Ralph and Bobby," and praise them with genuine affection, I would have shot him, too.

But this is what's so beautiful about my life. I have gotten to know the heroes of my youth, and the villains, and I have learned how thin the line is between them. In the late 1950s, when I worked for *Newsweek,* I used to hang out with Don Newcombe at a bar he owned in New Jersey, near the border dividing Newark and East Orange. Newcombe was a big drinker then.

Almost forty years later, he was my guest on a television show immodestly called *Schaap One on One* on ESPN Classic, and he told me that, in 1967, he got down on his knees, put his hand on the head of his four-year-old son and, with his marriage and his life in jeopardy, promised his wife on the child's life that "I would never drink another drop as long as I lived." As he recalled the moment, Don Newcombe struggled to hold back tears. He had not had a drink in more than thirty years.

One night in 1999, I took Bobby Thomson, who was a widower, and a woman he affectionately called "my lady friend," who was a widow, to dinner at Rao's, which is situated perhaps two miles due south of the old Polo Grounds. Thomson, making his first visit to the restaurant, loved the food and the ambiance. He and his lady friend met and chatted with Sidney Poitier, who was sitting at the next table. Sonny Grosso, a former New York City narcotics detective turned television producer, was seated nearby. Grosso, the real-life cop portrayed by Roy Scheider in the 1971 film *The French Connection,* grew up a Yankee fan. "Thank you for what you did," he told Thomson. "I hated the Dodgers."

Rao's is a place out of the past, owned and operated in the same building by the same family for more than one hundred years, and Thomson, soft-spoken, hair thinning, still trim, fit the setting perfectly. One woman came over to ask Bobby if he had known her father, who had pitched for the Giants, and several men simply wanted to shake Bobby's hand. I watched, beaming as happily as if, so many years earlier, Thomson had hit the home run *for* my Dodgers, instead of *against* them.

The following week, I returned to Rao's with Hank Aaron and his wife, Billye. Aaron and I had recently collaborated on an autobiographical essay for a book called *Home Run: My Life in Pictures.* Hank, too, received a hero's welcome at Rao's, the home run he hit in 1974 to break Babe Ruth's lifetime record of 714 as well remembered as Thomson's "shot heard round the world." Aaron also hit *his* milestone home run against the Dodgers, but by then they were the *Los Angeles* Dodgers, so who cared?

On consecutive Mondays, I had invited to a tiny restaurant in East Harlem two men who had hit two of the most significant home runs in baseball history. (Coincidentally, they had once been teammates. Thomson was traded from the Giants to Milwaukee, and when he broke his leg in 1954, the rookie Aaron replaced him in left field and in the Braves' batting order.)

The only way I could top myself was if, the following Monday, I brought the Babe himself to Rao's. I'm very good at collecting people, but I'm not that good.

Thomson and Aaron are among many people I have introduced to Rao's—from Bo Jackson and Joe Montana to Patti Lupone and Martina Navratilova. Open only for dinner, closed on weekends, the place serves incredible food and seats fewer than fifty customers. Everyone wants to go to Rao's because they can't. It's the toughest ticket in town. Frank Sinatra or the pope could walk in off the street and get a table, but neither has shown up lately.

I have a table for four every Monday night. Strangers and casual friends write and call and beg to borrow it. I offer it only to family and close friends, and I auction it off at charitable affairs. People have bid as high as $2,500 to use the table for one night, and that doesn't include the cost of food or drink. Once, at my golf tournament for the benefit of the Crohn's and Colitis Foundation of America, a woman stood up and turned to Frank Pellegrino, one of the owners of Rao's, and said, "Frankie, if you'll give me the whole restaurant one evening, I'll give fifty thousand dollars to the charity."

Pellegrino hesitated for a second, then said yes, and the woman wrote out a check. The check was good, and her daughter's birthday party—Frankie opened the restaurant on a Saturday—was great.

Thomson and Branca began bonding within weeks after *the* home run: They sang a duet—their own lyrics to "Because of You"—at the baseball writers' dinner and on *The Ed Sullivan Show.* "But come next spring, keep throwing me that thing," Thomson sort of sang, "and I will swing, because of you." Branca had by far the better voice. But Thomson had the National League championship.

Half a century later, Thomson and Branca, retired ballplayers and retired business executives, remained friends, prized septuagenarian celebrities at many of the charitable golf events held in the New York suburbs almost every Monday from spring to fall. Branca's golf game was better, too, but that didn't make up for the home run, either.

When I introduced them at dinners, I pointed out that if you had sought to pick the perfect men to survive the fame and infamy of the 1951 home run, you could not have chosen better than Branca and Thomson. A less religious or self-reliant man than Branca might have been destroyed by his momentary failure; a less humble or decent man than Thomson might have been destroyed by his monumental success. Branca kept up his self-confidence; Thomson kept down his ego.

I'd love to spend their golden anniversary with them—October 3, 2001.

Preferably at Rao's.

8

How I Stopped Jim Brown

My first week at Cornell, I wandered out of my Quonset hut to play touch football on the library slope, a gentle hill separating the campus quadrangle from the dormitories. Teams were chosen, and I said I'd like to play end. The only black student I had seen at Cornell—there were others in the early 1950s, but not many—played the opposite end. We were told to run ten yards straight ahead, turn, and crisscross. I followed instructions, but when I turned, the other end was far down the field.

I did not feel quite so leaden when I got back to the huddle and found out that the other end was a fifth-year engineering student named Meredith Gourdine. He was called Flash, for his last name and his speed. He was a world-class sprinter and long jumper, and the summer after we met, he won the silver medal for the long jump at the Olympic Games in Helsinki.

Flash Gourdine and I remained friends for almost fifty years, till his death in 1998.

* * *

I have always admired most the athletes whose interests and virtuosity extend beyond the playing field, and Gourdine was the first I ever met of that special breed. He came out of the Fort Greene projects in the Bedford-Stuyvesant area of Brooklyn, a scarred neighborhood where neither poverty nor violence was unusual. Encouraged by a math teacher, who saw a spark, Meredith took a competitive test that enabled him to enter Brooklyn Tech, one of New York City's elite high schools. At Brooklyn Tech, he was an outstanding student and one of the city's fastest scholastic runners *and* swimmers.

Meredith went on to Cornell to study engineering physics, arguably the university's most demanding academic discipline. He graduated near the top of his class, won his Olympic medal, became one of the first black officers in the history of the U.S. Navy, earned a doctorate in physics at the prestigious California Institute of Technology, and invented, among many things, an airport defogging system.

He had a zest for life and ladies that never diminished. At a party celebrating his selection to the Brooklyn Tech Hall of Fame, not long before he died, Meredith, robbed of his sight and one leg by a lifetime of diabetes, sat in a wheelchair, smiling at everyone, especially the women, trying to see if he could recognize them with his hands. I don't think one woman complained; I know my wife didn't.

When I was a freshman, reluctantly studying calculus, Meredith was an instructor in the subject. Once, the night before an exam, he agreed to tutor me. I went to his room and he told me to draw an x-axis and a y-axis. I did. Then he said, "Draw a parabola." I said, "What's

a parabola?" And he said, "Go home. I can't help you."
He was right. I got a 37 in the exam.

Meredith was hardly the only person smarter and
more gifted than I at Cornell. Richard Meier, who won
the Pritzker Prize, the Pulitzer of architecture, and designed the Getty Center in Los Angeles, arrived in Ithaca
the year after I did. Stephen Reich, the minimalist composer whose work has been performed by the New York
Philharmonic and orchestras throughout the world, was
my fraternity brother; he was a philosophy major, and I
never imagined that he had an interest in music. Gordon
Davidson, the longtime artistic director of the Mark Ta-
per Forum in Los Angeles and a Tony Award winner for
theatrical excellence, was a member, with Meredith
Gourdine, of Telluride, a quasi-fraternity for the intellectually advantaged. Sandy Weill, the financier, was my
classmate: I knew him only casually and did not re-
motely suspect that someday he would give the Cornell
Medical School a gift of one hundred million dollars.
The medical school now bears his name.

Thomas Pynchon, the novelist, was a couple of
years behind me, and although we had mutual acquaintances, I cannot recall ever meeting or seeing him.
Many people, of course, insist that the reclusive Pynchon does not exist, that he is merely a figment of his
own fertile imagination. I cannot vouch for his existence, but the year after *V,* his first novel, was published, I spoke to several people who claimed to have
known him during his Cornell years, then wrote a column about him for *Book Week,* emphasizing his
chameleonlike ability to alter his appearance and van-
ish from view. He hated my column and, in a letter to
his agent Candida Donadio, said that my report made
him sick, "almost homicidal."

Lesser critics have felt equally queasy about some of my work, but none that I can recall threatened ultimate bodily harm. I thank Pynchon for sparing me. He did not seem to notice, or care, that I called him "a hugely gifted and imaginative new writer," and said his friends considered him "a genius, a saint, an overly harsh self-critic, a letter writer without peer, and a master of every scholarly discipline from higher mathematics to Greek." Coincidentally, like Meredith Gourdine, Pynchon studied engineering physics.

I did not hang out with any of these extraordinary people at Cornell. I preferred playing gin and poker with Pismo, Jo-Jo the Dog-Faced Boy, Slick Willie, the Whale, and the Animal, whose real names now escape me. Lee Balter also played in the card games. I remember *his* real name because, in my junior year, he was my roommate. Forty years later, after he had enjoyed an enriching run on Wall Street, I saw him at a class reunion and learned he was operating a foundry, casting statuary.

In the spring of my first year at Cornell, I was persuaded to try out for the freshman lacrosse team as a goalie, not because I had any special skill at the position, but because the team did not have a goalie on its roster. I became the starting goalie, by default, and we went undefeated in a very short season. My sophomore year, I was a backup goalie on the varsity. I liked the position because it did not require much running, and, therefore, I did not have to give up smoking.

In the spring of my junior year, I skipped the lacrosse season—I was otherwise occupied, starting a one-year term as editor of the student newspaper, the *Cornell Daily Sun*—but in my senior year, I was the first-string goalie. I think the coach, Jim Smith, liked my writing.

I made second team All–Upstate New York—you can look it up—mostly because, in the big game against Syracuse, I made twenty-two saves. Three of them came on shots fired by my fellow Long Islander, Jim Brown. I never saw those three shots; they bounced off me. Brown took four other shots and scored four goals, and Syracuse won, in overtime. Once, when I blocked a shot and started running with the ball, Brown charged toward me, threatening destruction. Spurred by fear, I got rid of the ball with dazzling quickness.

Jim Brown was the best lacrosse player who ever lived. He played midfield, wielding a stick so short it bordered on the illegal, and protecting that stick so fiercely with his forearm that double- and even triple-teaming him did not slow him down. His legs brought to mind telephone poles, but telephone poles never moved so swiftly.

Still, the year I made second team All-Upstate, Brown earned merely honorable mention (I looked it up), probably because he played fewer than half his team's games. His lame excuse was that he was busy practicing the decathlon and playing spring football.

Brown became an All-American in football (and lacrosse). As a sophomore, he made the first start of his college football career against Cornell, and Syracuse lost the game. A couple of years later, the two schools terminated their football rivalry, presumably, I would like to think, because Syracuse feared Cornell.

By the time Brown was a senior, in 1956, I was at *Newsweek* and cast my first vote for the Heisman Trophy. I voted for Jim. When he finished fifth in the balloting—Paul Hornung of Notre Dame won the award; at that time, no black athlete had ever received the

Heisman—I swore I would never vote again. I waited a quarter of a century—till I voted for Marcus Allen in 1981. Times had changed. Allen's Heisman was the eighth in a row for a black running back.

I've known Jim Brown almost as long as I've known Jimmy Breslin, although not nearly so well. In 1968, when I wrote an article for *Look* magazine, "The Revolt of the Black Athlete," I interviewed Brown at the Arizona state penitentiary, where he was filming *Riot*. He was less than cooperative until he realized I knew him from the old days; then he warmed up considerably. Thirty years later, I interviewed him again, for ESPN Classic's *Schaap One on One,* and recalled the Heisman slight and the Cornell football victory. A few months after that, he and I cohosted a Super Bowl party for ESPN. More than forty years after he had last flicked a lacrosse ball at me, Brown remained in remarkable condition, not a hint of softness. His glare still intimidated me.

When I was editor of the *Cornell Daily Sun,* I shared a house with our managing editor, Philip Merrill Levine, and several of our friends. After we graduated, Phil went to work for Mike Wallace on a TV show called *Night Beat* and then for the diplomat Chester Bowles. He lost his last name somewhere and, as Philip Merrill, became publisher of a newspaper in Annapolis, Maryland, and of magazines in Washington, Baltimore, and Manhattan. He also served as an assistant secretary-general of NATO. I knew Phil was going to be a success because, during our senior year, he had an affair with an older woman, a member of the Cornell faculty who taught him French, among other things. I never knew the details of the relationship, but I was as jealous as a twenty-year-old virgin could be.

During our senior year, Phil perpetrated a cruel hoax. It started with a series of letters to me from a young woman in Brooklyn who had been a cashier in a restaurant not far from the offices of the *Cornell Sun*. As her letters grew progressively more ardent, I bragged about them to Phil and our housemates. Then I received a letter from an attorney, informing me that I was to be the defendant in a paternity suit.

I panicked, irrationally, considering that I was still a virgin. I called my father, who suggested I speak to a professor he knew in the Cornell Law School. The professor told me how to respond to the suit, and I got excused from classes to concentrate on my legal problem.

A few days later, Phil Levine said to me, "Get any letters lately?"

"No," I said.

"You sure?" he said.

I began to suspect that something was rotten in upstate New York.

Phil soon confessed, or boasted, that he had masterminded the plot. He had persuaded a young woman on the *Sun* staff to write the passionate letters, and she had sent them to a friend in New York to mail them to me. The lawyer was imaginary, his legal stationery bogus. I was conflicted. On the one hand, I wanted to kill Phil, but on the other, I took the fact that he thought I would believe the letters as a salute, however misguided, to my manhood. I swore revenge, but I'm not certain whether revealing his liaison with the French instructor is revenge or tribute.

Phil and I collaborated on another caper that was, to me, more satisfying. We decided in the fall of 1954 to invade the campus of Syracuse University, hijack the student newspaper, the *Daily Orange,* and substitute a bogus edition. Phil and I wrote many of the articles ourselves—one reported that the NCAA was suspending Syracuse for violating football recruiting rules; another detailed a predawn police raid that uncovered illegal drinking at fourteen fraternities and seven dormitories—and Phil found a printing plant not far from Cornell that could perfectly duplicate the typography of the real *Orange.*

As part of our scheme, Phil and I spent a night on the Syracuse campus, casing the joint, determining where the student newspaper was printed, when it went to press, the size of the printing staff, and when and where the paper was distributed. No problems: Only two or three printers to worry about, and not more than half a dozen distribution points, easy to chart.

On the appointed night, we led a small caravan of cars from Ithaca to Syracuse, an hour away. One car was filled with thousands of copies of our phony newspaper; two others with Cornell football players and wrestlers, just in case we encountered physical resistance. We also brought along a few bottles of whiskey and several copies of a new magazine called *Playboy* to keep the Syracuse printers amused.

The printers were amused, and the real student newspaper was not published on schedule. Our phony edition was delivered to the appropriate campus buildings. We stayed around long enough to watch the reaction of Syracuse students, few of whom noticed the difference.

* * *

Thirty-five years later, my older son, Jeremy, as the

sports editor of the *Cornell Daily Sun,* helped stage a similar coup in New Haven, victimizing the *Yale Daily News*, instead of the *Orange*. It is always gratifying to have a son who wants to emulate a father's success. Jeremy soon carried the process a step further; he is now a correspondent for my latest employer, ESPN. What I particularly like about his work is that he seems to feel the story is more important than he is; this is not a feeling universally shared by sportscasters. My younger son, David, who is in his teens, has indicated that he, too, might become a sports reporter. I think he reasons that if his father and his brother can do it, anyone can.

You might wonder how a cliché-ridden high-school sportswriter became the editor of a prestigious college paper once edited by E. B. White and enlivened by the prose of Kurt Vonnegut. In my junior year, the obvious candidate for editor in chief, a bright prelaw student who suffered from pomposity, fell into disfavor with the incumbent editor and managing editor. They urged me to switch from sports to news, so that they could groom me to be the editor. I agreed and have been journalistically schizophrenic ever since.

Equally important, a young woman named Anne Morrissy, a member of the *Sun* sports staff, wanted very much to be the sports editor. Not entirely because she recognized my skills, she joined the team championing my candidacy for editor in chief. My supporters prevailed. Anne became the first woman sports editor in the Ivy League, the center of considerable attention when she integrated the previously all-male Yale press box; with less celebration, I became the editor of a college newspaper that came out six days a week and proudly, and accurately, called itself "Ithaca's Only

Morning Newspaper." We covered national and international news as well as campus news. We carried stories that broke too late for the edition of the *New York Times* that found its way upstate.

We were a good training ground; my predecessor as editor, Stuart Loory, became a Moscow correspondent for the *Herald Tribune,* a CNN broadcaster and executive, and a professor of journalism. My successor, Keith Johnson, served many years as a writer and editor at Time Inc., then dedicated himself to updating a classic history of Cornell. *His* successor, Andrew Kopkind, who died too young, became a major and eloquent voice of dissidence for three decades, writing for *The Nation* and other liberal publications. (I spoke at a memorial service for Andy; so did Calvin Trillin and Joan Didion, among many who loved him.) One of the sports editors I served under, Ross Wetzsteon, a wise and kindly man, became an editor of the *Village Voice* and a respected theater critic, and when he died, also too young, he was working on a history of Greenwich Village. I don't remember once seeing Ross, who was a faculty brat, without a tie and a jacket during his undergraduate days; I don't remember once seeing Ross, in his Village days, wearing a tie or a jacket.

The Ivy League newspapers with which we attempted to compete were formidable rivals. During my editorship, David Halberstam was the managing editor of the *Harvard Crimson,* Anthony Lukas his associate managing editor, both of them Pulitzer Prize winners. Richard Kluger, who led the *Princetonian* a year later, edited my books-and-authors column at the *Herald Tribune,* wrote a massive biography of the *Trib* called

The Paper, and won a Pulitzer himself for his study of the cigarette industry, *Ashes to Ashes.*

The central political issue during my editorship was an attack on a Cornell professor of zoology, Marcus Singer, by the House Un-American Activities Committee, the McCarthyite congressional committee then led by Harold Velde of Illinois and sworn to flush out commies and pinkos. We called the HUAC the Un-American Committee.

Singer told the committee he had been a member of a Marxist study group during his graduate-school days at Harvard and had considered himself a communist, even though he had never formally joined the party. But he refused to tell the HUAC the names of other members of the group, on the grounds of "honor and conscience." When he was cited for contempt, the university declined to champion him and relieved him of his teaching duties. The *Cornell Daily Sun,* which was flatteringly but inaccurately sometimes called "the Upstate Daily Worker," rallied around Dr. Singer, a pioneer in studying regeneration who, long before he was cited by Congress, was cited, in a far more laudatory way, by the American Cancer Society.

Dr. Singer, who was Jewish, grew up on "the Hill" in Pittsburgh, a predominantly black neighborhood. One day, he told me, his mother went to the local butcher shop, and the butcher's wife said, "Mrs. Singer, how's your oldest boy?"

"He's wonderful," Mrs. Singer said.

"Vat's he doing?" the butcher's wife asked.

"He's at Harvard."

"Vat's he doing at Harvard?"

"He's studying zoology," Mrs. Singer said.

"Zoology?" the butcher's wife said. "Vat does he do?"

"Vell," Mrs. Singer said, "he cuts up salamanders."

The butcher's wife looked incredulous. "Does it pay vell?" she asked.

While I wrote news stories and editorials about Dr. Singer—sometimes, I'm afraid, it was hard to distinguish one from the other—I also completed my Cornell studies. I had started in the School of Arts and Sciences, planning to major in English, but after my freshman year, with money running low, I transferred to the New York State School of Industrial and Labor Relations, which did not charge tuition for New York State residents. I majored in the *Sun,* but got a bachelor of science degree in industrial and labor relations. I certainly did not realize then that it would be the perfect preparation for covering professional sports in the last third of the twentieth century.

For a journalist, there is no such thing as useless knowledge. Every fact from every discipline has the potential to brighten style or strengthen substance. Journalism is a profession whose practitioners should know everything and pretend to know nothing. Too many people in the profession know nothing and pretend to know everything.

As part of my ILR training, I spent the summer of 1953 working in Pittsburgh in the labor relations department of Crucible Steel, a company that is now extinct. I wrote a training manual advising foremen in the steel mill how to deal with new employees. Show them their lockers, I counseled, show them where they clock in, where they pick up their paychecks; explain to them the importance of their work, how it fits into the assembly-line process. I thought it was a terrific manual. I asked one of the foremen what he thought. "What do you want me to do?" he said. "Take every nigger that comes in here by the hand and lead him around the place?" That response had not been covered in my textbooks.

On weekends, I received further education. I worked as a short-order cook in a drive-in restaurant called Eat N' Park. I worked on the grill between a seminarian and an English teacher. I dated carhops, to no avail. I tried to get a night job working in the sports department of either Pittsburgh paper, the *Press* or the *Post-Gazette,* but both turned me down. I lived in a rooming house called Bachelor's Quarters, near Carnegie Tech and Forbes Field, the home of the Pittsburgh Pirates. One of my housemates was, during the school year, attending Drexel University in Philadelphia. We hit it off. We both played lacrosse and he played the ukulele. He was a trainee for Westinghouse Electric. His name was Chuck Barris, and several years later, he created *The Dating Game, The Newlywed Game*, and *The Gong Show*, among other gold mines.

In the summer of 1953, when the Brooklyn Dodgers came to Pittsburgh, Roger Kahn came with them. He was a young reporter for the *Herald Tribune.* Twenty years later, he wrote *The Boys of Summer,* a stunningly successful account of his days with the Dodgers. A couple of years earlier, he had been covering high-school sports for the *Trib,* and I had been his Long Island correspondent.

Roger invited me to the Schenley Park Hotel, the Dodgers' headquarters in Pittsburgh, to have dinner with him and three more of my heroes, Jackie Robinson, pitcher Joe Black, and infielder Jim Gilliam. I thought I was in paradise, not Pittsburgh. During the dinner, the conversation turned to the young star of the New York Yankees, Mickey Mantle, and Kahn told a story he had heard about how dumb Mantle was.

"Shit," Jackie Robinson said, "we got plenty of guys that dumb, but we don't have anybody that good!"

Two years later, in the fall of 1955, as the Grantland Rice Fellow at the Columbia School of Journalism, I was assigned to cover the seventh and final game of the 1955 World Series between the Dodgers of Jackie Robinson and the Yankees of Mickey Mantle. A young left-handed Dodger pitcher named Johnny Podres shut out the Yankees, 2–0, and for the first and last time in the history of their life in Brooklyn, the Dodgers won the World Series. I wrote a workmanlike report, but at the time, I thought it was the greatest story ever told.

(The summer before the 1955 World Series, between college and graduate school, I worked at *Sports Illustrated,* which celebrated its first anniversary during my three-month stay. I worked on what was called "the clip desk," cutting out sports stories from newspapers.)

The Grantland Rice Fellowship was awarded in memory of the poetic sportswriter who wrote, "Outlined against a blue-gray October sky, the Four Horsemen rode again," and "When the One Great Scorer comes to mark against your name, He marks not that you won or lost, but how you played the game." Rice's prose was often purplish, yet frequently memorable.

The three-man panel that chose the Grantland Rice Fellow included Bill Corum, sports columnist for the *New York Journal-American* and president of Churchill Downs racetrack (they don't make conflicts of interest like they used to); Ralph McGill, the distinguished editor of the *Atlanta Constitution;* and John Kieran, sports columnist for the *New York Times,* ornithologist, and a regular on *Information Please,* a radio quiz show that required its panelists to be knowledgeable in a wide variety of fields. (Mike Lupica, my associate throughout the 1990s on *The Sports Reporters,* would have been perfect for *Information Please;* Mike does not quite know everything about everything, but he does know almost as much as he thinks he does, which is considerable.)

When I received the fellowship at a luncheon in Manhattan, my father sat between Jimmy Cannon, the columnist, and Willard Mullin, the cartoonist, two of his heroes, and mine. Cannon told my father that if I was getting a fellowship named after Grantland Rice, I would have to major in martinis.

I did not became an alcoholic during my year at Columbia. I did, however, become a workaholic, an addiction that has driven me during my lifetime to great productivity and considerable alimony. Besides going to classes, and covering the World Series, I worked nights at the *Long Island Press,* was a campus stringer for the *Times,* and served as the assistant sports information director for Columbia. Our prize athlete at the time was a basketball player named Chet Forte, who later became the director of ABC's *Monday Night Football* and a degenerate gambler, a calling that led him to commit fraud and to serve time in prison. Forte, who was no more than five-foot-seven, made the 1957 All-American team alongside Wilt Chamberlain. I would like to think my glowing press releases contributed to his selection.

At Columbia, I took a class in magazine writing, and as part of the course, I was required to write a potentially salable article, several thousand words long. I wrote about the recruiting of high-school basketball players in New York City. I spent days and nights prowling the gyms of Manhattan and Queens and Brooklyn, talking to players and to recruiters, men with nicknames like "Spook" and "the Garf."

The class of 1956 was an exceptional basketball class; three of the city's high-school stars that year went on to become first players and then head coaches in the National Basketball Association: Tom "Satch" Sanders, Doug Moe, and the winningest coach in NBA history, Lenny Wilkens. Wilkens was also named one of the fifty greatest players in the history of the NBA, but in 1956, he was not even the best player on his Boys High School team in Brooklyn. That distinction went to Tommy Davis, who never played college basketball but did play for the Los Angeles Dodgers and, in 1962, led the National League in hitting and in runs batted in.

I wrote about the often sleazy pursuit of these prize athletes, and my Journalism School professor, a literary agent named Sterling Lord, sold my thesis for $1,000 to *Sports Illustrated,* which edited it heavily and ran it for six full pages under the title "Basketball's Underground Railroad." Not surprisingly, when I turned pro, Sterling Lord became my agent. With the fellowship, the *SI* sale, and three part-time jobs, I made more money during my year at Columbia than I made in my early years in the real world. A few days after I graduated, I went to work at *Newsweek* for $67.50 a week.

I had no complaints. I had always assumed that choosing a career in journalism was like taking a vow of poverty. I had also assumed that it would be great fun. I was correct on the second count.

9

Pogo and the Idiot Prince

I spent my twenties at *Newsweek*—from 1956 through 1963—and in those years I polished my craft, wrote dozens of freelance magazine articles, published my first three books, and advanced from assistant sports editor to sports editor to general editor to the youngest senior editor in the history of the magazine. I also initiated and sustained friendships with four of the more significant people in my life (Cassius Clay, Bobby Fischer, Lenny Bruce, and Herb Gardner), did irreparable damage to a marriage I had entered pure at the age of twenty-one, and, perhaps by way of explanation, engaged in the first two affairs of my life, one with a wonderful French woman who remained a friend for decades and one with a flirtatious Swede who didn't. I was a boy wonder in my profession, a late bloomer in my social life.

At *Newsweek,* everyone had affairs. Secretaries and researchers were equally fair game. It was considered one of the perks of the job, and too often and too loudly, editors and writers boasted of their conquests. My best friend at the magazine, for instance, had an affair with an admirably endowed secretary, and one night he asked me to keep her company until he could join her late in the evening. I took her to see Lenny Bruce perform at the Village Vanguard. Lenny talked dirty, by the standards of the day, and either his words or his hip manner, or my hand on her knee, aroused the young woman. Me, too.

I took her back to her apartment to wait for my friend, her boyfriend, to arrive. She gave me a drink and showed me her bookcases. She had one shelf to commemorate each of her relationships at *Newsweek*. One editor had given her a collection of naval books. My friend, she told me, had contributed the F. Scott Fitzgerald shelf. I put my arm around her and kissed her. She kissed back, and the phone rang. My friend said he had been delayed and asked to speak to me. "You sure you want me to come over?" he said. "If you just want to be alone with her, it's all right." He was a true friend.

So was I.

"Don't be ridiculous," I said. "Get here as soon as you can."

I went back to his girlfriend. We had another drink, another kiss, and, as lust surfaced, the phone rang again. "You positive you want me to come over?" my friend said. My body said no, but my lips said, "I'm positive."

Eventually, he showed up, my ardor, and his friend's, wasted. I never got a shelf. I might have given her Hemingway, or perhaps a set of the lesser-known Russian novelists.

It was Roger Kahn, the same person who had introduced me to Jackie Robinson, who introduced me to the wonders of *Newsweek*. In 1956, he had not yet written *The Boys of Summer,* but he had left the *Herald Tribune,* paused briefly at *Sports Illustrated,* then moved to *Newsweek* as sports editor. We had stayed in touch, and when he needed an assistant sports editor, he offered me the job. When I started, I told people I was the number two man in the *Newsweek* sports department. It was a two-man sports department.

Four months after I went to work for Roger, the Yankees and the Dodgers reprised the 1955 World Series. I was a newlywed, and on October 8, 1956, with our summer sublease expiring, my wife Barbara and I went apartment hunting. I passed up the baseball game that day. I did not see Don Larsen strike out Dale Mitchell for the final out. I did not see Yogi Berra leap into Larsen's arms after the strikeout. I missed the first, and only, perfect game in World Series history. I think my marriage was in trouble from that day on.

Roger cared about the English language, almost as much as he cared about Roger Kahn. His mother was an English teacher, his father, according to Roger, one of the creators of *Information Please.* Roger taught me how to use the language as a weapon, how to listen for the rhythm of a sentence, how to use punctuation to slow down a reader, or speed him up—or stop him. He taught me to ration adjectives and value transitions. He made me care about every sentence I wrote. He also made me sit and write down the amounts of money he was earning from various sources as a freelance writer and then add them up and let him know how much he was making. Roger was not a great human being, but he was a good teacher.

And *Newsweek,* with all its intrigues, with all its self-justifying editorial second-guessing, was a great place to learn. You covered only the top of the news, only major events, or feature stories with an irresistible angle. You wrote short and tight. The end of the world? Give me eight hundred words. The end of the World Series? Maybe five hundred. You learned to strip away excess verbiage, extraneous detail. You were a minimalist, and even though you made jokes about the bizarre nature of "group journalism"—one editor actually insisted and probably believed that Shakespeare was the first newsmagazine, his plays written by committee and consensus—you took pride in mastering the medium.

The chief danger was that, instead of writing for the reader or, even better, for yourself, you wrote for the editor who was going to run his pencil through your copy. We had one editor who was not terribly bright. He was the heir to the magazine, and his secretary called him the Idiot Prince. They were not having an affair. Once, when the postal service announced that the price of first-class stamps was going up, from four cents to five, as I recall, one member of our staff wrote a reasonably amusing story about a man in the Midwest who, hearing that the price of first-class postage was rising from four to five cents, sent his secretary out to buy as many four-cent stamps as she could. When the story crossed the desk of our Prince, he told *his* secretary to go out and buy as many four-cent stamps as she could.

My favorite editor was the managing editor, Gordon Manning. His picture belonged in the dictionary next to the word "indefatigable." We all worked uncommon schedules at *Newsweek,* with three lazy days of gearing up, then two grueling ones of grinding out. Sleep was an elusive luxury in those last two days, the short gap between leaving the office and returning filled generally by Scotch. By late in the fifth day, I was usually battling exhaustion and migraines, and losing. Gordon was as fresh as he was on the first day. A former sports-writer, later an executive at NBC and ABC, Manning wrote memos by the dozens, and you had to read them all, because one out of every twenty-five ideas would be a beauty.

Manning's boss, the editor in chief, was John Denson, a Louisiana Republican with all the prejudices of both. Denson wore dentures that clicked, and once Manning and a researcher straight from one of the Seven Sister colleges were called into his office and bawled out for some editorial indiscretion. As they emerged, the young woman turned to Manning and said, "Are those nuts Mr. Denson is chewing on?"

"Yeah," Gordon said. "Mine."

I once covered a boxing news conference at which Sugar Ray Robinson, accused of being purely a mercenary, said, "That's not true. There's one guy I'd fight for nothing."

Who?

"Faubus," Robinson said.

I thought it was pretty clever, Ray's reference to the segregationist governor of Arkansas, Orville Faubus, but when I used it in my article, Denson summoned me to his office. "You can't run this," he said, "unless you get Governor Faubus's side."

What could the governor say: "Okay—if it's eight-ounce gloves?"

Robinson's bon mot came out of my story.

When Roger Kahn decided to leave *Newsweek,* I desperately wanted to be his successor. But I was only twenty-five and knew the odds were against me. Denson and Manning took me to lunch at the Park Sheraton Hotel, the hotel in which Albert Anastasia of the Murder Incorporated Anastasias, while having his hair cut, fell victim to ballistics, a scene modified and immortalized in *The Godfather*. Our visit was less exciting. We discussed the job, and at the end of lunch, it was my distinct impression that they had not come to a decision. But as we were leaving the hotel, the venerable Columbia University football coach, Lou Little, happened to be entering. I knew him from my tour as assistant sports information director. Little gave me a big greeting, and Denson and Manning, I surmise, were impressed enough to give me the job.

Incidentally, the best line in the previous paragraph is stolen from its originator, the gifted and erudite son of Ring Lardner, John Lardner, who wrote a weekly column for *Newsweek*. One of my most pleasant and enlightening chores was to fact-check Lardner's column. In three years, I think I found only two factual errors, and Lardner insisted that in one of those cases, despite empirical evidence, he was correct. In one column, John alluded to a lesser Mafia light named Willie Moretti, "who later fell victim to ballistics." Checking Lardner afforded me the opportunity to learn a new word almost every week. John contributed "antepenultimate," among others, to my vocabulary.

Lardner also wrote the best lead, the best opening sentence, I ever read in a magazine article about sports, maybe about anything. "Stanley Ketchel was twenty-four years old," Lardner wrote in *True* magazine in 1954, "when he was fatally shot in the back by the common-law husband of the lady who was cooking his breakfast." He told a complicated dramatic story in one sentence, deftly saving the clincher for the last word. If he had said, "lunch" or "dinner," the story might have been slightly ambiguous. But "breakfast" left only one meaning.

Working for John gave me the opportunity to join him and his friends one day a week at their regular lunch at Bleeck's. A speakeasy during Prohibition, Bleeck's had a sign hanging in front that read, "Artist & Writers Restaurant." Underneath the name, smaller lettering read, "(Formerly Club)."

Naturally, Lardner and his friends formed the Formerly Club, dedicated to drinking and gambling, their vices of choice. Lardner and his closest friend, Walt Kelly, the creator of the comic-strip character Pogo, used to take nitroglycerin pills, for heart conditions. They would lift their pills and say, "Don't anyone move, or we'll blow up this place." Then they would swallow the pills and wash them down with Scotch.

Their corner of the saloon was decorated with framed winning daily double tickets once held by members of the club and framed drawings of "The Match Game" by the humorist James Thurber, an ex officio member. "The Match Game" involved two players or more, equipped with three matches apiece. Each player would then surreptitiously put zero, one, two, or three matches in one fist and hold that fist out in front of him. Then, in order, each of the players would guess the total number of matches in the outthrust fists. The player closest to the correct answer would be eliminated, and the game would go on until only one player remained. He paid for the drinks.

Lardner had a gambler friend, a handicapper in Detroit, whom he called the Wizard. At one meeting of the Formerly Club, Lardner soberly announced that he and the Wizard, mostly the Wizard, had figured out a system to beat the horses, a system that could not lose. The day after the announcement, before he had a chance to reveal the system, Lardner died of a heart attack, only forty-seven years old. The next day, the Wizard died. The members of the Formerly Club were greatly saddened, but not surprised.

None was more saddened than Walt Kelly. Kelly was among the handful of geniuses I have known. He drew and wrote a comic strip that had immense political and sociological significance, composed nonsense songs that made incredible sense ("Deck Us All with Boston Charlie"), and authored two of the more memorable lines in the English language: "We have met the enemy—and he is us" and "We are the people our parents warned us against." I have rarely been prouder than when Kelly used me as the model for a character in *Pogo* named Mr. News Life ("You can leave all the details to me, Mrs. Beetle," Mr. News Life told the insect he was interviewing, "I can arrange all in exchange for exclusive pictures"), when he had two of his swamp creatures invoke my name in a discussion of a football strike ("We write book 'To Have and Hold Out,' no?" says one, and the other replies, "Dang right! And we'll slip it under Schaap's door!"), and, the ultimate acceptance for his friends, when Kelly drew my name on the stern of a boat drifting through the Okefenokee Swamp.

When Lardner, who leaned toward the taciturn, died, I assisted Roger Kahn on the *Newsweek* obituary, and the most beautiful comment came from Kelly. "To be alone with John Lardner," Walt said, "was to enjoy solitude in the best of company."

Among the people I interviewed for the obituary was a man named Stanley Walker, who had been the youngest city editor in the history of the *Herald Tribune.* Walker told me he had hired John as a reporter over the objections of the paper's managing editor, who had inquired, "Is he any relation to that guy who *thinks* he writes funny?" When Walker confirmed the managing editor's suspicion that John Lardner was indeed the son of Ring Lardner, the managing editor said, "I hope he writes better than his old man."

Walt Kelly outlived Lardner by more than a decade, coping gamely and grumpily with heart disease and diabetes. Kelly believed strongly that groaning was good for you. One day, after Kelly lost a leg to diabetes, Jimmy Breslin and I visited him at his home not far from Gracie Mansion, the residence of the mayor of New York City. Kelly had moved into a bedroom at the front of the first floor of the brownstone in which he lived. When we walked in, Walt lay on his bed, deliberately exposing his stump. He looked at us and shook his head. "I can't do anything," he said. "I can't get up. I can't walk. I can't go anywhere. Until it grows back."

During my early years at *Newsweek,* I rarely interviewed anyone younger than I. Probably the first was the boxer Floyd Patterson, a gentle man outside the ring who had overcome a troubled childhood to become an Olympic gold medalist and then the heavyweight champion of the world. He was my junior by ten weeks, and he won the title six months after I joined *Newsweek.*

Floyd let me, and other reporters, into his life, shared his dreams and fears with us, opened up the way wary athletes no longer open up to the media. The day of one of his most important fights, his third title bout against Ingemar Johansson of Sweden, he permitted Gay Talese and me to hang out with him, first in his rented home in Miami Beach, then in his dressing room. Only a few hours before the bout, Floyd and I played tonk, the five-card rummy game, and as the fight approached, and the tension built, Patterson appeared increasingly tired. He yawned as he played his cards and, perhaps an hour before the fight, he dozed off. I don't think I ever met another athlete who reacted to nervousness by going to sleep. I was a couple of dollars ahead at the time.

I admired Floyd, and liked him, and suffered with him when, later in his career, he took harsh beatings from Sonny Liston and Muhammad Ali. After forty years of our friendship, when Floyd entered his sixties, I saw his memory fade and his mind begin to betray him, and I was reminded of how much I liked so many boxers and how much I hated their cruel game. I do not understand how a civilized society not only tolerates but rewards a sport in which the object is for one man to separate another from his senses. Boxing, not coincidentally, has inspired brilliant writing, from Ring Lardner to Bill Heinz to Ernest Hemingway to Norman Mailer to Joyce Carol Oates, but the literature of the sport does not compensate for its barbarism.

In 1958, when I was twenty-three, I met a sports champion fully nine years younger than I. I watched Bobby Fischer, at the age of fourteen, win the U.S. chess championship, and I was fascinated by him. He became a prized piece in my people collection, at least a bishop, maybe a rook. He could anticipate countless chess moves, but he sometimes forgot which subway took him from the Manhattan Chess Club to his home in Brooklyn. I helped him find his way and, occasionally, played tennis with him on the Brooklyn College courts not far from his apartment. I told people I beat Bobby Fischer, but I failed to mention at which game.

I took Bobby to watch the New York Knicks play basketball and the Rangers play hockey. At one especially dramatic Knicks game, we sat courtside, and as

the home team rallied and the partisan crowd behind us
grew louder and more frenzied, Bobby, accustomed to
the reverent silence of a chess battle, turned to me and
asked, "Are they dangerous?"

After the game, I guided Bobby to the Knicks'
locker room and introduced him to Dave DeBusschere,
the gifted forward who happened to be a chess buff.
"How'd you like the game?" DeBusschere asked.

"It was good," Bobby said.

"Was it exciting?" DeBusschere said.

"Yes," Bobby said.

"As exciting as a chess match?"

"No."

I often watched Bobby play chess. He taught me that
it was a blood game. "You crush your opponent's ego,"
he said. Once, I saw Bobby, playing the white pieces,
start a game by moving pawn to king four, a pre-
dictable opening. His opponent visibly began to trem-
ble. Twenty minutes passed before he could get his
nerves under control and make *his* first move. Not unlike Mike Tyson, a later world champion from Brooklyn, Bobby loved to intimidate.

I rarely saw Bobby in the 1960s. Not many people
did. I didn't get to any chess tournaments, and he didn't
get to many. After a few abortive bids for the world
championship, trying to fight his way through chal-
lengers' rounds against large fields, Bobby gave up in
disgust and distrust. He was convinced that in the chal-
lengers' tournaments, the Russians, eager to keep the
world championship in the Soviet Union, ganged up on
him, played lackadaisical draws against each other, and
saved their mental and physical strength for games
against him. Bobby believed, beyond doubt, that he
was the best player in the world, but was convinced the

Russians would never let him prove it. He withdrew from competition, but not from chess. Ten, twelve hours a day, he studied, practiced, polished his game.

Then, at the start of the 1970s, over the objections of the Russians, the system for selecting a challenger for the world championship was changed. The size of the field in the early rounds was reduced; the survivors would meet in head-to-head elimination matches. Bobby stormed through the competition, crushing everyone's ego, at one point winning twenty-one matches in a row, not a loss, not a draw, one of the most remarkable winning streaks in any sport at any time. By then, I was delivering the sports news at 6 and 11 P.M. on WNBC in New York, and I devoted considerable time to the matches and marveled at the results. The denizens of the chess world appreciated the coverage and when Bobby returned to the United States, after earning the right to face Boris Spassky for the world championship, he and I renewed our friendship.

I invited him to a party I gave in my apartment in New York, and Peter Falk was fascinated by Fischer—"An absolutely straight line," Peter said, "just one thing on his mind"—who was fascinated, in turn, by Jerry Lucas, a basketball player for the New York Knicks who had a photographic memory, and, for the pleasure of himself and others, had memorized sizable chunks of the Manhattan phone book.

Bobby's own memory, away from the chessboard, had not noticeably improved. We went out to lunch one day, accompanied by a friend of mine, and Bobby promptly sat down at a table for two.

Bobby's paranoia, his suspicion that the worlds inside and outside chess plotted against him, blossomed. He saw a cloud in every silver lining. He rejected generous offers. He issued unreasonable ultimatums. He delayed his departure to Iceland, the site selected for the match against Spassky for the world championship. He forced the competition to be postponed. He detected conspiracies everywhere. The Russians were trying to poison his orange juice; they were telephoning his hotel room at ungodly hours to disturb his rest; they had sabotaged his chair to make him uncomfortable.

I covered the story from New York, and at one point, I called Dr. Reuben Fine, the former vice president of the American Institute for Psychoanalysis and himself an international grand master of chess. He had written an intriguing book, *Psychoanalytic Observations on Chess and Chess Masters,* which proved beyond reasonable doubt that every world champion who was deceased had been crazy. Dr. Fine did not analyze any living world champions, who might have reacted litigiously.

"Dr. Fine," I said, "I realize you can't psychoanalyze someone who is two thousand miles away, that wouldn't be ethical, and I know you haven't seen Bobby in a while, but I'd like to interview you on television just about the psychological stress of high-level tournament chess."

Dr. Fine said that would be acceptable. I went to his home in Connecticut, and my crew set up in his yard. He came out and, on camera, I repeated what I had said on the phone, that Dr. Fine hadn't seen Bobby lately, that he could not ethically analyze anyone thousands of miles away. "Doctor," I said, "considering the current situation in Iceland, where Bobby Fischer is threatening to pull out of the Spassky match, where he is accusing the Russians of every conceivable tactic to disconcert him, where Fischer seems to be endanger-

ing his chances to win the championship he has sought
for so many years, could you tell us a little about the
psychological stress of championship chess?"

Dr. Fine took a short breath, stared straight into the
camera, and said, "Bobby is obviously schizophrenic . . ."

The funny part was that Dr. Fine's diagnosis was remarkably accurate.

Fischer, however, did eventually focus on the match,
and as the end approached, as the championship
seemed to be within Bobby's grasp, I went to Iceland
for NBC. When I arrived, Bobby needed to win only
one more game to capture the title. I watched the decisive game on closed-circuit TV in an anteroom in the
chess hall in Reykjavik, flanked by three American
grand masters—William Lombardy, Larry Evans, and
Robert Byrne. I followed the early moves, but the strategy was far too sophisticated for me to comprehend. I
turned to the grand masters for counsel. One assured
me Spassky had the stronger position, another assured
me Fischer did, and the third said a draw seemed likely.

The game was suspended after forty moves, standard procedure, with Spassky sealing his forty-first
move. That night, I went to dinner with Lothar Schmid,
a West German who refereed the championship match,
and Dr. Max Euwe, the president of the World Chess
Federation and a former world champion. To our surprise, Bobby Fischer walked into the same restaurant,
accompanied by William Lombardy and a pocket
chessboard. Fischer kept studying his options, and
Spassky's. "Bobby has a sure win," Lombardy said.

Euwe nodded, and Schmid said, "Spassky is lost. I
would not be surprised if he resigned tomorrow without appearing."

The next day, Spassky resigned without appearing.

He conceded game, match, and championship to Fischer. When I saw Bobby an hour later in his hotel room, he was still studying the game he had already won. "Would you have resigned if you had been in Spassky's position?" I asked him.

"No," Fischer said, convinced that he, and no one else, would have figured out a way to win.

When Fischer returned from winning the championship, in the fall of 1972, the mayor of New York, John Lindsay, honored him at a reception in front of City Hall. I was the master of ceremonies, presumably because I was the only person who had covered both City Hall and chess. I saw Bobby infrequently after that day. He discarded me, as he discarded so many friends, as if we were lower than pawns.

Once, after Bobby moved to the West Coast and paranoia led him to forfeit his championship, I was in Los Angeles visiting Wilt Chamberlain at Wilt's palatial home on a hill above the city. I sent word to Bobby, through a friend of his, that I would like to see him and that I was reachable at Wilt's. I left the phone number.

Bobby soon called back. "Are you really at Wilt's house?" he asked.

I assured him I was. "I'd really like to see that house," Bobby said.

"Would you like to join us for dinner?" I said.

"I'd like to," Bobby said, "but I'm not seeing people."

I haven't seen Bobby since then, not since he added virulent anti-Semitism to his store of neuroses and psychoses. Once, I tried to reach him for an article I was writing for *Games* magazine and was told, through an intermediary, that Bobby was now charging $25,000 an interview. I asked if he would take a check.

10

The Greatest of *My* Time

In 1960, within weeks after I became sports editor of *Newsweek,* I met Cassius Marcellus Clay, eighteen years old and brash and wide-eyed and naive and shrewd, a bubbling young man without a serious thought in his head, without a problem that he didn't feel his fists or his wit would eventually solve.

I was hanging around the New York hotel where the American Olympic team had assembled, picking up anecdotes and background material I could use for long-distance coverage of the Games in Rome. I had a couple of friends on the team. One was a long jumper named Bo Roberson, who was, I always maintained, the best pure athlete ever to compete for Cornell. He followed Meredith Gourdine, and their track-and-field skills were similar; like Gourdine eight years earlier, Roberson won a silver Olympic medal in the long jump in Rome in 1960. Later, Roberson played football for the Oakland Raiders. He starred in basketball, too, for Cornell. The other 1960 Olympian I knew was

Ira Davis, a triple-jumper from Philadelphia who had played on the same Overbrook High School basketball team as Wilt Chamberlain. Roberson and Davis told me I had to meet this kid Cassius Clay.

He was a light-heavyweight, fresh out of high school. He was supposed to be one of the two best pro prospects on the U.S. team; the other was a light-middleweight named Wilbert "Skeeter" McClure, a college student from Toledo, Ohio. I offered to show them, and a couple of other American boxers, around New York, to take them to Harlem and introduce them to Sugar Ray Robinson. Young Cassius leaped at the invitation, the chance to meet the man whose extraordinary skills and style he dreamed of matching. Sugar Ray meant big money and fancy cars and flashy women, and if anyone had told Cassius Clay then that someday he would choose a course of action that scorned those values, the teenager would have laughed and laughed and laughed.

I wasn't just being hospitable, offering to escort the boxers. As usual, I was looking for a story. I never dreamed I would find one so monumental, so enduring.

On the ride uptown in a taxi, Cassius turned the conversation into a monologue. I forget his exact words, but I remember the message: I'm great, I'm beautiful, I'm going to Rome, and I'm gonna whip all those cats, and then I'm coming back and turning pro and becoming the champion of the world. I'm pretty sure he did say, "I am the greatest." He didn't add "of all time" until a few years later.

I'd never heard an athlete like him; he had no doubts, no fears, no second thoughts, not an ounce of false humility. (Bobby Fischer was similar in one way: Each believed he was the best who ever played his game,

and each was probably right.) Clay was outrageously
bold, and yet his wink and his smile let you know that
he wasn't a megalomaniac, he was a showman.

"Don't mind him," McClure, more serious, more
thoughtful, said amiably. "That's just the way he is."

We were kids in the car, all three of us. Clay was
eighteen, McClure twenty-one, and I twenty-five. It
would have been ridiculous to think that almost forty
years later, when Dr. McClure was a graying psychologist practicing in Chestnut Hill, Massachusetts, and
Clay/Ali an internationally beloved figure suffering
from Parkinson's syndrome, we would all still be
friends, sharing rides and meals and laughs—Ali still
insisting he was the greatest, McClure and I still con-
curring.

Barry Gottehrer, who was my assistant sports editor
at *Newsweek* and eventually my successor, accompanied us on the trip to Harlem. (Coincidentally, almost a
decade later, as an aide to Mayor Lindsay, Gottehrer
was responsible for keeping the streets of Harlem from
erupting in violence.) Barry and I made a modest bet
the night we met Clay and McClure. I said Clay would
become a world champion first, Barry picked McClure.

Skeeter gave it a good run. He won his first fourteen
professional fights, and Teddy Brenner, the knowledgeable boxing matchmaker for Madison Square Garden,
told me years later that McClure, at that stage of his career, was a better prospect than Sugar Ray Leonard was
almost two decades later. But then McClure, poorly
managed, was thrown in with three seasoned fighters
who were too strong for him, two of them world champions, Jose Torres and Luis Rodriguez. All three
whipped him, and Skeeter's career declined. He never
won a championship, and Gottehrer never paid me.

When we reached Sugar Ray's bar on Seventh Avenue, near 124th Street, Robinson hadn't shown up yet, and Cassius wandered outside. At the corner of 125th Street, a black man, perched on a soapbox, preached to a small crowd. He was advocating something that now seems remarkably mild—his message, I recall, was buy black, black goods from black merchants—but Cassius seemed stunned. He couldn't believe that a black man would get up in public and inveigh against white America. He shook his head in wonderment. "How can he talk like that?" Cassius said. "Ain't he gonna get in trouble?"

A few minutes later, when a purple Cadillac pulled up in front of the bar, Cassius literally jumped out of his seat. "Here he comes," he shouted. "Here comes the great man Robinson."

I introduced them to each other, the once and future kings of their sport, and Sugar Ray, in his bored, superior way, autographed a picture of himself, presented it to Cassius, wished the kid luck in the Olympics, smiled, and drifted away, handsome and lithe and sparkling. In the previous decade, Sugar Ray Robinson had been the biggest name in boxing; in the following, Cassius Clay would become infinitely bigger.

Cassius clutched the precious picture. "That Sugar Ray, he's something," the youngster said. "Someday *I'm* going to own *two* Cadillacs—and a Ford for just getting around in."

Within a couple of days, Clay and McClure and the rest of the U.S. Olympians flew off to Rome, and soon reports filtered back to me, from *Newsweek* correspondents, that young Cassius was the unofficial mayor of the Olympic Village, the most friendly and familiar figure among thousands of resident athletes. He strolled from one national area to the next, trading greetings, snapping pictures with his box camera. He took hundreds of photographs—of Russians, Chinese, Ethiopians, Italians, anyone within camera range. And when reporters from Europe and Asia and Africa lured Clay into discussions of racial friction in the United States, he would say, "Oh, we got problems, man, but we're working 'em out. It's still the bestest country in the world."

Cassius Clay won the Olympic light-heavyweight boxing championship, Skeeter McClure the Olympic light-middleweight championship. When Cassius flew home, I met him at New York's international airport, which was then called Idlewild. Within five years, both the airport and the fighter had changed their names. Jimmy the Greek would have given me terrific odds on that.

I took the new Olympic champion to the Waldorf-Astoria Hotel. He was staying in the Waldorf Towers, the elite section of the hotel, in a sprawling suite halfway between Douglas MacArthur's and Herbert Hoover's, provided by Billy Reynolds, who lived in Louisville, belonged to the Reynolds aluminum family, and wanted to become Clay's manager.

(At one point, I contemplated investing in the young fighter, a small investment, perhaps a thousand dollars. My first wife, Barbara, vetoed the idea. She thought it too risky. She is a good person, but I have never forgiven her for that.)

Clay and I had dinner at the Bull and Bear restaurant in the Waldorf, and he ordered steak with all the trimmings. When he finished, he asked if it would be all right if he had seconds, of everything. He had worked up a hunger in Rome, and I had an expense account.

After dinner, we went out to celebrate his Olympic

victory. Cassius was an imposing sight, not only for his developing light-heavyweight's build, 180 pounds spread like silk over a six-foot-two frame. He was wearing his blue Olympic blazer, with USA embroidered upon it, and dangling around his neck was his gold Olympic medal, engraved PUGILATO. For forty-eight hours, ever since an Olympic dignitary had draped the medal on him, Clay had worn it, awake and asleep. "First time I ever slept on my back," he said. "Had to, or that medal would've cut my chest."

We started our victory tour in Times Square, and, almost immediately, a passerby did a double take and said, "Say, aren't you Cassius Clay?"

Cassius's eyes opened wide. "Yeah, man," he said, "that's me. How'd you know who I is?"

"I saw you on TV," the man said. "Saw you beat that Pole in the final. Everybody knows who you are."

"Really?" Clay said, fingering his gold medal. "You really know who I is? That's wonderful."

Dozens of strangers recognized him on Broadway, and Cassius swelled with delight, spontaneous and natural. "I guess everybody do know who I is," he conceded.

At a penny arcade, Cassius had a bogus newspaper printed with the headline: CLAY SIGNS FOR PATTERSON FIGHT. "Back home," he said, "they'll think it's real. They won't know the difference."

He took three copies of the newspaper, jammed them in his pocket, and we moved on, to Jack Dempsey's landmark restaurant. "The champ around?" Cassius asked a waiter.

"No, Mr. Dempsey's out of town," the waiter said.

Cassius turned and stared at a glass case, filled with cheesecakes. "What are them?" he asked the waiter.

"Cheesecakes."

"Do you have to eat the whole thing," Cassius said, "or can you just get a little piece?"

Cassius got a big piece of cheesecake, a glass of milk, and a roast beef sandwich. When the check arrived, and I reached for it, he asked to see it. He looked and handed it back. The three items came to something like three and a half dollars; this was 1960. "Man," he said, "that's too much money. We coulda gone next door"—there was a Nedick's hot dog stand nearby— "and had a lot more to eat for a whole lot less money."

From Dempsey's, we went to Birdland, a jazz shrine that died in the 1960s, and as we stood at the bar, with Cassius holding a Coke—"and put a drop of whiskey in it," he told the bartender—someone turned to him and said, "You're Cassius Clay, aren't you?"

"*You* know who I is, too?" Cassius said.

Later, in a cab cruising through Manhattan, Cassius had to admit he was famous. "Why," he said, leaning forward and tapping the cabdriver on the shoulder, "I bet even you know that I'm Cassius Clay, the great fighter."

"Sure, Mac," the cabbie said, and Cassius took that as positive identification.

In Harlem, after a stroll along Seventh Avenue, Cassius and I paused in a café on 125th Street, and a young woman there knew who he was, too. She twirled his gold medal in her fingers and said she wouldn't mind if Cassius would like to take her home. She had a girlfriend with her, and first we walked the girlfriend to her apartment house at 135th Street. I walked with the friend, Cassius behind me with *his* friend. Cassius and his friend kept falling farther behind. It was Harlem, and late and dark, and I was white. "Please try to keep up," I called to Clay. We dropped the first young lady off, then took Cassius's friend home, the three of us in a cab. We stopped in front of her home on a Harlem side street, and Cassius walked her to her door. "Take your time," I said. "I'm in no hurry. I'll wait in the cab."

He was out in thirty seconds.

"That was quick," I said.

"Man," he said, "I'm in training. I can't fool with no girls."

Finally, well past midnight, we wound up in Cassius's suite at the Waldorf Towers. He insisted I look at the hundreds of photographs he had taken in Rome, and I was too tired to argue. After an hour of snapshots, Clay gave me one of the bedrooms in the suite and said good night. "Cassius," I said, "you're gonna have to explain to my wife tomorrow why I didn't get home tonight."

"You mean," he said, "*your wife* knows who I is, too?"

A few months later, after Clay turned professional, I traveled to Louisville to spend a few days with him as he prepared for his pro debut against a West Virginia sheriff named Tunney Hunsaker.

In 1960, segregation still flourished in Louisville, backed up by Jim Crow laws that kept whites and blacks apart. Cassius Clay and I could not eat together at any restaurant in downtown Louisville. We ate every night at the same place, a small restaurant in the black section of town, and every night Clay ordered the same main course, a two-pound sirloin. Nothing larger than a one-pound sirloin was mentioned on the menu.

"How'd you know they served two-pound steaks?" I asked Cassius the third or fourth night.

"Man," he said, "when I found out you were coming down here, I went in and told them to order some."

While I was in Louisville, Jackie Robinson came to town to appear at a Nixon-for-president rally. Clay and I went to the rally. Robinson shared the spotlight with Kentucky's two Republican senators, John Sherman Cooper and Thruston Morton. Each of the three endorsed Richard Nixon. Robinson said that when he was a child, his mother told him not to trust anyone who couldn't look him in the eye, and John F. Kennedy, he said, couldn't look him in the eye. Years later, I used to tease Rachel Robinson by reminding her that I had seen and heard her husband at a Nixon rally. She insisted it was only a brief aberration.

A decade later, I almost wrote the autobiography of Muhammad Ali. I received a phone call late one night from California, from Bob Gutwillig, a fellow Cornellian who had edited three of my earliest books, *Instant Replay, Turned On,* and *RFK,* one on football, one on drug addiction, and one on politics. "I've got someone who wants to talk to you," Gutwillig said.

He put Ali on the phone. "My man," Muhammad said, "I have had my choice of all the nigger writers in America, and I have chosen you to write my book for me."

I told him I was delighted. "It's about time you picked a good white man," I said.

"You ain't no white man," Ali said. "You a Jew. You half-nigger."

Ali's humor may sound sometimes as if it borders on the racist, but, if you listen carefully, you can hear him mocking and skewering ethnic stereotypes. ("Didja hear about the black man, the Mexican, and the Puerto Rican sitting in the backseat of a car?" he asked me many years later. "Guess who's driving." I said, "Who?" And Ali said, "The police.")

The Black Muslims who surrounded Ali at the time eventually persuaded him to use an African-American coauthor, which disqualified me. I was disappointed, of course. I wanted to write his story, but not as much as I wanted to write DiMaggio's, or Sinatra's. The difference was that Ali had never kept secrets. He had little new to reveal, which probably explains why his autobiography turned out to be a commercial dud.

11

"The Wit in the Mirror"

Less than two months after I met Cassius Clay, I met Lenny Bruce. At the beginning, I didn't notice any similarities. I had no idea they both would take unpopular stands based on principle. They both would go up against the Establishment and the law, and both be convicted of violating conventional beliefs. They would become Causes.

In October 1960, *Newsweek* dispatched me to cover the World Series between the Pittsburgh Pirates and the New York Yankees. The Series went seven games, and the first two, and the last two, were played in Pittsburgh. In those days, World Series games were played in daylight, as God and Abner Doubleday, if either of them ever existed, intended. The nights were free, giving the players time to think about the game, and me the chance to go to a nightclub on the outskirts of town where Lenny Bruce was appearing. I caught his act the night before each of the four games in Pittsburgh.

I had heard of Lenny Bruce. *Time* magazine had labeled him the sickest of the so-called sick comics, a label *Time* justified by quoting Bruce's comment on the Loeb and Leopold murder case. "Bobby Franks was a snotty kid, anyway," Bruce said. You had to be sick to take that remark seriously; Bruce, as usual, was eviscerating clichés and stereotypes.

But I had never seen Bruce perform, and didn't realize that he and I had spent a good part of our teens in the same town—he, too, lived in Freeport—and had attended rival high schools. I went to Freeport, Lenny to Mepham; his name then was Leonard Alfred Schneider; mine was Dick Schaap.

The first night I saw Lenny work, the crowd was slim, but the performance stunning. I had never heard anyone like Lenny. He had a straight man traveling with him, a young black musician named Eric Miller, and the act began with a dialogue mocking the hypocrisies of the time.

"Are you in show business?" Lenny asked.

"Yes, I am," Eric said.

Lenny paused. "Do you know Aunt Jemima?" he finally asked.

"No, I don't."

"How about the fellow on the Cream of Wheat box?" No luck there, either.

"You're a nice fellow," Lenny decided. "I'd like you to come over to my house. When my sister's not there, of course."

Pause.

"You understand," Lenny said.

Lenny took on segregation, conventional morality, the Catholic Church, sexual mores, everything. He dialed VAT 69 to call the pope; to the beat of a bongo, he gleefully contemplated and conjugated the verb "to come"; he counted the house as if it were a bridge hand, "There's four dykes, three kikes, two spades— double." He threw in jazz talk and Jewish words, and said Eleanor Roosevelt had great tits, and the Jews didn't crucify Christ, they drove a silver stake through his heart. "We did it for his own good," Lenny said. "He was a werewolf." At that point, a few uneasy Jews, wary of offended gentiles, usually walked out of the nightclub.

After his performance each night in Pittsburgh, Lenny sat down with me, probably because I had listened and laughed. Each night, I brought a sampling of sportswriters to the club, and since most of us were New Yorkers and Jewish and thought we were hip, we made up a receptive audience. We outnumbered the other patrons.

The locals in the audience did not seem to get Lenny. Or maybe they got him and didn't like what they got, with one exception. At the time, the mantra for Pirate fans was "Beat 'em Bucs." The slogan was everywhere, on billboards and banners. As part of his act, Lenny broke open his mezuzah—the symbol of his religious faith that he wore around his neck—pulled out a small parchment scroll, and read, "Beat 'em Bucs."

They got that one in Pittsburgh.

The night before the Series ended, I invited Lenny to go with me to Forbes Field for the seventh and final game, and he accepted. He told me he had never been to a big-league baseball game.

Fittingly, the 1960 World Series was a bizarre one. In the first six games between the Yankees of Mickey Mantle and Yogi Berra, and the Pirates of Roberto Clemente, the favored Yankees outscored the Pirates, 46–17. Incredibly, Pittsburgh won three of those games, by one run, two runs, and three. The Yankees won the other three, 16–3, 10–0, and 12–0. Never were two dead-even teams so uneven.

In the seventh, the decisive game, the Yankees threatened to bury the Pirates again. They led, 7–4, going into the bottom of the eighth inning, three runs coming on a home run by Berra. But as Yogi knew instinctively, and as I was reminded that day, it ain't over till it's over.

In the bottom of the eighth inning, after a pinch-hit single, Pittsburgh's Bill Virdon cracked a ground ball to shortstop that looked like a certain double play. But the ball took a weird hop, and instead of slamming into Tony Kubek's glove, skipped into his larynx, leveling him. Both runners were safe, igniting a rally that cut the Yankees' lead to one run, 7–6, with two out and two men on base.

Then a catcher named Hal Smith—one of two Hal Smiths who caught for the Pirates during the 1960s; this one played the guitar and wrote one of my favorite country songs, "I Got a Stomach Full of Chitlins and a Bellyful of You"—drove a home run over the left-field wall, and Pittsburgh led, 9–7, going into the ninth inning. Lenny roared with the rest of the Pittsburgh crowd. "Beat 'em Bucs," he said.

In the top of the ninth, with one out and the tying runs on base, Mickey Mantle came to bat. Mantle drove in one run with a single, and then on the next play staged a nifty bit of base running that enabled the tying run to score.

The crowd was subdued, but only briefly.

Leading off in the bottom of the ninth inning, the Pittsburgh second baseman, Bill Mazeroski, hit Ralph Terry's second pitch high over the head of Yogi Berra, who was playing left field, high over the left-field wall. One of the most dramatic games ever played, in any sport, came to an abrupt end: Pirates 10, Yankees 9.

It was the first time in baseball history that a World Series, and a season, had ended with a home run.

When the ball cleared the fence, Mazeroski, rounding first base, jumped in the air, whipped off his batting helmet, and began whirling his right arm, like a cheerleader gone berserk. For a moment, Mazeroski was the only Pirate on the field, a solitary symbol of happiness among nine gray-suited symbols of gloom.

Then fans and teammates exploded onto the field, bursting past a cordon of policemen so wildly happy themselves they barely slowed the tide. Mazeroski was mobbed, crushed, embraced, adored. Downtown, the streets swelled with people and paper, celebrants and confetti. Car horns honked, and strangers hugged in a blast furnace of joy.

"C'mon," I told Lenny, "let's go."

We made our way from the press section to the locker room. The mayor of Pittsburgh was having trouble getting in. Lenny and I breezed past him with our press passes, one legitimate, the other borrowed. Dick Stuart, the Pittsburgh first baseman, later known as Dr. Strangeglove, for ample reason, sprayed both of us with champagne and beer. Lenny loved the theatricality of the game and of the locker-room celebration.

Lenny, wisely, never went to another baseball game.

Ten weeks later, after I saw him work at Basin Street East in New York, the same place where I later saw Bill Cosby and Barbra Streisand for the first time (she was the opening act for Benny Goodman and she sang a song that went, in its entirety, "You better not shout, you better not cry, you better not pout, I'm telling you why, Santa Claus is dead"), I wrote a profile of Bruce for *Newsweek.* "Lenny Bruce, slim and catlike in a blue sports shirt and tight black slacks," I began the article, "paced back and forth across his small New York hotel room, punctuating his words with long pauses and constant gestures. 'Sometimes,' he said, 'I look at life in the fun mirror at a carnival. I see myself as a profound, incisive wit, concerned with man's inhumanity to man. Then I stroll to the next mirror and I see a pompous, subjective ass whose humor is hardly spiritual.' "

I suggested a headline for the story, "The Wit in the Mirror," and John Denson, the editor who had spared Governor Faubus from Sugar Ray Robinson's jab, changed it to "The Ass in the Mirror." I argued, strenuously, and for once I won.

"How does [Lenny] work?" I wrote. "He stands on the periphery of the major problems of the time, darts in, jabs his needle, draws blood and then darts away. Mixing bop talk, multisyllabic erudition and four-letter obscenities, he moves back and considers the damage. Sometimes, mumbling and snapping his fingers, he rushes in and opens the wound wider. Sometimes, he closes it partially."

Lenny liked the story. He loved the headline.

On February 4, 1961, only four months after I'd met him, on the night of a twenty-inch snowstorm that staggered New York City, Bruce gave a midnight performance at Carnegie Hall. To my astonishment, and his, the audience filled every seat in the historic hall. Lenny paid the fanatics back with one of his best performances. Forty-five minutes into his act, he mentioned me by name. In one sentence, he spoke of Arthur Gelb from the *Times,* a gossip columnist from *The National Enquirer,* and—"Dick Schaap, *Newsweek.*" I was sitting in the balcony, and even if I did get third billing, I felt I had achieved the ultimate in recognition.

The following day, Bruce and I were walking down Forty-sixth Street in Manhattan, between Sixth and Seventh Avenues, near his low-rent suite in the Hotel America. Only a narrow path had been shoveled through the sidewalk snow. A black delivery boy, a teenager, came toward us on a bicycle, filling the path. Lenny jumped out of the way, and at the same moment, the young cyclist swerved. Accidentally, he ran into Lenny and pinned him to the wall. Lenny didn't hesitate for a second. "That's why they don't let you people on the buses," he said.

Even the kid laughed.

Lenny and I spent a good deal of time together during the last six years of his life. I visited him at a variety of aging New York hotels, the America in midtown, the Earl in Greenwich Village. I liked to watch Lenny listening to himself on tape. He recorded many of his performances, then studied them, trying to figure out what he should add, what he should cut, what he should refine. He was not a tough audience. For instance, every time he said "fuck," he laughed. I was sitting in one of Lenny's hotel rooms when Allen Ginsberg, the beat poet, called to say he had seen Lenny's act the night before and had loved it and knew that he couldn't really do anything in return, but that if Lenny ever needed a great blow job . . .

Once, I picked Bruce up after his late-night second show at the Village Vanguard, and we went out to eat. We went to an East Side spot called the Brasserie, which was new then, and in, and stayed open twenty-four hours a day. Lenny was typically disheveled—black pants, black shirt, unshaven, haunted—and the maître d' took one look at him and led us to a corner table, so that we would not blight the view of more fashionable customers.

A few minutes later, a young comedian named London Lee came in, dressed formally and impeccably, with an equally impeccable blonde on his arm. They were ushered to a choice table. Lee sat down, spotted Lenny, and came over to our table. "Excuse me, Mr. Bruce," he said, "but my name is London Lee and your mother gave me my start in show business and I'm opening Monday night at the Living Room and I'd love you to come and see my act."

Lenny barely looked up. "I never watch anyone else work," he said.

End of conversation.

A few years later, after Lenny died, I played golf one day with Buddy Hackett at his club in Englewood, New Jersey, a sporting haven for comics. Buddy lived close by in Fort Lee in a house that once belonged to a godfather, the head of the Anastasia crime family. When Buddy moved in, a sign by the front door warned strangers, "If you are found here in the evening, you will be found here in the morning." Buddy did not take the sign down.

When we finished our round, Buddy and I went into the clubhouse for lunch. A couple of minutes later, London Lee walked in, and Buddy introduced us. "I met you once before," I said to Lee. "It was about three o'clock in the morning at the Brasserie, and I was with Lenny Bruce."

"Oh, yes, I remember," London Lee said. "Lenny got up and came over to my table and wished me luck with my act."

I would not be the least surprised if London Lee actually believed that that was the way it happened, just as, a few years later, when I was covering the Sam Sheppard murder retrial, Sheppard, after a decade in prison, actually seemed to believe that, contrary to all evidence, he had not murdered his wife. (Most of us know what it's like to have a dream in which you commit a terrible act, a dream so real that when you wake up and realize you were dreaming, you feel incredibly relieved. Similarly, I think some people who truly commit terrible acts convince themselves they were only dreaming.) The mind is a wonderful thing.

I suspect my mind, too, might play a few tricks on me in recalling the events and conversations recounted in these pages, and even though I have not intentionally altered, distorted, or exaggerated, I am prepared to plead guilty to an occasional misdemeanor in these areas. Like Sam Sheppard, however, I am not prepared to plead guilty to capital crimes.

When I finished my *Newsweek* tour at the end of 1963, Lenny's career was at risk, not because he had become any less witty, or clever, or incisive, but because the police and the courts had decided he was a threat to decency and had begun to harass him, to monitor his appearances and arrest him for obscenity. (If the same laws against obscenity were enforced similarly at the end of the twentieth century, no more than two or three comedians would be walking the streets free.)

My brother Bill, then a law student at the University of Chicago, helped one of his professors who was defending Lenny against obscenity charges in Chicago. I returned to Lenny's cause when I got to the *Herald Tribune*. We Freeport guys stuck together.

12

"What a Strange Face to See in the Nuthouse!"

Early in my *Newsweek* days, I was granted a six-month leave of absence to fulfill my obligation to serve in the United States Army. Thanks to the Reserve Officers Training Corps at Cornell, I was a second lieutenant serving in a time of peace, between wars and police actions. I spent my active duty in Petersburg, Virginia, stationed at Fort Lee, the headquarters of the Quartermaster Corps.

For six months, I had no real responsibilities, deadlines, or pressure, no one to answer to except my commanding officer in the public information office, a relaxed captain who came from Tennessee and every day at lunch guzzled a pint of Jack Daniel's bourbon, to support what he said was the only industry worth saving in his native state. I wrote for the local newspaper, the Petersburg *Progress-Index,* and for the base newspaper, the Fort Lee *Traveller,* named after Robert E. Lee's horse, who was not a spelling purist. I covered the Second Army baseball and golf championships.

At the baseball games, I met Bill White, a bright man, a college man, who had played one full season for the New York Giants before being drafted, and we became friends for life. Once, as we were driving in segregated Virginia, Bill turned to me and said, "You know, I believe in Hammurabi's Code, an eye for an eye and a tooth for a tooth. For every Negro who's lynched, one white man should be lynched." Later, when Bill, after a successful playing and broadcasting career, became the highest-ranking African-American official in baseball, the president of the National League, he was considerably more circumspect. I preferred his earlier spontaneity.

When I came out of the Army, I was obligated to spend seven and a half years in the reserve, with two-week tours of active duty each summer. One summer, I served two weeks with the 101st Airborne at Fort Campbell, Kentucky. Almost every day, I went up in a plane with a platoon of paratroopers and everyone jumped except me. Deep into the night, I drank and played cards with the pilots, who, only a few hours later, would fly in precariously tight formation.

I was a public information officer, ground-bound, a "leg," in the vernacular of the paratroopers. The commanding officer of the platoon was a lieutenant named William Carpenter, who had played football at West Point in the late 1950s and had become known as the Lonely End because, following orders from Coach Red Blaik, he kept out of his team's huddles, stationed himself near the sidelines, and received the plays through foot signals from his teammates. Carpenter later won the Silver Star in Vietnam for calling in artillery fire on his own position.

Carpenter was the best soldier I ever saw, a quintessential leader, never asking his men to do anything he wouldn't do first. He rose to general, and in 1988, when the Olympic Games were held in Seoul, and he was the second-ranking American officer in Korea, and I was covering the Games, I phoned him to say hello. "General Carpenter," I said, "my name is Dick Schaap and I'm with ABC, and you probably don't remember me, but I was assigned to your platoon at Fort Campbell in the early sixties."

"You're right," General Carpenter said. "I don't remember you."

In the fall of 1962, I was sent to the Pentagon for two weeks to serve my country as a public information officer for the Conseil Internationale du Sport Militaire, a sort of military Olympics. When I reported to the Pentagon, I was startled to see senior officers, generals and admirals, scurrying about, carrying beds and bedding. I couldn't understand why. The next day, President Kennedy announced the Cuban blockade. The threat of Russian missiles made the Conseil Internationale seem remarkably insignificant.

One summer, as an officer in a reserve public information unit from New York, I bivouacked in Wellfleet, Massachusetts, a lovely Cape Cod village. My troops stormed the beach at every opportunity. Usually, they hid behind the dunes, catching up on sleep and tans and reading.

My troops included Avery Corman, the novelist who wrote *Oh, God!* and *Kramer vs. Kramer,* both of which inspired popular films, and Herb Gardner, the playwright, the author of *A Thousand Clowns, I'm Not Rappaport,* and *Conversations with My Father.* Herb became and remained one of my dearest friends, nursing me through two divorces—three, if you count his—and numerous columns and books. (My third marriage took place on the patio of Herb's Manhattan penthouse apartment, a charmed setting; marriages at Herb's—mine and Judd Hirsch's—tend to endure.)

I was supposed to teach writing to the enlisted men. Corman and Gardner and a few others should have been teaching me, but I was the officer. Each week, I would ask Herb to sit in front of the group and pretend to be someone, and the other men would interview him and write stories based on their interview with an imaginary person. Herb had a genius for being someone else. Once he announced that he was the public relations man for the Atlantic Ocean. Nicholas Monsarrat had just written a bestselling book called *The Cruel Sea,* and Herb feared the ocean was getting a bad press.

Herb often reminds me that Sergeant Mario Puzo was also attached to our unit, employed as sort of the godfather of the Army reserve. If you wanted to get into the unit, and stay out of active duty, you had to slip him a small bribe. Kissing his ring didn't hurt, either. Herb says Puzo kept an unpublished manuscript in the right-hand bottom drawer of his desk, which he occasionally asked chosen reservists to read. It wasn't bad, but it wasn't *The Godfather;* it was called *The Dark Arena,* and, eventually, it was published. Several years later, I reviewed *The Godfather* for the *New York Times Book Review* and did not praise it lavishly, probably because I had forgotten that Puzo and I had served together.

When Herb and I were still in our twenties—he also belonged by birth to the class of 1934—he wrote *A Thousand Clowns,* a classic of poignant comedy that starred Jason Robards and featured Sandy Dennis,

Gene Saks, and a child actor named Barry Gordon. I wrote a story about the show for the *Saturday Evening Post,* and when I interviewed Barry, who was eleven or twelve at the time, he began many of his answers by saying, "When I was young . . ."

Herb told me he didn't expect *A Thousand Clowns* to be a hit. He said he had prepared himself for failure. "I was all ready to sell out," he said. "I had a whole list of things I was going to sell out as."

Herb has never sold out, although he has listened to offers. He has remained loyal to Broadway and to his craft, painstakingly writing funny plays about serious matters, half a dozen plays since *A Thousand Clowns* ("prolific" is the adjective least used to describe him). He has always written lovingly and wittily about old Jewish men, hardly suspecting that we would become two.

Herb was a sculptor, a cartoonist, a short-story writer, and a novelist before he turned twenty-five, and his hand-lettered scripts are works of art, in appearance and content. I don't think he has ever written a bad sentence. He is also a marvelous actor. The best performances I ever saw of two of his plays, and I have seen them all, were readings at which Herb read all the parts.

As good a writer and artist as Herb is, he is an even better friend. Offstage as well as on, he makes you laugh *and* think. Breslin *forces* you to reveal yourself; Gardner *invites* you to.

During my *Newsweek* days, I rose from sports editor to general editor to senior editor, at twenty-seven in charge of the sports, press, theater, movies, books, music, medicine, and education departments. I got the job because I lobbied for it, petitioned Gordon Manning for a chance. I blew my own horn—and not everyone was thrilled by the sound.

One of our writers, a talented and troubled Princeton man named Richard Boeth, a critic by profession and inclination, considered my promotion a disastrous mistake. He phoned me to share his opinion and, for more than half an hour, vilified me, attacking my intelligence, character, and ability. I listened, mostly because I respected him. Boeth once wrote a review of a movie called *Wind Across the Everglades,* which concerned itself with flamingoes, and the review in its entirety said, "This is a movie about the birds and for them." He reviewed a television series based on the play *Bus Stop* and wrote, of TV, "Give them an Inge—and they'll take a mile." I liked his acid wit. I didn't particularly like being its target.

When I left *Newsweek* two years later, the writers and researchers in my departments presented me with a farewell note: "The undersigned do not want Dick Schaap to leave without collectively and ceremoniously letting him know what a profitable pleasure it has been to transact business and friendship with him. . . . In a spot where it is almost impossible to balance pressure, people and prose, Dick Schaap's performance was a remarkable success. He apparently had no ax to grind except doing the best possible job and getting the most quasi-clean fun out of it. Both of these axes he honed to glittering edges, with no bloodstains." A dozen people signed the note, but Richard Boeth wrote it. Naturally, I thought it was his best review.

The editors and writers who signed the note included Barry Gottehrer, who followed me to the *Herald Tribune;* Mel Gussow, who went to the more stable

Times and wrote understandable books about such complex playwrights as Beckett, Pinter, Stoppard, and Albee; David Slavitt, who reviewed films for us and, on the side, wrote serious poetry and salable porn such as *The Exhibitionist* and *The Voyeur,* and Leslie Hanscom, an intelligent book and theater critic, who had rare skills as an editor.

Many editors can take a bad manuscript and turn it into a passable one; only a few can take a good manuscript and turn it into a better one. I remember Leslie taking a pretty decent story I had written about Joan Baez and Bob Dylan and the folk-singing surge and brightening the piece with a delightful sentence, "Never before have the songs of the shoeless been so popular among the well-shod." (Not long afterward, I wrote a story revealing that Bob Dylan's real name was Bobby Zimmerman, that friends and neighbors had heard him sing for the first time at his bar mitzvah in Hibbing, Minnesota, and that rather than being estranged from his parents, as he claimed, he had flown them to New York to one of his concerts. Dylan didn't like the story. I found him surly. I liked his songs but didn't like him.)

When personal problems drove Hanscom to a brief stay at Payne-Whitney, the mental hospital, I visited him and brought him a couple of books by Russian authors. When I walked into his room, he said, "Dick Schaap, what a strange face to see in the nuthouse!"

David Slavitt once took me to lunch with Peter Lorre, the pop-eyed Hungarian-born Viennese-trained actor who oozed menace, right from his early film, Fritz Lang's classic *M*. We ate at the Four Seasons, at a choice table next to the pool, and after a few pleasantries, Slavitt went to work. "Mr. Lorre," he said, "I was reading an article this morning in which you said, in 1936—"

Lorre interrupted. "You spent the morning in the morgue?" he said, in his unmistakable nasal voice. "I love to spend mornings in the morgue."

When Slavitt's lunch arrived, Dover sole handsomely presented, Lorre inquired, "How do you like your dead fish?" When the subject of people doing impressions of Lorre came up, he said, "I can do a Peter Lorre impression, too." He squeezed his nostrils, exaggerating his nasality, and croaked, "Do you have the information? Yes, I have the information."

A sleazy new magazine called *Confidential* had published a story about Lorre, in which the magazine charged that the actor had taken a prostitute to his room in Great Falls, Montana, and had refused to pay her. "It was a vicious lie," Lorre said. "I have never been to Great Falls, Montana."

"Could it have been Missoula?" I asked.

"It could have been Missoula," Lorre replied.

As we were leaving the dining room, we passed a magnificent tapestry. Lorre stopped to look at it and spotted a cockroach crawling across the top.

"Miss," Lorre said to the hatcheck woman on our way out, "there is a cockroach on your tapestry."

The woman laughed. "Oh, Mr. Lorre," she said. "You're so funny."

I never saw the cockroach again. I did see Lorre. He frequented a French restaurant around the corner from *Newsweek,* and often he held court at the bar. He talked about his youth in Vienna, working with Karl Jung in psychodramas, and I told him how much I loved the cult film *Beat the Devil, Casablanca* with a funny bone, that he had made with Humphrey Bogart and

Sydney Greenstreet, directed by John Huston.

"For one week," Lorre said, "we tried to make it as a serious film, and then Bogey and Huston and I went out and got drunk and decided that it was a piece of shit, and Huston brought in a new writer to work on the script. His name was Truman Capote, and when we met him at the airport, I wanted to flush him down the toilet. But then I got to know him and he is such a funny man."

Mel Gussow specialized at *Newsweek,* and later at the *Times,* in feature stories about the theater world, and sometimes he took me with him to interviews. Once we sat with James Earl Jones, who was then appearing in Jean Genet's *The Blacks,* and Jones talked about how much he would love to play Othello. But, Jones said, he felt that he had to live another ten or twenty years to acquire the maturity the role demanded. The following week, he signed to play Othello in a production of Shakespeare in the Park.

Years later, when my daughter and Jones's son attended the same nursery school—the sound you hear is of worlds colliding, again—Jimmy's wife told me that he was going to play a major role in a film version of W. P. Kinsella's wonderful novel *Shoeless Joe.*

"Who's he going to play?" I asked.

She looked sheepish. "J. D. Salinger," she said.

I said, "Oh."

When the film came out, *Shoeless Joe* had become *Field of Dreams,* and J. D. Salinger, played by Jones, had become a black activist.

13

Inside Rocky's Head

I supplemented my *Newsweek* income with freelance writing, first magazine articles, primarily for *SPORT* and *Cavalier* magazines, then books. I was twenty-three when my first article appeared in *SPORT,* "What Makes a Bonus Kid Worth $110,000," a study of a teenage baseball prospect named Dave Nicholson. "Take it easy the first few days," his mother told him, when he reported to the Baltimore Orioles. "Don't start throwing the ball around right away."

"Don't worry, Mom. I'll wait until I'm real loose."

"And don't forget to get to sleep early," his mother said. "You'll need the rest."

In the table of contents, my name was spelled, "Schapp"; forty years later, it was still being misspelled, in magazines, books, even in an ad for my health club. The misspelling, like the more than occasional mispronunciation, has helped to keep my raging ego in check, along with, "I know you. Who are you?"

I am frequently called Curt Gowdy, especially at

baseball games. I am sometimes called Larry Merchant, usually at boxing matches. And I have even been called Gene Shalit, presumably because we once worked together on the *Today* show. My hair, gray or silver, does bear a resemblance to Gowdy's and to Merchant's; it bears no resemblance to Shalit's.

I first met Shalit when I was at *Newsweek,* and he was a public relations man, half of Barkas and Shalit, a firm that represented, among other clients, American Machine and Foundry, AMF, which was, at the end of the 1950s, big in the bowling business. Shalit once arranged for me to interview Jack Benny, who had just invested—reluctantly, I assumed—in a bowling alley. The interview took place on the telephone—with Shalit listening on an extension—and I lobbed up questions to Benny, giving him every opportunity to be funny about the bowling business ("I guess it's changed a lot since your childhood" was one of my more probing questions) or about his trademark tight-fistedness. Most of Benny's answers were one word long: "Yes" was a favorite. Sometimes, he babbled, "I suppose so." When I got off the phone, I turned to Shalit and said, "I've got nothing," and Shalit said, "Next time, I'll have you interview his writers."

Gene used to take me to lunch once a month at the Four Seasons, one of the city's most pricey restaurants; I would eat very lightly for a few days before feasting on Shalit's largesse. I'll never forget the first time he showed up at the Four Seasons with frizzy hair piled high on his head, the wild and woolly "do" later emulated by the boxing promoter, Don King. A few of us, friends of Shalit, threatened to do to his hair what Delilah did to Samson's, a move that ultimately might have cost him millions. Years later, I told King, who had served time for manslaughter, "Your body got ten years, and your hair got the electric chair." I think he laughed.

Early in the sixties, someone proposed that Shalit, Gloria Steinem, and I host a radio show together. Nobody would buy the idea. Nobody knew who we were. Now everybody knows who they are.

While I was still in my twenties, I wrote profiles of Pancho Gonzales, Oscar Robertson, and Wilt Chamberlain for *SPORT.* I visited Wilt at his home at 6205 Cobb's Creek Parkway in Philadelphia—I reported that the nine-room house cost less than $15,000—and I asked him if he'd rather not be seven feet tall. "I'd rather be seven feet than six feet," Wilt said. "Maybe there's a happy medium, six-six or six-seven." Only a seven-footer would think six-six or six-seven is a happy medium.

On the team bus from Philadelphia to New York— they didn't fly on chartered jets then—I played tonk with Wilt and beat him, just as I had beaten Floyd Patterson earlier. Wilt got even, however. I once took my Swedish friend from *Newsweek* to his nightclub in Harlem, Big Wilt's Small's Paradise, and Wilt joined us and started talking Swedish to her, and I knew my relationship with the young woman was in jeopardy.

My relationship with Wilt survived. My second wife, Madeleine, and I once stayed at his mansion in the Hollywood Hills, with the ceiling in his bedroom that slid back to let in the sun, or the moon, with the television set that rose out of the floor at the foot of his bed, with the sunken tub that could be programmed to fill up at a certain time to a certain height at a certain temperature, with the swimming pool that started in the living room, flowed to the patio, and ended in a whirlpool. Wilt showed us a guest bedroom that was, from wall to wall, an ocean of a water bed. Then he told us that he didn't waste the room on married couples. We slept on a conventional bed in a conventional room.

In the late 1950s and early '60s, I was able to get close to my subjects, to get to know them, to share their lives in a way that seemed mythic a generation later. My son Jeremy, who is a diligent reporter, envies the rapport that once existed between the media and the athletes, a rapport that has been replaced by mutual distrust. Money contributes to the gap, the incredible incomes of the athletes. So does race. Most of the best professional football, basketball, and baseball players in America today are African-Americans, or in the case of baseball, Latin-Americans; most of the people who cover them are not. Yet when I was in my twenties, I seemed to have little trouble bridging ethnic gaps.

When I went to interview the tennis champion Pancho Gonzales, a Mexican-American, I had been told that, one, he distrusted reporters and, two, he loved automobiles. I walked up to Gonzales's locker after a long and dramatic match against the great Australian Lew Hoad in a small arena in upstate Corning, New York—I had never met Pancho before—and after congratulating him for his victory mentioned that I had seen his car parked outside the arena. I knew nothing, and cared nothing, about automobiles or engines. "Some car," I said, trying to appear interested. Gonzales lit up. "You like it?" he said. I said I did, and he explained to me that it was a 1955 Ford Thunderbird with a modified 1950 Cadillac engine, that he had two sets of spark plugs, one for driving in town, one for the open road, and I just listened. Then we went out for a postmatch snack and Gonzales invited me to travel with him the next day in his souped-up Thunderbird from Corning to the next stop on the low-budget pro tennis tour, Clinton, New York, 160 miles away.

The next morning, just before we pulled out of Corning, Gonzales stood in pouring rain and replaced his city spark plugs with the country ones. Two miles out of town, he ran out of gas.

My story on Gonzales began: "When Richard Alonzo Gonzales stretches to the top of his toes, whips his right arm high in the air and serves a tennis ball at 112 miles an hour, he is more than simply powering the swiftest shot in tennis history. He is swinging at every Southern Californian who ever called a Mexican 'Pancho,' flailing at every tennis official who ever barred a youngster from a tournament, and whacking at every father who ever ordered his daughter to stop dating the kid from the wrong side of the tracks."

Like Gonzales, Oscar Robertson shared his time with me and his feelings. I hung out in his room in French Dorm at the University of Cincinnati, and when we wanted to listen to music together, we went across the river to Newport, Kentucky, to the black clubs where he, and I, could feel comfortable. "In the three years since he entered Cincinnati," I wrote, "Oscar has been called 'The Big O,' 'The Wonderful O,' 'the greatest sophomore basketball player ever' and 'the greatest junior basketball player ever.' He has also been called 'redcap,' 'porter,' and other ugly, humorless labels."

But the story was not all about race. "Some people say that Pete Dawkins, the Army football player, stands a chance of becoming the most famous graduate in West Point history," I wrote. "All he has to do is be-

come a general, win a war, run for President, and be
elected. Oscar Robertson has a chance to become the
most famous graduate in Cincinnati history. All he has
to do is graduate."

During my *Newsweek* days, I ghosted an article for the
first time, I traveled with the first Russian hockey and
track-and-field teams to visit North America, and I
made such disparate friends as Stirling Moss, the ur-
bane Grand Prix racing star from Great Britain, and Jose
Torres, the precocious boxing star from Puerto Rico.

My first collaborator—on my first "as told to"
story—was Rocky Graziano, who had a few years earlier shifted his talents from the ring to show business.
He had been the subject of a ghostwritten (not by me,
unfortunately, for me) autobiography called *Somebody
Up There Likes Me,* a hugely successful book that became a hugely successful film starring Paul Newman
as Rocky.

Rocky agreed to work with me on an article for
SPORT, called "For $50,000, I'd Fight Any One of
Those Bums," lamenting the depressed state of the
middleweight boxing division Rocky had abandoned. I
met him for the first time in the office of his theatrical
agent, and I commented on how fit he looked. "You
still work out?" I asked.

"Oh yeah," Rocky said. "I woik out uppa Goddem."

It is hard to capture in print the way Rocky spoke. He
sounded naturally the way Jimmy Breslin sometimes
sounded deliberately, only more so. I think Rocky owed
some of his diction to Tony Zale, Sugar Ray Robinson,
and others who had pounded him in the head.

I had a blank look on my face. "He says he works
out at the Gotham Health Club," his agent translated.

"What do you do there?" I asked.

"Oh, I woik out wid Paul Newman, Ben Gazzara, Tony Franciosa," Rocky said, naming three actors whose careers were flourishing.

I made a passing reference to Franciosa's wife at the time, the actress Shelley Winters.

"Shelley got a fat ass," Rocky said. "She oughta be in a gym herself."

"With friends like that," I said, "do you ever go to the Actors Studio?"

At the time, the Actors Studio, Lee Strasberg's school of method acting, was at its peak, its most celebrated student, Marlon Brando, a soaring star.

"Oh yeah," Rocky said. "Funny ting you should axt me that. I went over da Actors Studio de udder day, and I walk up da stairs and I go inside and dere are four guys standin' in da corner learnin' how to be actors, and you know what?"

"What?" I said.

"Dey're all tryin' to talk like me," said Graziano.

Somehow, I managed to write the article coherently, yet in Rocky's voice, which is the key to credible ghostwriting. You have to put yourself inside your subject's head. I had never before been anyplace like Rocky's head.

When I first met Jose Torres, his English was no better than Rocky's, but his accent was considerably different. Torres was not long out of Ponce Playa, Puerto Rico, and he, like his stablemate Floyd Patterson, both of them managed by Cus D'Amato, seemed much too gentle to be a fighter. Their gentleness disappeared in the ring and both became world champions. (Later, of course, D'Amato managed Mike Tyson, who never seemed too gentle to be a fighter.) Torres became very friendly with Norman Mailer and, understandably, became enamored of the written word. Jose wrote books about Ali and about Tyson, and when I interviewed him on television, he laughed and said, "When we met, I couldn't speak English, and now I'm a bestselling author."

In 1957, in the days of the repressive Batista government, I went to Havana to cover the first Gran Premio de Cuba, a Formula One auto race. I interviewed Juan Manuel Fangio, the great Argentine driver, exactly one year to the day before, on the eve of the last Gran Premio de Cuba, he was kidnapped by the rebel forces of Fidel Castro. I asked Fangio if he ever thought about death, and he replied, "Death? I give it only a quick glancing thought."

I took several race drivers out to lunch in Havana one day, but before we could choose a restaurant, Stirling Moss, as tightfisted as he was talented, had to check out the prices. Even though I was picking up the check, he abhorred the thought of overpaying. He ran into one restaurant, a steak house, and came out shouting, "They want seven-fifty for a steak. What do they think my bloody name is, John D. Rockefeller?" A less affluent driver, a Swede named Joachim Bonnier, came out of the restaurant with Moss, shouting, "What do they think my bloody name is, Stirling Moss?"

Of the six drivers I took to lunch that day, four were dead within a couple of years. Moss was one of the survivors. Years later, when we renewed our acquaintance in London, Stirling began quoting an article that referred to him as, among other things, "a shilling-pinching Englishman." He didn't realize that I had

written the article. Not until he said he was flattered by
the reference did I confess that I was the author.

I saw him most recently in London, in the spring of
2000. I had known him for more than forty years. He
had survived his demanding sport in large measure because, in his thirties, he had almost died in a crash that
left him in a coma for a month and cut short his career.
He handed me his business card, which said, "Sir Stirling Moss, OBE."

Late in the 1950s, I traveled in Canada with the Soviet
national hockey team, led by a coach named Anatoly
Tarasov ("Call me Phil") and a defenseman named
Nikolai Sologubov (we called him "Kolya"). I had
never seen an athletic team drink the way the Russian
hockey team drank, especially vodka and especially
Sologubov. He had stepped on a land mine during the
Siege of Leningrad and had been told he would never
walk again. He became captain of the Red Army
hockey team. He deserved a drink.

I joined the Russians in Montreal and traveled with
them to Kingston, Ontario, where I was met by a freelance photographer who was shooting for *Newsweek*.
"You should have been here last night," the photographer said.

"Why?" I asked.

"We shot a porno film," he said.

I could have been the masked marvel.

I settled for a lesser role. When I accompanied the
Russian players to a reception in Kingston, they invited me to pretend I was a member of their team. I
walked down the receiving line, and each time a Canadian slowly said to me, "Very . . . nice . . . to . . .

have . . . you . . . in . . . our . . . country," I replied, *"Spaseba, spaseba,"* Russian for "Thank you."

I did mention to a Soviet official that I was sorry they didn't have a player named Chekhov, the perfect name, I felt, for a hockey player. "But," he said, "we have our goalie, Pushkov."

When the Russians came to New York, I walked with Pushkov from his hotel near Broadway to the old Madison Square Garden on Eighth Avenue and Fiftieth Street. "What is *medicine*?" Pushkov asked me during our walk.

"Penicillin," I suggested.

"No, no, no," he said. *"Medicine."*

I tried to explain about doctors, hospitals, nurses. "No," Pushkov said. *"Medicine. Medicine* Square Garden."

The hockey players were the second Russian team in the cold war days to visit the United States. The first was their national track-and-field team, which competed against the United States in Philadelphia. The meet produced one of the most poignant moments I ever witnessed in sports, the end of the 10,000-meter run, the American distance runner so exhausted, so spent, but so determined to finish, that he sometimes staggered backward as he wobbled toward, and finally reached, the finish line.

The meet also introduced me to a charming young Soviet athlete from Kiev, Igor Ter-Ovanesyan, who looked like a Yalie, spoke flawless English, and long-jumped almost as well. He and I and a monumentally self-righteous American athlete all competed for the attention of a bright and beautiful woman who was working as an interpreter at the track meet. When Igor won the competition, and her attention, I was almost as happy as if I had won. Almost.

Later, in New York, I took Igor to a nightclub called Basin Street East where a singer named Jaye P. Morgan was appearing. We sat at a banquette, next to an elderly gentleman accompanied by a blonde who was young enough to be his granddaughter. It was evident from their behavior that she was not. She ordered a champagne cocktail, a shrimp cocktail, and a sirloin steak, and Igor turned to me and, in his flawless English, said, "Sugar daddy?"

Sitting in a cab on Fifth Avenue, heading back to his hotel, Igor said, "After New York, Moscow is like a village." I quoted him in *Newsweek,* and once the article appeared, the KGB agents traveling with the track-and-field team made it difficult for Igor to socialize with me. I did get Igor a date one night with a young woman who worked at *Newsweek,* and she and I waited in his hotel lobby for more than two hours before we conceded that the KGB was not going to permit Igor to join us. The young woman later married Kenneth Tynan, who also spoke flawless English. Tynan was a superb theater and movie critic and was, as I recall, the first person to say, "Fuck," on television. He said it on the BBC, flawlessly.

I didn't see Igor for almost twenty years, and when I saw him again, he was coaching the Russian national track-and-field team and had matured into a boring bureaucrat.

The articles I contributed to *Cavalier,* which also enlisted such writers as Breslin, Mickey Spillane, and William Bradford Huie, were not about people so famous as Rocky, Oscar, Pancho, and Wilt. I profiled the

irst man to jump off the Brooklyn Bridge, Robert Od-
um, who died in the attempt, and a fellow nineteenth-
century daredevil named Sam Patch, who loved to leap
into raging waters. He jumped off Niagara Falls and
survived, but the Passaic Falls in New Jersey were his
downfall. I toured with an air show, the Cole Bros. Fly-
ng Circus, and visited a stripper.

Patti Waggin (not her real name) went to San Jose
State, was billed as the Coed with the Educated Torso,
and was married to a pitcher for the Chicago White
Sox named Don Rudolph. Don picked me up at the airport in Louisville, drove me to the Savoy burlesque
theater, and invited me to stand in the wings and catch
his wife's wardrobe as she discarded each item. As
soon as the last garment came off and the curtain came
down, Don dashed onstage and wrapped Patti in a
bathrobe. The editor of *Cavalier,* a delightful man
named Bob Curran, titled my story of the Rudolphs
"The Pitcher and the Twitcher."

Curran had a way with titles. My favorite was a
cover line that posed the intriguing question "Did a
Woman Die with Custer?" If you read the article, you
found out that the answer was no, but by then you had
paid for the magazine. Curran, who mastered the rare
art of being able to talk with his teeth clenched, was a
conservative politically and morally. When the owners
decided to change *Cavalier* from an adventure book to
a girlie book, Curran resigned on principle.

I wrote my first three books before I left *Newsweek,*
before I turned thirty. The first two were paperbacks,
part of a series called the Sport Magazine Library,
30,000-word portraits of superstars. I started with
Mickey Mantle: The Indispensable Yankee, which came

out in 1961, after Mantle's first decade in the big
leagues. Mantle was accessible—he let me follow him
through a day in spring training—and scatological. I
wrote a large chunk of the book—sanitizing his crude
humor—on the train from Florida back to New York. (I
had temporarily abandoned flying, essentially out of
cowardice; like any good control freak, I find it difficult to trust anyone else at the controls. But a few
months later, when I was invited to Israel to cover the
opening of the country's first and only golf course, I
submerged my fears and returned to the air.)

I saw Mantle often over the next few decades, sometimes socially, sometimes professionally. Once, years
after he had retired, I read a story in which he said he
desperately missed playing, regretted that he had
abused his body and his skills, and suffered a recurring
nightmare in which he showed up at Yankee Stadium
and was refused entrance. I interviewed him and asked
him if he could do anything in the world, what would
he do? I expected him to recount his dream of playing
baseball again, but Mickey grinned at me and the camera and said, "Fuck Raquel Welch."

My second book, the following year, was called
Paul Hornung: Pro Football's Golden Boy, and after I
flew into Green Bay on a now-extinct airline that
called itself the Route of the Flying Goose, I found
Hornung to be more than cooperative. He shared his
lifestyle with me, and I still have not fully recovered.
Paul was a bachelor, a drinker, and a gambler, and
worked at all three with the same dedication he
brought to the football field. I spent a week with him in
Green Bay and lost count of both his drinks and his
conquests. I didn't really lose count, but the numbers,
even a third of a century later, still boggle the mind.

Paul has changed. In 1999, my wife Trish and I spent a few days with Paul and his wife Angela at a golf tournament in Idaho, and his idea of carousing was having an ice cream sundae before he went to bed, long before midnight. His old Green Bay roommate, and running mate, Max McGee, who once shared Paul's vices and his fear of sleep, was also in Idaho. He was into sundaes and an early curfew, too.

The book about Hornung was the first of six I've written about the Green Bay Packers, the start of a requited love affair between me and the state of Wisconsin. I am, to my amazement, a hero in Oconomowoc and La Crosse, in Appleton and Madison. I now own one share of stock in the Packers. It is nonnegotiable and utterly worthless, but I take almost as much pride in it as I do in my Monday-night table at Rao's.

My first hardcover book was commissioned by the distinguished publishing house of Alfred A. Knopf. It was called *An Illustrated History of the Olympics,* and when the first edition came out, in 1963, Knopf insisted that the byline be the proper "By Richard Schaap." In later editions, after I had acquired a small following, Knopf relented and changed "Richard" to "Dick." Many years later, when Trish and our son David were browsing in a used-book store, looking for copies of books I had written, many of which I had left behind in divorces, David spotted a first edition of *An Illustrated History of the Olympics.* "I don't see any books here by Dad," he announced, "but there's one by somebody named Richard Schaap." At least Knopf spelled it correctly.

I had published a book a year in 1961, 1962, and 1963, a pace that I managed to sustain through the sixties and sought to maintain throughout my career. I have come up short—full-time jobs tended to get in the way—only thirty-three books in the last thirty-nine years of the twentieth century.

When I left the security of *Newsweek* to become city editor of the *Herald Tribune,* I was given a copy of *City Editor,* the work of Stanley Walker, perhaps the most celebrated of the breed. I was given the book, with a generous inscription, by a *Newsweek* researcher named Joan Walker Wenning, who was the daughter of Stanley Walker, who had been the youngest city editor in the history of the *Herald Tribune,* until I boarded that sinking ship.

14

"Greetings from Mecca"

My first day at the *Herald Tribune,* I slipped into *Newsweek* habits. Every story that came across my desk, I edited, heavily. I rewrote leads, altered transitions, scratched out adjectives. At *Newsweek,* writers accepted abuse of their copy as part of the system. At the *Trib,* I almost sparked a rebellion. My two assistant city editors, a pair of relatively young but knowledgeable newspapermen, Don Forst and Danny Blum, both native New Yorkers, gently informed me that it was neither wise nor politic to edit the copy of veteran reporters.

I holstered my pencil and settled into a job for which I was clearly not prepared. For instance, I did not know where New York City Police Headquarters was. I was not, however, a complete moron. I did know where City Hall was, and I did know that Robert F. Wagner Jr. was the mayor. I even knew that his father, Senator Robert Wagner, had also fathered the Wagner Act, a pro-labor law with which I was at least vaguely familiar from my studies of industrial and labor relations.

During my days as city editor—my reign lasted slightly more than ten months, from the start of 1964 through Election Day—I brought in my friend and associate from *Newsweek,* Barry Gottehrer, to organize and oversee a lengthy series called "City in Crisis," which I thought of as bold journalism, but which my employer, John Hay Whitney, the former ambassador to the Court of St. James's and an affable millionaire, viewed, more realistically, as a means to discredit the Democratic Wagner administration and bring Whitney's fellow Republicans to power. I wrote the first sentence of the "City in Crisis" series: "New York is the greatest city in the world—and everything is wrong with it." Gottehrer wrote most of the rest.

The city room of the *Herald Tribune,* even in the summer, with no air-conditioning and heat steaming up from the presses a floor below, was a wonderful place to work. Perhaps because we all realized the paper's chances for survival were slim, there were no petty intrigues, no jockeying for position, no infighting, no sniping. We might have been going down, but we knew we were going down in good company.

The rising star of my cityside staff was Tom Wolfe who had already put in two years at the paper. He was obviously, a stylist—his use of words and punctuation as distinctive as his dandy attire—but he was also a magnificent reporter, painstaking and perceptive, with a dazzling eye and ear. Wolfe made his mark at the *Tribune* before I arrived, most noticeably with his story of a debutante party in the Hamptons that turned into a mansion-trashing brawl. I did not have him on my staff for long—Clay Felker, the editor of the paper's Sunday supplement, *New York* magazine, spirited him away—

out while I did, I assigned him to cover the first coming
of the Beatles to the United States, and his vivid report
began with a description of the quartet's waiting fans,
"transistors plugged in their skulls."

Later, I assigned Wolfe to cover the first wedding
ever held at the nightclub El Morocco, a union between a wealthy and elderly businessman and a
woman poorer and younger. The bride and groom were
so flattered by our straight-faced coverage of their lu-
bricious nuptials that they invited Wolfe to join them
and their entourage on their honeymoon in Paris.
Wolfe filed daily reports and frequently referred to the
bride as "ravishing," which, according to Webster's,
means "extremely beautiful." Also, according to Webster's, it can mean "raping, violating, seizing and carrying off by force, or plundering." The woman basked
in the first definition.

Wolfe's articles in *New York* brought him a devout
and growing following, and when his first book, *The
Kandy-Kolored Tangerine Flake Streamline Baby,* surfaced in 1965, he was as hot as a young writer could
be. One day early in the Wolfean frenzy, Tom was sitting at his typewriter, only an inch or two of copy paper jutting out of the carriage. Forst, the assistant city
editor, surreptitiously walked behind him, to sneak a
preview of Tom's latest effort. All that was visible was
"Dear Mommy and Daddy . . ."

If Wolfe was the champion of my staff, he had a
challenger in a younger writer, Bill Whitworth, who
looked as though he came from Arkansas and did.
Whitworth crafted exceptional articles, but wrote them
slowly and meticulously, and as accomplished a journalist as he was, he did not seem, or feel, best suited to
daily deadlines. He soon switched to *The New Yorker,*

and the hayseed with the aw-shucks mien was quickly being mentioned as a possible editor in chief of the sophisticated weekly. But before he could be elevated Whitworth left *The New Yorker* and became the editor of the *Atlantic Monthly,* a position he filled, with distinction, for two decades.

Wolfe and Whitworth were the core of a staff so undersized that on Fridays, when we prepared the Saturday paper, our smallest edition in pages and in circulation, we employed only a handful of reporters and one, a police reporter named Milt Lewis, often was called upon to write four or five bylined stories, which he did with world-class speed and printable grace. Milt tried to sneak into each story his favorite word, "quondam," an awkward synonym, in my opinion, for "former" or "onetime." I deleted the word regularly, until, of course, I became the quondam city editor.

We had another reporter, who, after many years on the *Tribune,* still thought the Tombs, the ancient New York City prison, was spelled "Tooms." He sat near another veteran who could pound out stories only until it was time for his liquid lunch at Bleeck's. When he returned, he settled in at his typewriter, fingers poised for action, but eyes glazed, as immobile as Mount Rushmore.

Terry Smith, the son of Red Smith, the *Trib* sports columnist who could make words twinkle, joined the paper at about the same time I did. I immediately began assigning frothy feature stories to him, assuming he would have the light touch of his father. Terry's features were dreadful. But when he shifted to City Hall and began writing hard news stories, he shined. Clearly, he didn't want to work the same territory his father had worked so brilliantly for so many years

Terry moved to Washington and covered presidents and congressmen, and in the 1980s, I did a story for ABC on father and son, a mutual admiration society, Red and Terry, "The Wordsmiths."

The editors of the *Herald Tribune* were as diverse and talented as the reporters, starting at the top with Jim Bellows, who mumbled every word he spoke yet managed to communicate perfectly. Bellows had an instinct for a story, and loved good writing, which meant that good writers loved him, which meant that he was popular among the *Tribune* staff.

Bellows was a superb editor (he ran the *Washington Star* and the *Los Angeles Herald-Examiner* after he left the *Tribune*) and a formidable drinker of vodka martinis. Every day at lunch, he drank two, on the rocks, with a twist, and without perceptible effect. Many years later, when Bellows was recovering from a stroke, his doctor ordered Jim to cut down to one martini a day. He did, but doubled the size of the glass.

Bellows's associates on the *Tribune* also flourished after the paper folded. The managing editor, Dick Wald, became the president of NBC News; my predecessor as city editor, Buddy Weiss, the editor of the Paris *Herald Tribune;* my successor, David Laventhol, the publisher of *Newsday;* my assistant city editor, Don Forst, the editor of the *Village Voice;* and the deputy foreign editor, Harry Rosenfeld, the metropolitan editor of the *Washington Post.* In the early 1970s, Harry helped steer a pair of young reporters named Woodward and Bernstein through a collaborative investigation of the president of the United States.

One of my stronger journalistic peeves is the use of the phrase "investigative reporter," as it was often applied to Woodward and Bernstein. It is redundant: If a reporter is not investigative, he is not a reporter. I object almost as strongly to the use of the word "objective" to describe reporting or journalism. There is no such thing. Every story is subjective; the choice of lead, the choice of verbs, the choice of adjectives, the choice of information to include and to exclude, all are, and must be, subjective judgments. I prefer "honest" journalism, which seems to be a dying or at least ailing art, in my subjective, but honest opinion.

As city editor, I oversaw the coverage of the opening day of the 1964–65 New York World's Fair. For that occasion, Abe Rosenthal, the metropolitan editor of the *New York Times,* deployed more than one hundred of his reportorial troops. I dispatched everyone I had, fewer than twenty men and women. But our skeleton force included Breslin, Wolfe, Whitworth, and Red Smith, and I still believe our coverage, though not nearly so comprehensive as the *Times*'s, was more readable.

I did try to reduce the size of the *Times*'s staff. I convinced Bellows and Jock Whitney that I should offer jobs at the *Tribune* to Gay Talese, Bob Lipsyte, and McCandlish Phillips, three of the opposition's stars. I argued that a successful raid would strengthen both our image and our meager staff. Bellows and Whitney said try, with a caveat: I had to hire all three, or none.

I offered each of the *Times*men a considerable raise. Lipsyte, an idealistic young sports columnist, showed little interest. Phillips, who worked the streets of the city both as a police reporter and as an evangelical Christian preacher, indicated he would leave the *Times* only for an editorial position on the Bible, with powers of revision. Talese was tempted, but insisted that the display and frequency of his column match or surpass Breslin's. The raid collapsed.

A little more than a year later, I had occasion to write a column about McCandlish Phillips, a decent and gentle man who, at six-foot-five, was known as "Long John." He had revealed in the *Times*, in a splendid and well-documented story, that Daniel Burros, the viciously anti-Semitic King Kleagle of the Ku Klux Klan in New York State, was, by birth and religious training, a Jew. The day Phillips's story was published, Burros killed himself.

Phillips had, appropriately, kept himself out of his story. But he was the central character in mine. Two days before his article appeared, Phillips told me, he met Burros face-to-face for the first time and told him what he had learned about his background. "If you publish that," Burros said, "I'll come and get you and kill you. I don't care what happens. I'll be ruined. This is all I've got to live for."

Phillips took Burros's threat seriously, yet the next day sat down and wrote the article that appeared in the *Times* the following morning. The story said that Daniel Burros was Jewish. Burros spared Phillips. He fired one bullet into his own chest, then one into his head. "Daniel Burros was a living soul, a human being of infinite worth," Phillips said afterward. "I felt sad. I felt it was a consummate tragedy."

His story had set off the suicide, yet Phillips solemnly explained, "I never felt it was up to me, but if it had been, I certainly would have published the story. You can't pull in your journalistic horns just because someone threatens you. I have no regrets at all about having written the story."

If I had been able to hire Phillips, I would have assigned him the desk next to Tom Wolfe's, Phillips wore black suits and kept the Bible on his desk. Wolfe wore white suits and kept *Esquire* on his desk. They were both terrific newspapermen. I suspect they would have gotten along famously.

While I was city editor, just as when I was a senior editor at *Newsweek,* I felt compelled to write at least an occasional story, to maintain my typing skills. One of the first was the newspaperman's dream—a scoop. I broke the story that Cassius Clay, courted by Malcolm X, had decided to become a Black Muslim. Through a friend, whose cousin was Malcolm X's secretary, I learned that Clay had interrupted training for his first fight against Sonny Liston to fly to New York to attend and address a Muslim rally.

At the time, the *Herald Tribune* employed a reporter from the *Amsterdam News,* New York's black newspaper, to be our eyes, ears, and bodyguard in Harlem. His name was Jimmy Booker, a bright and well-informed newspaperman who, when I paid my visits to Harlem, scolded me for overtipping the cabdrivers. "You're spoiling it for us," he said.

Through Booker, I got to know Malcolm X, who, holding court in his office on the mezzanine of the Hotel Theresa on Seventh Avenue, could be as disarming as his street rhetoric could be disquieting. Sleek, tall, and handsome, with a winning smile and matching charm, Malcolm contradicted his own sermons of hatred and separation of the races. "My idea of the ideal guest list for a cocktail party," I wrote, "would be one that started with Malcolm X and William Buckley." (Buckley was also a contradiction, far too intelligent to

believe many of the things he wrote and said. David
Merrick, the theatrical theatrical producer, once insisted to me, only half-kidding, that Buckley was "a
closet liberal.")

When Malcolm X made a pilgrimage to the Middle
East in the summer of 1964, he sent me a postcard
with the message, "Greetings from Mecca, the holiest
and most sacred city on earth, the fountain of truth,
love, peace, and brotherhood." He signed it, "Bro.
Malcolm X."

Six months later, a photo of the card and Malcolm's
message ran on the front page of the *Tribune*. It was
the morning after he was assassinated at the Audubon
Ballroom on upper Broadway. I wrote his obituary and
mentioned in it that, during his younger days, serving
as a pimp, he had provided black women for white
men and white women for black men. My story was
picked up by several newspapers; at least one deleted
the reference to white women for black men.

I attended Malcolm's funeral—as I recall, I shared a
limousine to the Harlem church with Percy Sutton,
who became the borough president of Manhattan, and
Michael Olatunji, the Nigerian musician—and listened
to the actor Ossie Davis proclaim in his eulogy, "Malcolm was our manhood, our living black manhood."

Malcolm was buried with his head facing east toward Mecca, "the fountain of love, truth, peace, and
brotherhood." He had been murdered by followers of
Elijah Muhammad, the Black Muslim leader with
whom he had dramatically split.

The week after Malcolm was murdered, I attended a
party at Buddy Hackett's house, and when the other
guests, many of them comics and singers, discovered
that I had written Malcolm X's obituary and attended

his funeral, they flocked to hear what I had to say. For the first time in my life, I was a minor celebrity, and I liked it. I still enjoy celebrity, being recognized, being complimented, being asked for my autograph, probably because those things happen only often enough to nurture my ego, not so often that they become bothersome. I watch Bo Jackson and Billy Crystal and Muhammad Ali, see them stripped of all anonymity and marvel at how each reacts to it, Bo warily, Billy politely, and Ali delightedly.

15

From Mississippi to Watts

In September 1964, I started writing a column twice a week for the *Tribune*. The first column featured Ali, but the first to have any impact focused upon the opening-night party for *Golden Boy,* a Broadway musical adapted from the Clifford Odets drama. Sammy Davis Jr. played the protagonist, a young would-be boxer. The show had opened out of town to mostly unfavorable reviews. The word of mouth was equally unkind.

The opening-night party was held at a popular saloon called Danny's Hideaway, and several hundred of Sammy's most intimate friends showed up for the occasion, most of them anticipating disaster. They hung around until the early reviews came in; the *Times*'s and the *Tribune*'s were unmistakably favorable, to the astonishment, and dismay, of most of Sammy's well-wishers. The saloon quickly emptied; the party died out. "There are some people who cannot stand the sight of no blood," I wrote.

I love hypocrisy. I mean, I love writing about it. Peo-

ple responded to the Davis column, especially Jim Bellows. He granted my wish to give up the city editorship,
just when I was starting to possess the knowledge, and
reflexes, the job demanded. "My low opinion of editors
was never elevated by being one," I often said. (As
usual, I couldn't resist a good line; actually, I had a
high opinion of many editors, but not of the institution,
which is similar to my feelings about religion.)

Bellows allowed me to become a full-time writer,
turning out three columns a week, which appeared directly underneath Breslin's and alternated with Art
Buchwald's. I was flattered by the play and fulfilled by
the job, which gave me more freedom and satisfaction
than I had ever had.

The *Golden Boy* column led to a friendship with
Sammy Davis. I was, in fact, Sammy's best friend in
the whole world for a few weeks in the mid-1960s.
During those few weeks, I watched him work simultaneously on a Broadway show (*Golden Boy*), a television series (*The Sammy Davis Jr. Show*), and a feature
film (*A Man Called Adam*), playing the title role in all
three. He also found time to perform at Mayor John
Lindsay's Inaugural Ball, and he appreciated, and
used, a line I offered him. The day Lindsay took office,
a strike shut down the subways, and I suggested that
Sammy say, "Look, only one day in office, and he's already eliminated crime in the subways."

I had to miss a party Sammy threw at the Rainbow
Room in Rockefeller Center, celebrating the anniversary of his marriage to the beautiful blond Swedish actress, May Britt. I was in Philadelphia, Mississippi, at
the time, covering the arrest of twenty-one men in connection with the murder of three civil-rights workers
during the summer of 1964.

I was not exactly comfortable in Philadelphia, Mississippi. My first day in town, I was eating lunch in the only local restaurant when two men in uniform walked in. "Is that Sheriff Rainey and Deputy Price?" I asked a waitress. Lawrence Rainey and Cecil Price were two of the murder suspects.

She said yes, and I got up and walked to their table and told them I was Dick Schaap from the *New York Herald Tribune*—I deliberately swallowed my name and the newspaper's, hoping they would miss both—and asked if I could join them. They said yes, and as I sat at their table, a stream of good ol' boys came up to the sheriff and his deputy and shared a good laugh about them being indicted for murder. The next day, I went to a local church, met the minister, who was recommended to me as the most liberal man in Philadelphia, and told him that I had dined with Rainey and Price. "They'd as soon kill you as look at you," the minister said. I heard the minister's words and prayed that neither Rainey nor Price had seen my column about our lunch. "In Mississippi," I had written, "murder is a laughing matter."

I decided to send a telegram to Sammy from Mississippi, explaining why I would miss his party. I was nervous, with reason. I went to the local Western Union office and told the clerk I wanted to send a telegram to Mr. Sammy Davis. I felt better when he said, "Is that S-A-M-M-I-E?" I wired my regrets and concluded, "Everyone here in Philadelphia, Mississippi, joins me in wishing you and May love and happiness."

In Mississippi, I missed a deadline for the first and only time in my newspaper career. I was sharing a car with Joe Lelyveld, then a reporter for the *Times,* later its executive editor, and as we pulled out of Philadelphia, I started writing my column with my typewriter on my lap. As we approached Jackson, the state capital, the deadline for the first edition also approached. I spotted a gas station with an open-air telephone, and asked Joe to pull in so that I could call in my column. Just as I started dictating, three young men—Confederate flags adorning their black leather jackets—formed a small circle around me. I knew they would not be amused by my column. "I think I'm going to miss the first edition," I told the typist. "I'll call you back in half an hour."

I wrote an article about Sammy for *New York,* which began:

> The cats on the corner recognized him right away. Of course, they had a few hints. His chauffeur-driven Rolls-Royce limousine sat at the curb. His beautiful wife, May, stood next to him. He wore a custom-tailored tuxedo. . . .
>
> The cats stared at him—he was buying cigarettes in a (Harlem) candy store on his way to a benefit—and they stared at the big car and at the blond wife and at the expensive clothes, and then one of them spoke up to Sammy Davis.
>
> "Ease up on us, baby," he said. "You too strong."

When that article came out, Sammy and I were like brothers. Then he went out of town and I neither saw him nor heard from him for ten years. When we met again, at a golf tournament he hosted in Connecticut, he resumed our previous conversation as if it were yesterday. We were once again best of friends, for several hours.

* * *

The middle 1960s, the dying days of the *Herald Tribune,* were a period of remarkable turmoil, presaging the upheaval of 1968, the year that Robert Kennedy and Martin Luther King were assassinated and the Democratic National Convention transformed Chicago into a battlefield. Bellows stretched his small staff by using columnists as reporters, a strategy that took me first to Mississippi, and then, in the summer of 1965, to the Watts riots in Los Angeles.

I went to Watts by accident. Breslin had just left for Saigon, to cover the Vietnam war, and I had written a column reporting the reactions of his friends and neighbors. "He couldn't go two years ago?" one of the neighbors said. "Is he there permanently?" said another, hopefully. His friend Pepe the Gambler, co-owner of Pep McGuire's, a watering hole in Queens, suggested, "Just get on the beach at Waikiki and make it all up. Steal from Norman Mailer. Do anything, but just come back to us." Pepe was very emotional; after all, Breslin still had a tab to settle at Pep McGuire's. Jimmy's friend Marvin the Torch, a made-up name for an arsonist whose real name was Bert the Torch, fretted, too. "I am going to burn candles for him," Marvin said. "Or something like that."

While Breslin flew to the Far East, I flew to the West Coast, for a change of pace and a few laughs, to accompany the futile New York Mets on a road trip that started against the Dodgers. The first night, Sandy Koufax beat the Mets. "The Mets opened their final 1965 visit to the West Coast on a positive note," I wrote. "They showed up. There is some question as to whether they can keep up that pace." The second night, Don Drysdale shut out the Mets, their tenth consecutive defeat. "There is something about the Mets that strikes courage into the hearts of opposing pitchers," I reported.

But the night Drysdale stopped the Mets, the arrest of a black motorist in Watts, the sprawling Los Angeles ghetto, provoked an ugly confrontation between police and local residents. Stories of police brutality quickly circulated, and resentment festered in the community for the next day. Bellows and I decided that instead of following the Mets to Houston, I should follow the uneasiness in Los Angeles.

That night, Friday night, I had an early dinner at a Polynesian restaurant with a friend, the black actor and comedian Godfrey Cambridge, then headed for Watts. As a newspaperman, I could have stayed on the outskirts, interviewed cops and civilians, pieced together a reasonable account of the eruption in the ghetto. That would have been sensible. Instead, I made the mistake of hooking up with a local television crew. Once I got into their van, I realized they couldn't take pictures from the outskirts.

The next thing I knew, a police blockade halted our van inside the war zone and the cops ordered us out. As soon as we emerged, bullets started flying, from rioters or national guardsmen, I didn't check. I lay down on the street and all I could think, as the bullets whistled overhead, was that I had made fun of Breslin, and he was probably in an officers club in Vietnam, far from violence, drinking a beer.

Eventually, deep into the night, I abandoned the camera crew and made my way to a firehouse on 103rd Street, which had flamed into Charcoal Alley, the heart of the devastation. I spent hours in the firehouse, pinned down by sporadic sniper fire, lying under a fire engine, sometimes chatting with Los Angeles policemen who wondered how a New York reporter had reached the scene so rapidly. "They called me and told me there was going to be a riot," I said. "Didn't they call you?"

Saturday morning, as the first rays of sunshine hit Watts, I tentatively made my way out of the firehouse, half running and half crawling to a pay phone across the street. I deposited a dime, called collect to the *Herald Tribune*, and crouched as I talked. I told the desk I thought I would have a pretty good story for the Sunday paper. Then I retreated to my hotel, the Chateau Marmont in Hollywood, set up my typewriter by the swimming pool, watched the smoke billowing out of Watts, and, in that strange setting juxtaposing reality and unreality, wrote a story that ran on the front page of the Sunday *Trib:*

> Blood stained the broken glass strewn on the sidewalk outside 8201 San Pedro Ave. A 27-year-old policeman crouched behind Patrol Car 12522, a gaping hole cut into its windshield, the motto "To Protect and to Serve" printed on its side. The policeman clenched his 12-gauge sawed-off shotgun, a riot gun, and every time a car cruised by, he tensed. "The snipers scare you," he said.
>
> In all directions, the sky glowed red with fresh flames, from the Friendly Furniture store and the White Front discount house and a Mexican food stand, sacked and then burned, and the screams of police sirens played counterpoint to the burglar alarms ringing unheeded up and down the street.

I reported from Watts for a week, driving in and out of the scarred neighborhood, ducking involuntarily when I heard sudden noises, scanning the rooftops for possible snipers, observing the return of an uneasy calm. A month later, I went back to Los Angeles, to watch baseball once again, to cover the Dodgers in the last week of the pennant race, and to revisit Watts. It did not strike me as at all strange that one day I was asking people about fast balls and curves and the next about looting and shooting.

The journalistic principles are the same for covering a pennant race or a race riot. You use your eyes, your ears, and, as Jimmy Breslin has always preached, your legs. You go to the scene. You talk to the people involved. You ask questions. You look for the small details that illuminate the larger story and reinforce credibility, and then, using those details, using quotes, using the richness of the English language, you tell the story as vividly, as honestly, as compellingly as you can. Your story has a beginning, a middle, and an end, and each leads seamlessly to the next. But the beginning, the lead, and the ending, the denouement, must be especially strong.

When I went back to Watts, I met a courageous and militant black woman named Bobbi Hollon, who came out of Harlem and Morgan State College and worked for the Westminster Neighborhood Association. She wore sneakers still caked, six weeks later, with the blood of the riots, and she wore them like a badge. She said she would never wash them. "I'm glad the riots happened," she insisted. She said they gave pride to people who, previously, had no hope. Bobbi Hollon was aggressive—and attractive. "I'll do anything I can to help here with the kids, with their mothers," she said. "I'll be fine and foxy if I have to be, or I'll be articulate, or I'll wear pants and bloody sneakers. But I won't forget who I am. I'm just a little black girl."

The next night, I had dinner at the home of Budd Schulberg, the author of *On the Waterfront* and *What Makes Sammy Run?,* and his wife, the actress Geraldine Brooks, and I told them about Bobbi Hollon. Budd was so intrigued he arranged to meet her, and their meeting led him to create the Watts Writers Workshop, a program that transformed rioters into writers.

A couple of days later, I watched the Dodgers clinch the National League pennant. "Sandy Koufax, the best advertisement for a sore elbow, set out to pitch the Dodgers into the World Series yesterday," I reported. "Poor Sandy. He was pitching with only two days' rest. Poor Milwaukee." Koufax overcame fatigue and the Braves, 3–1.

Then I left baseball and violence behind, and returned to New York to concentrate on the race for mayor among Abe Beame, the Democrat; John Lindsay, the Republican; and William F. Buckley, the maverick.

16

Mailer Versus Dostoevsky

When William Buckley announced he was running for mayor, I attended his news conference. The Conservative Party candidate made it clear that he not only did not expect to win, but he would be appalled if he did. "What will you do if you're elected?" someone asked.

"I will demand a recount," Buckley replied.

That was vintage Buckley, and so was his retort to a question from a man clearly not a journalist who had infiltrated the conference. "Mr. Buckley," the man shouted out, "in the last issue of the *National Review,* you said that it was time to forgive the Germans and to forget about the six million Jews who were killed during World War Two. Did you mean that, Mr. Buckley?" And Buckley, at his obfuscating best, replied, "Sir, if you have come here to debate the validity of ultimate charity . . ."

Buckley's cleverness can be as confounding as his politics, but, even if you reject his beliefs, it is difficult not to be charmed by him. He is droll, always with a twinkle in his eye, and he is a talented organist and pianist who loves entertaining even liberals in his Park Avenue home.

Buckley was one of the more distinguished writers I persuaded to contribute to *SPORT* when I was its editor. Bill wrote about the Olympics. Robert Coover, the novelist, wrote about soccer. I tried to get Norman Mailer, who told me, "I'm like a fighter. If the purse is right, I go into the ring." I couldn't meet Mailer's price. But I was able to meet Pat Conroy's, in the days, long before *The Great Santini* and *Prince of Tides,* when Pat still considered a couple of hundred dollars honest pay.

Politics is the most demeaning trade I know. Not even prostitution demands that its practitioners surrender so many pieces of themselves. I've known politicians who launched their careers with intelligence and ideals and, as they rose, as being elected and reelected became obsessively important, gave away so much of themselves that all that remained was a caricature.

The 1965 New York mayoral campaign cried out for caricature: the accountant Abe Beame, short and Jewish, against the congressman John Lindsay, elegant and Protestant, and the writer William F. Buckley, haughty and Catholic. Who could ask for a more entertaining race?

On the eve of the election, I wrote:

Of the three men who have campaigned strenuously during the past few months for the right to live in Gracie Mansion, only one, Abraham Beame, seriously and deeply wants to be mayor of New York City. This alone should be enough to cast grave doubts on Beame's judgment.

One of the candidates, William F. Buckley, doesn't even want to live in New York City, much less be mayor. . . . Buckley really wants to be a journalist, which casts even graver doubts on his judgment.

The third man, John V. Lindsay, actually wants to be President of the United States. It is indicative of the silly state of politics that this ambition, which is a totally reasonable one, cannot even be mentioned in the campaign. Lindsay, instead, must pretend that all through his life he has dreamed of being mayor of New York.

Lindsay won, and a week later, literally, not figuratively, the lights went out all over New York City. A blackout, originating at a power plant near Niagara Falls, paralyzed the city and much of the Northeast. I was sitting at my desk at the *Trib,* in the office I shared with Breslin, and as the lights dimmed, I succumbed to paranoia. "The *Times,*" I thought. "The *Times* did this to us."

As soon as I determined that the *Times* was innocent, that they, too, were cursing the darkness, I set out to explore the moonlit city. I started on the West Side, on Broadway, worked my way up past the northern end of Central Park and into Harlem, then stopped at a 125th Street restaurant where the owner was giving away shrimp cocktails before they spoiled. Harlem was peaceful. "Baby," I was told, "we didn't know the lights were going to be out this long."

I resumed my trip, down the east side of Central Park till I reached Sardi's East, the restaurant where, in a back room, John Lindsay and his campaign aides were celebrating their victory by candlelight. I walked in, and Bob Price, his campaign manager, greeted me,

"What the fuck are you doing here?" The mayor-elect was more cordial. Price suggested that Abe Beame, the incumbent controller of New York City, had forgotten to pay the electric bill. Lindsay suggested that maybe he should take a tour of his powerless town.

I wound up the evening at the downtown apartment of a young woman I knew who graciously offered to share her bed with me. She had already graciously offered to share the bed with one of her girlfriends. To avoid an argument, I suggested that the three of us share the bed. I lay in the middle, just as I had often fantasized. All of us remained fully clothed; my companions, apparently, did not share my fantasy.

The next day, after little sleep, I sat down and described the city by moonlight:

> In the cockpit of his TWA airliner coming into Kennedy Airport from Pittsburgh, Capt. William Brown began his approach to runway 4-right. "Captain," said his co-pilot, "the runway lights are starting to dim."
>
> On the elevator leaving the lobby of the Winslow Hotel, on Madison Ave., a 91-year-old woman, Mrs. Edgar Moyes, began to relax for the ride up. Before the car reached the second floor, it rocked to a halt. . . .
>
> Everywhere lights flickered, died, glowed again and died. Television screens sputtered, then went blank. And electric clocks stood still.
>
> The time was 5:28 P.M. EST. . . .
>
> The brightest city in the world had gone dark. . . .

The story ran on for three thousand words, an epic by newspaper standards, certainly the longest I ever wrote for the *Tribune*.

One year to the day after the blackout, I went to Queenston, Ontario, on the Canadian side of Niagara Falls, and visited the Beck power plant where, on November 9, 1965, a tiny relay had shut down without warning, stripping two provinces, nine states, and twenty-five million people of their electricity. I wanted to see if it would happen again. I also wanted to see if I could talk to John Lovering, who was the shift foreman in the plant when darkness descended.

"Lovering entered the elevator on the main floor of the Beck plant," I reported, "and, in a few seconds, descended 245 feet to the control room where he would sit, for eight hours, and stare at dozens of small dials on the wall in front of him. A year ago, the dials . . . dropped to the bottom when the electric energy burst out of the plant, and Lovering had been the first man to know that something had gone wrong.

"He would not talk about 1965 yesterday. . . . 'You can understand,' said Bert Bloome, superintendent of the Beck plant. 'He still feels badly about it.' "

Many of my stories, notably the reports on Watts and the blackout, were samples of the so-called New Journalism of the 1960s, journalism that ignored the old rules of "who-what-why-where-when" and the inverted pyramid (facts revealed in descending order of importance) and, instead, used novelistic techniques to re-create scenes, to establish atmosphere and characters. Tom Wolfe, Jimmy Breslin, and Gay Talese were among the earliest journalists to practice this art, and in their hands, at their best, it truly was an art. I was more of a craftsman.

Wolfe, in an essay on "The New Journalism," wrote of the feature writers on the *Tribune:*

[Charlie] Portis had the desk behind. Down in a bullpen at a far end of the room was Jimmy Breslin. Over to one side sat Dick Schaap. We were all engaged in a form of newspaper competition that I have never known anybody even to talk about in public. Yet Schaap had quit as city editor of the *Herald Tribune,* which was one of the legendary jobs in journalism— moved *down* the organizational chart in other words— just to get in this secret game. . . .

Here was half the feature competition in New York, right in the same city room with me, because the *Herald Tribune* was like the main Tijuana bullring for feature writers . . . Portis, Breslin, Schaap . . . Schaap and Breslin had columns, which gave them more freedom, but I figured I could take the both of them. [I figured Breslin had a puncher's chance.]

I always considered those mentions more flattering than accurate. Not that I've ever been exactly self-effacing. My ego does permit me to think of myself as only a notch below the best of the New Journalists, and as being capable of doing some things the others can't. What those things might possibly be, I can't imagine.

I was in the perfect place at the perfect time, in the dizzying company of writers who cared and stories that mattered. I worked for the *Herald Tribune* for only the last two and a half years of its existence, but I covered enough major stories to last a lifetime.

Not long after the 1964 election, before Lyndon Johnson was sworn in for a full term, the vice president–elect, Hubert H. Humphrey of Minnesota, invited Breslin and me to have breakfast with him in the Presidential Suite at New York's Carlyle Hotel. Senator Humphrey asked us serious questions, and took our answers seriously. Until that morning, I had an idealized conception of the people who ran the country. I assumed they were smarter than the rest of us, better informed, more articulate, and, in almost every conceivable way, superior human beings. I was wrong. Breslin knew more than Humphrey about the causes and cures of crime in the streets, and didn't hesitate to tell him. I mostly listened. So did the vice president–elect.

A few years later, I wrote a story for *Harper's* magazine about the man who was not elected vice president:

> Brenda, the friendly waitress in Jaeger's Restaurant on Main Street in the heart of Lockport, New York, heard the question and glanced up from the bacon and eggs she was serving. "Who's the most famous person in Lockport?" she repeated. She thought for half a minute. "Gee," she said. "I don't know."
>
> "Is there anybody particularly famous in Lockport?" she was then asked.
>
> Brenda shook her head. "Nobody that I can think of," she said.
>
> "Anybody who ever did anything spectacular?"
>
> "I've only lived here fifteen years," she said.
>
> *Only three years ago, in the election of 1964, Congressman William E. Miller of Lockport, New York, missed becoming President of the United States by one heartbeat and sixteen million votes.*

I called the story "Whatever Happened to What's His Name?" but the editor of *Harper's,* Willie Morris, changed the title to "Whatever Happened to William E. Miller?" I thought it was one of Willie's few lapses in editorial judgment. Willie was the youngest editor in the distinguished history of *Harper's*. He was born, like me, in 1934, and enjoyed a similar celebrity, his on a larger, and more literary, scale.

Some of my best friends were editors, including Paul Krassner, the outrageous overseer of an outrageous (but funny) publication called *The Realist*. Once Paul accompanied me to a party at Norman Mailer's home in Brooklyn Heights, and when I introduced him to James Baldwin, Paul sweetly asked the author, "Is it true that LeRoi Jones is the black James Baldwin?" The man who wrote *The Fire Next Time* quietly burned.

I knew Baldwin, and Jones, because early in my *Tribune* days, while I was still city editor, Richard Kluger, the editor of *Book Week,* the newspaper's Sunday literary supplement, gave me the opportunity to contribute a column about books and authors.

The best part of writing the column was that it forced me to read a book every week. At the time, I also read a dozen daily newspapers and perhaps as many weekly and monthly magazines; I read rapidly. As I got older and slipped out of the habit of reading so many newspapers, magazines, and books, I slowed down. I'm still not certain whether I read less because I slowed down, or I slowed down because I read less.

During the four years I wrote for *Book Week*—the supplement survived in the *Chicago Sun-Times* after the *Herald Tribune* perished—I met, and cultivated, dozens of writers, from Terry Southern and William Burroughs to Ralph Ellison and James Jones. I had read and loved *Catch-22* and met Joe Heller when I was at *Newsweek,* but when I was writing the *Book*

Week column, he told me that I had almost read *Catch-18,* which was his original title. But Leon Uris's *Mila 18* beat him to the bookstores, and Heller's publisher did not think the public was ready for two "18" books in the same year. At first, Heller resisted, certain that "18" was the only suitable number, but eventually he relented. "After all, twenty-two is a funnier word," he told me.

I visited James T. Farrell, who had written *Studs Lonigan* three decades earlier, in his apartment in New York's Beaux Arts Hotel, and he showed me 32,000 pages of unpublished work, novels and short stories and essays, and talked about his friends Ernest Hemingway and H. L. Mencken and his heroes Paul Waner and Shoeless Joe Jackson, and he said that his favorite baseball book was Ring Lardner's *You Know Me, Al,* his least favorite, Bernard Malamud's *The Natural.*

Farrell's low opinion of *The Natural* delighted me. Once, at a party in the home of the book publisher Roger Strauss, someone asked me if I would like to meet Malamud, and I said I would. When we were introduced, I said, "Mr. Malamud, I'm a great admirer of your work, but as a former sportswriter, I always had some questions about *The Natural.*"

Before I could ask one, Malamud said, "Well, obviously, you didn't understand it."

I conceded the possibility.

"You see," Malamud said, "it's the telling of the story of Sir Percival in modern terms."

He turned away, saying, "If you have any more questions, ask me later."

I checked out Sir Percival. He was the youngest and purest of King Arthur's knights. When Arthur was dying, he asked Sir Percival to return the sword Excalibur to the Lady of the Lake. That explained it.

Robert Lowell, the poet, treated me with similar scorn. I interviewed him about the odds against a poet earning a living, and my questions were obviously too crass for him. He would have preferred that I address the intellectual challenges of his poetry, but I wasn't certain that I comprehended his work, and he was certain that I didn't.

When Norman Mailer, the finest American writer of my generation, wrote *An American Dream,* a novel about crime and more, I interviewed him over a drink at Bleeck's. "Who's reviewing the book?" he asked me.

"Tom Wolfe," I said.

"What does he say?" Mailer wanted to know.

"I don't know," I said, "but I do know that he compares the book to *Crime and Punishment* and you to Dostoevsky."

"Guess who wins that match," Mailer said.

Once I was invited to be a panelist on a radio show discussing books and authors, and a man named Bernie Geis, the publisher of Jacqueline Susann, the author of the potboiling bestseller *Valley of the Dolls,* argued that Susann was a great novelist, perhaps in the tradition of Proust and Jane Austen. I said I agreed. "I think she has a lot of Balzac in her," I said. In those innocent days, I was bleeped off the air.

I hit the literary jackpot one night. I took three novelists from three countries—the German Gunter Grass, the Irish Edna O'Brien, and the American Calder Willingham—to watch the second Ali-Liston fight on closed-circuit television at the Hotel Astor. The national anthem lasted almost as long as the fight, and after Ali knocked out Liston in the first round, Grass, who later won the Nobel Prize, came out whistling "The Star-Spangled Banner." "It's a very catchy tune," he said.

I met dozens of authors, obscure and famous. I did not meet J. D. Salinger.

17

"A Friend in Need Is a Pest"

In 1966, Peter Falk was the star of a TV series called *The Trials of O'Brien*, which was admired by most of the critics and ignored by most of the public. Peter played a lawyer, and the excellent cast included Elaine Stritch and Joanna Barnes. When the show was about to expire, I decided to write a column about its final day.

The shooting took place at an old movie studio in East Harlem. Everyone knew it was the last show, but that did not stop Falk, speaking softly, believably, from delivering his lines over and over until he met his own demanding standards.

I was reminded of Falk's perfectionism two decades later when Jonathan Pryce, the British actor, told me what it was like to work with Robert De Niro on Terry Gilliam's film *Brazil*. "When we did the first take," Pryce said, "De Niro was the worst actor I had ever seen. By the twenty-fifth take, he was the best."

I had met De Niro when he and Michael Moriarty

and Danny Aiello—all unknowns—made the baseball movie *Bang the Drum Slowly*. De Niro played the catcher. At the beginning, De Niro was the worst catcher I had ever seen. By the end, he wasn't bad.

De Niro, who grew up in Manhattan, had never played or followed baseball. Years later, when he and Billy Crystal teamed up for *Analyze This,* Billy invited the Yankees' David Wells to the set the day after Wells pitched a perfect game. "That's David Wells," Crystal told De Niro.

"Who the fuck is David Wells?" De Niro said.

"He pitches for the Yankees. He pitched a perfect game yesterday."

"What the fuck is a perfect game?"

"No hits, no walks, no base runners," Crystal explained.

"Sounds fucking boring to me," De Niro said.

While Falk was shooting his scenes in the East Harlem studio, an attractive and playful blonde was standing in for Elaine Stritch and Joanna Barnes, representing them for the purpose of setting the proper lights. She finished her stand-in duty late in the afternoon, just as I was preparing to go downtown. For some strange reason, I offered to share a cab with her. She accepted, for a good reason. She knew that after the final scene was shot that evening, on the corner of Park Avenue and Fifty-fourth Street, I was going out with Peter Falk. She had been trying to seduce Peter for weeks, trying without success to add him to an impressive list of celebrity conquests, and she figured this was her final chance. Of course, I thought she wanted me.

I invited her to have a drink at the Lombardy Hotel,

across the street from the final location, half an hour before the shooting was to begin. She arrived promptly, with a friend. The purpose of the friend was to distract me. I was distracted.

After Falk finished shooting, he and I and the two women went out. It was a weird evening. We went to the Andy Warhol Cinematheque, a midtown theater operated by the pop artist to showcase his own films. As I recall, we sat through a Warhol triple feature. One of the films was about Salvador Dalí, who was in the audience. I knew Warhol slightly, and between films, I introduced him to Peter. They talked for fifteen minutes, and I am reasonably certain that neither understood one word the other said.

When we escaped from the movies, Peter and I and the two women went to Joe Allen's, a popular spot for the show business set. We sat around a red-and-white-checkered tablecloth, ordered hamburgers and drinks. I think Peter ordered a Coke. When he finished, he put a twenty-dollar bill on the table, stood up, and said, "I got to get out of here. I got a pool game at McGirr's at two o'clock."

McGirr's was a billiards parlor around the corner, on Eighth Avenue. It was ten minutes before two. Peter walked out and left me with both women. I got a cab, dropped the blonde at her home, and accompanied the friend to hers. I did not get home before daylight.

The next day, I saw Peter, and he said to me, "Stay away from those broads, they're crazy."

I thought he was kidding. A little more than a year later, I married the distraction. I found out Peter wasn't kidding.

However, the evidence suggests that I was crazier.

* * *

The same week that I met the woman who would become my second wife, a New York City policeman, searching for heroin, opened the trunk of a rented red Chevrolet and discovered, instead, the dead body of a nineteen-year-old girl named Celeste Crenshaw. Her arms were tracked with needle scars. Her boyfriend, Robert Friede, who was twenty-five, had been found sitting at the wheel, blue eyes dazed by heroin. Friede was the nephew of Walter Annenberg, the multimillionaire newspaper publisher who became Richard Nixon's ambassador to the Court of St. James's. Crenshaw, it developed, had been high on amphetamines, and Friede had injected a double dose of heroin to bring her down. The heroin overdose killed her, and Friede, terrified, kept her body in the trunk of his car for thirteen days, until the police found him parked on East Second Street, between Avenue A and Avenue B, lost in a heroin nod.

As soon as I read about the death of Celeste Crenshaw, I wanted to write a book about it. I wanted to write the book because Truman Capote had recently published *In Cold Blood*. Capote claimed that he had invented a new literary form, the "nonfiction novel." Of course he hadn't. He had simply used the techniques of the New Journalism, the form Wolfe and Breslin were already practicing at a high level, the form that Norman Mailer would lift to an even higher level in *The Executioner's Song*. If Capote had invented anything, it was simply a new way to sell books. "A boy has to hustle," he once said. Still, with his considerable talent and imagination, Capote had fashioned an irresistible story, an instant bestseller, a book that made millions. Many journalists were jealous—of Capote's success, his skill, and, not least, his claim to have invented a new literary form. We wanted to show that we, too, could write compelling nonfiction novels about true crimes.

Turned On: The Friede-Crenshaw Case was my small contribution to the genre. ("Schaap then, with less artifice and more instinctive empathy than Truman Capote, details the lives and shadowy drug world of both victim and her lover-executioner," said the *New York Times Book Review*. The review was written by Jack Newfield of the *Village Voice,* who was, and is, a friend. It was nice of Jack to be so kind, but *In Cold Blood* was, and is, a better book.)

I wrote *Turned On* in a strange way. Usually, you write a book and, if you're lucky, you sell excerpts to magazines and newspapers, whetting a reader's appetite. I did it backward. First, I wrote a magazine article for *Look,* which was called "Death of a Hooked Heiress," and was reprinted in *Best Magazine Articles: 1967,* in company with stories by Wolfe (his classic on New York City in a state of "behavioral sink"), Talese (*the* profile of Joe DiMaggio), John McPhee, Joan Didion, and Gore Vidal. Then I expanded the magazine article into a series of fifteen newspaper articles called "Turned On," and finally I expanded the newspaper articles into a book with the same title. Interestingly, while I was working on the project, Walter Annenberg, then owner of the *Philadelphia Inquirer,* wrote a letter to his fellow publisher, Jock Whitney, my boss at the *Herald Tribune,* warning Jock that a member of the *Trib* staff was working on a scurrilous story about a member of the Annenberg family. Whitney wrote back and said, in essence, "I know."

My unpaid research assistant on *Turned On* was Pe-

ter Falk, who was between engagements and fascinated by the drug culture and the cop culture in New
York City. Peter accompanied me on several excur-
sions into both worlds. He always asked intelligent
questions—"Just one more thing"—and his familiar
presence often encouraged people to speak more
freely.

The first time Peter joined me, we walked up four
littered flights to the dingy loft of a college-educated
junkie whom, in the book, I called Art English. When
we entered the loft, "Art" was pacing back and forth,
clearly agitated, on the brink of sickness because his
next fix, his next shot of heroin, was overdue. Earlier in
the day, he had purchased from an unfamiliar connection several tiny glassine envelopes that had been ad-
vertised to contain heroin. He had removed the white
powder from a few of the envelopes and had shot it
into his veins, and it had not affected him at all.

"It looks just like heroin," he said, "but I don't know
what the hell it is. It doesn't do anything, damn it. It's
garbage. I had three junkies taste it, and none of them
knew what it was." He swore, furious that he had been
cheated out of money and, worse, out of his fix.

Suddenly, he reached into his back pocket and
pulled out a glassine envelope. He strode to a small
table, lifted a switchblade knife, triggered it open, and
slit the envelope. He poured the white powder onto a
torn copy of *Life* magazine, then turned to me. "Taste
it," he said.

I hesitated. I was reasonably certain that it was not
heroin; he would not give heroin away. But the white
powder could have been anything. "Art" could have
been paranoid; he could have thought I was a detective.
He had already told me I looked like a cop, and I had

asked him how he could trust me. He had shrugged and said, "I might as well," without further explanation.

"No, thanks," I said.

He waved the switchblade knife and pointed it at the powder. "Taste it," he repeated.

I dipped my index finger into the powder and licked the tip of my finger. The powder tasted sweet.

The junkie turned to Peter Falk. "You taste it," he said.

Falk, too, went through the motions of sticking his finger into the powder and onto his tongue. "A little bitter," he said.

The next few minutes passed slowly. One selfish thought occurred to me. "Peter's shorter than I am," I figured, "and if it's poison, it'll affect him first. I'll have a warning."

Nothing happened. Half an hour later, Peter and I left the loft. "Did it really taste bitter to you?" I asked.

"How the fuck would I know?" he said. "I palmed it."

Another time, I introduced Peter to a junkie who, after several minutes, said, "Ain't you an actor?"

Peter confessed that he was.

"I seen you on television," the junkie said. "I seen you when I was in the joint. You're a terrific lawyer."

The persuasive power of television is remarkable. Once, when Peter and I were at a bar, a young man walked over, told us he was an arsonist, and offered to turn himself in if Peter would represent him.

Of course not everyone was consumed by television. When I lived in an East Side apartment building in the late 1960s, the only person my doorman ever stopped from coming up to my apartment unannounced was Peter Falk. He was wearing a frayed trench coat.

When "Turned On" ran in installments in the *World*

Journal Tribune, the bastardized successor to the *Trib,*
Peter agreed to film a television commercial to publicize the series. He stood by the trunk of a car, not unlike the car in which Celeste Crenshaw's body had
been found, and summarized the story. His first take
was very good. His second was better. "We've got it,"
the director said. Falk didn't think so. He did fifteen
takes before he was satisfied, and he wasn't being paid.

A few years later, when Falk was playing Columbo,
a friend of mine in the advertising business asked me if
I would ask Peter about doing a commercial for Tuborg
beer. He said Peter would get something like $50,000
for one day's work. I passed the offer along, and Peter
said, "That's for people on the way down."

Peter and I had a falling-out in the mid-1970s, a dis-
pute that was entirely my fault. At the time, I was editor of *SPORT* and hosting a dinner to honor
Muhammad Ali. The writers George Plimpton and
Neil Simon were going to speak. The singer Melba
Moore was going to perform. The unknown Billy
Crystal was going to entertain. I asked Peter if he
would emcee the dinner. He said no, he was busy, he
couldn't make it, but I didn't give up. I pestered him,
beseeched him, told him how much it would mean to
me, tried to lay obligation and guilt on him. We didn't
speak for a few years after that.

The next time I saw Falk was at the Polo Lounge of
the Beverly Hills Hotel. He was having breakfast with
Neil Simon. I was having breakfast with Trish, whom I
was about to marry. We all chatted for a few minutes.
Peter had warned me about my second marriage. "Is it
all right this time?" I asked.

"It's a definite maybe," he replied.

Our friendship revived, but he was so busy in the

late seventies and eighties, with television and films and theater, we saw each other rarely.

I learned a lesson the time I antagonized Peter. I learned not to lean too heavily on friends. I learned to be considerate of the demands upon them. As Breslin puts it, "A friend in need is a pest."

In recent years, hardly a week has gone by without someone asking me to intervene in some way with Billy Crystal. Ask him to read a screenplay. *It's a great script.* Ask him to appear at a charity affair. *It's a terrific cause.* Ask him to autograph a photograph. *Tell him to write, "You look mahvelous."* On rare occasion, if the request seems reasonable enough, I will pass it along to Billy. But I try, very hard, not to put any pressure on him. I can see, when I'm with him, how much pressure there already is.

Many of my columns for the *Herald Tribune* touched on show business, and two that I remember vividly sprang from observing Broadway auditions. One was an audition for the Anthony Newley–Leslie Bricusse musical *The Roar of the Greasepaint, the Smell of the Crowd.* A young African-American, barely out of his teens, stepped onstage and sang Martin Luther King's "I Have a Dream" speech set to music. I was sitting behind Newley and the producer, David Merrick.

"He's too young for the part," Newley said, "and he's too tall for the part. All he's got is the greatest bloody fucking voice I've ever heard." Gilbert Price got the part.

Gilbert and I became friends. I was awed by his talent, his warmth; he was pleased to be noticed. Gilbert went to Erasmus Hall High School in Brooklyn, a con-

temporary of Streisand, and he was so sweet class-
mates called him "The Subway Saint."

The day after Trish and I were married, our friend
Ed Downe hosted a magnificent party for us, and I
knew that Trish was going to sing a song to me, "I'll
Walk Beside You." She has a pure and beautiful voice,
and I cannot carry the simplest tune. I responded to her
song by standing up and pretending that I was going to
sing. She was terrified. Then I stepped back, and
Gilbert Price, whom Trish had never met, stepped in
and began to sing "You Are My Beloved." Gilbert sang
with his arms around both of us and with a smile that
ranged from beatific to mischievous. He thundered and
purred. He hit notes that I did not know existed. Trish
cried. I cried. Gilbert was the star of our wedding.

A few years later, my parents celebrated their fiftieth
wedding anniversary. For their party, Gilbert recorded
the Erasmus Hall fight song on videotape. My parents
cried.

Gilbert was an enormously gifted performer who
traveled with Harry Belafonte and appeared on Broadway. He had everything he needed to become a huge
star, except he was driven by neither ego nor greed. He
sang at his church. He sang at fund-raisers. Once, he
sang at a New York State prison and, even after being
warned that the inmates were not receptive to songs
that stressed religion or patriotism, he opened his program with "God Bless America" and sang with such
vigor and conviction that the inmates began singing
along with him.

Gilbert did not have an easy life. He suffered from
juvenile diabetes and regularly had to inject insulin. He
developed psychological problems, saw angels and
devils dueling for his tortured soul, and, despite his tal-

ent, rarely earned much money. For a while, he lived with me and my family, and he would sing "Puff the Magic Dragon" to my children. But Gilbert was HIV-positive and used needles intravenously and sometimes, in his confusion, forget to put away his needles. I hated asking him to move, but had to.

He did not develop full-blown AIDS. He tried to revive his career, but his religious intensity frightened people. He was invited to Vienna to sing, and one night, as he was using a gas heater to warm a rented flat, something went wrong, and the gas escaped, and he was asphyxiated. Gilbert died far too young. I presided over the memorial service at the Actors Chapel off Broadway. Geoffrey Holder, the flamboyant dancer, swept into the chapel wrapped in a cape, delivered a eulogy, and swept out.

At a "cattle call," an open audition, I met a young woman three months out of Juilliard whose name was Susan Cohen. She came from Boston, where her father was an attorney, and she had previously auditioned, unsuccessfully, for four Broadway shows. She had earned $80 in three months, $45 for teaching modern dance to a group of suburban children, $35 for posing as a battered woman to illustrate a *Modern Romance* story called "I Was a Teenage Mental Case." Her parents did not applaud her choice of career.

My story of Susan's struggle to succeed in show business concluded:

> A few months ago, Susan was dating a young actor who had a show opening in Boston, so she took the young actor to meet her parents. The parents liked him right away. He was intelligent, polite, a good conver-

sationalist. He was just, from the parents' point of view, in the wrong business. On the way to the airport, after the visit, the young actor, who got the picture clearly, turned to Susan's mother and needled, "I'll call you when I go into medicine."

Mrs. Cohen brightened perceptibly. "Oh," she said, "are you interested in medicine?"

Several years after the column appeared, I was at Madison Square Garden, watching the New York Knicks. After the game, a guy who sat regularly behind the Knicks' bench said to me, "Do you remember the story you wrote about the girl who wanted to be an actress and had a boyfriend who wanted to be an actor?"

"Sure," I said.

"Well, I was the boyfriend," said Dustin Hoffman.

Susan Cohen's relationship with Dusty, as she called him, lasted several years. My friendship with Susan was more enduring, but less intense.

Whenever I was strapped for a column, I called Herb Gardner and, invariably, he fed me wit:

Herb Gardner is finally approaching the end of his second play. Yesterday, he started writing thank-you notes for the opening-night telegrams. Any day now, he is going to begin work on the third act.

"With my first play," Gardner explained over the phone, as he sat in his studio and struggled to avoid writing, "I didn't know what the business was all about. I just wrote a play and they put it on. Now I know how the system works. The play isn't important.

"Right now, I'm very busy on the pre-post-production. For instance, I'm preparing rejoinders to all the critics. I'm also getting ready a diatribe against the whole Broadway system. I'll burn it, of course, if the play is successful. My integrity carries me about ten blocks.

"It's very important now for me to figure out what my play is all about, so that, after the reviews appear, I can have my defense ready. I'm teaching my friends to say, *They don't understand you,* every time they see me."

"They don't understand you," I offered.

"Thank you," said Herb Gardner.

"Look," I said, "I don't want to keep you from working."

"Please, please, don't hang up," Gardner responded. "How is the play itself coming?"

"Very well," he said. "I go to work at 7 a.m. every day. I'm asleep by 8 a.m. Then I stop for lunch. I have my heart and a glass of milk."

I don't think Herb has ever spoken a bad sentence, either.

When I covered the First Annual Spring Revel of *The Paris Review*, the literary quarterly edited by George Plimpton, I watched Norman Mailer and William Styron and a couple of others compete for the title of top celebrity. The competition ended when Frank Sinatra walked into the Village Gate, the site of the party. Plimpton had invited Sinatra only because he knew his address, never expecting him to show up. Sinatra towered over the more lettered guests. "Now, finally, the trinity is complete," I wrote, "the saints of *The Paris Review*—Hemingway, Faulkner, Sinatra." I described Sinatra's departure—"Frank's splitting," one of his henchmen explained—and, as the party visibly sagged, I concluded, "It must have been like that at the Mermaid when Shakespeare split."

Sinatra's press agent hated my piece, until he found out that Frank liked it.

My favorite topic in my newspaper columns was John Lindsay. At the start of his administration, I introduced the nickname Fun City to describe New York. Lindsay himself inspired the phrase. The subways went on strike his first day in office, and after he toured the gridlocked city in a helicopter, someone asked him if he was still glad that he had been elected mayor. "I still think it's a fun city," Lindsay said.

I grabbed the words, capitalized them, and ran with them. I think my first reference to Fun City came in a paraphrase of the mayor's comment (" 'New York's a Fun City'—John Lindsay") followed by a gibe (" 'Same here'—the Mayor of Da Nang"). The name caught on, and regularly, as often as once every week or ten days, I called my column, "What's New in Fun City?"

Lindsay himself always gave me credit, and in a letter to William Safire, the *New York Times*'s formidable essayist and etymologist, Woody Klein, the mayor's first press secretary, wrote, "It was Dick Schaap . . . who publicized the term with his regular columns entitled, 'What's New in Fun City?' "

A third of a century after I first used the expression, the *Times* put its official imprimatur on my creation: "Though the term is commonly associated with Mayor John V. Lindsay and his eight years in office [1966–1973], it was Dick Schaap . . . who coined and popularized the vaguely sarcastic term . . . the term still carries with it the none-too-faint scent of derision."

"Fun City" was derisive, and sarcastic, but it was also affectionate. I liked John Lindsay, I respected the dedication and idealism of his administration, and I believed New York *was* a fun city. Lindsay encouraged me to use the nickname. He got angry with me only twice, once when critics attacked him for telling mugging jokes to Johnny Carson—they said that was beneath the dignity of the mayor of New York City—and I defended him by saying that nothing was beneath his dignity, and once when Muhammad Ali returned from exile, and I suggested that an Ali-Lindsay title match might pack Madison Square Garden, but might not be sanctioned because Lindsay was not a real heavyweight.

The rest of the time, the mayor and I got along fine. We went head-to-head only once. The occasion was the First Annual Softball Game between City Hall and the City Hall reporters. I pitched for the reporters. Lindsay batted for City Hall. It was not exactly Seaver versus Aaron.

"John V. Lindsay, the Mayor of Fun City, stepped up to home plate, tall and loose and confident," I wrote. "Only the faintest trace of a sneer curled across his lips. . . . His teammates cheered. . . . One of the Mayor's sides, from force of habit, said, 'Now, here's what we've got to get John to do.' "

The catcher came to me and offered counsel. "Don't pitch fast to him," the catcher said. "I promised them you wouldn't pitch fast to him." I was appalled by the thought of giving anything less than the athlete's standard, if mathematically improbable, 110 percent. Still, it was Lindsay's turf. It was Central Park. I pitched slow.

The first pitch floated in low and inside, near the mayor's knees, and Lindsay skipped deftly out of the way. It was at that moment that I was truly glad that Lindsay had won the mayoral race, because, I wrote, "the pitch might have hit Abe Beame in the head."

Incumbent mayor Lindsay thought the last line was pretty funny. Future mayor Beame did not.

City Hall won the game, but I got even when my friend Barry Gottehrer decided to leave the Lindsay administration. I was asked to emcee his farewell dinner. I introduced everyone on the dais and insulted all of them impartially. The only one who was offended was Burton Roberts, the district attorney of the Bronx. I said that Roberts arrived at the dinner late because he was busy writing his memoirs, *Mein Kampf*. Roberts called me the next day to complain. "That's not a nice thing to say about a Jewish boy," Burt maintained.

Let me make up to Roberts by pointing out that he was an excellent district attorney and, later, a fine judge, always energetic, informed, passionate, and intelligent. I should also mention that I never met a man who more enjoyed seeing his name or, preferably, his picture in the newspaper, preferably on the front page.

Sometimes I searched for columns; sometimes I stumbled on them. Once, after a speech in Syracuse in upstate New York, I took a midnight Greyhound bus back to the city. A man in work shirt and creased trousers sat next to me, opened a brown paper bag, took out a white turnip, and bit into it. Soon he started singing a college fight song. "Your school?" I asked.

"Oh, no," he said. "It's just football season."

He told me that he was on his way to New York City for a reunion. "College?" I asked. "High school?"

"No," he said. "My orphanage."

He told me he was employed as a custodian, a janitor, at a YMCA in Syracuse, but many of the people who had been raised in the orphanage with him had become lawyers and doctors and successful businessmen, and he was proud of them. He couldn't wait to see them.

The next day, I called the orphanage and asked about the reunion. (I should have used my legs; I should have gone to the reunion.) I mentioned the name of the man who had been eating white turnips and singing football songs on the midnight bus. "Did he attend?" I asked.

"Oh, yes," I was told. "He was very nice. He stood by himself in a corner and just looked at everybody."

I wrote a column that day about the YMCA custodian who had traveled all night to attend a reunion at his orphanage, and when the paper came out, Jimmy Breslin gruffly paid me his ultimate compliment. "Stick to your own set," he said. "Stay away from my people."

18

Deaths in the Family

Not long before the *Herald Tribune* succumbed to economics, my old boss, Roger Kahn, came to visit the paper that had given him his start. He wrote about the visit in *The Boys of Summer* and concluded that the paper had declined disastrously after his departure. He looked in the office that Breslin and I shared, and he wrote: "A fat columnist bulged over his typewriter, cursing and reeking of beer. A hungry-eyed columnist sat nearby, squirming in his chair. . . . Between the two, a fat hungry-eyed secretary slouched on a table, her short skirt hiked high on enormous thighs. . . ."

I was offended. Why didn't Kahn notice that Breslin's eyes were as hungry as mine and the secretary's? Actually, I didn't mind Roger sneering at me and Jimmy, even if, in all my years of sharing an office with Breslin, he never once reeked of anything except sweat. At least Breslin and I were legitimate targets, big enough to fight back. The remarks about the secretary were just plain cruel. Breslin wrote a note:

Dear Roger:
Your body needs cheap shots the way other people's
bodies need blood.

I mailed it for Jimmy. He was lousy on addresses.

Late in the life of the *Trib,* Jimmy Breslin, Walt Kelly,
and I decided to form our own labor union in opposition to the American Newspaper Guild, which we felt
did not properly represent the editorial worker. This
decision, I recall, was made late at night, and announced at a news conference early in the morning, at
Gallagher's, a favorite saloon.

The news conference began at 10 A.M., and every
other newspaper and every television station elected to
cover it. Damon Stetson, the labor reporter for the *New
York Times,* asked how many of the editorial workers
supported the revolution, and Breslin said, "Seventy-
five percent."

"How did you arrive at that figure?" Stetson asked.

"With an abacus," Breslin said.

When the news conference ended, Jack Newfield reported in the *Village Voice,* Breslin and Kelly "lurched
toward the bar, and Dick Schaap, the most thoughtful
of the rebels, wore an expression recalling [then Lyndon Johnson's press secretary] Bill Moyers' when the
President displayed his scar to the world."

In March of 1966, John Hay Whitney, and his adviser
and hatchet man, Walter Thayer, announced that the
Herald Tribune was going to merge with two afternoon newspapers, the *Journal-American* and the
World-Telegram and Sun. Whitney and Thayer agreed
this was the only way the *Tribune* could stay alive.

Many *Trib* staffers felt that merging with a Hearst paper and a Scripps-Howard paper was a fate worse than death. They argued that such extreme life-sustaining devices should be abandoned. They preferred to die with dignity.

The planned merger triggered a newspaper strike, which began the day the *Herald Tribune* died, the final edition appearing on Sunday, April 24, 1966—not quite twenty-eight months after I joined the paper. I liked to tell people that I was the penultimate city editor of the *Trib;* I said it was like being the next-to-last mayor of Pompeii. The joke was wry, the pain real. I had never worked at any place I liked better, and never expected to again. It's hard to explain what it was like to work in a place where people had such great respect for what they were doing and such great respect for the people who were doing it with them. There was talent, commitment, integrity, professionalism, wit, and a wonderful touch of lunacy. Some of the people who ran the institution could have easily passed as inmates. All we lacked were sufficient readers and sufficient advertising to sustain a major newspaper; the unions, who took too large a share of the blame, did their damage, too, but, as the *Times* proved, you can coexist with the unions if you have the circulation and the ad revenue.

The strike delayed the start of the *World Journal Tribune* for five months, until Monday, September 12, 1966. On Sunday night, as we prepared to go to press for the first time, William Randolph Hearst Jr. himself roamed the city room. He read Breslin's column over Jimmy's shoulder and laughed in the wrong places.

Jimmy's story, on two thousand construction workers attending a dress rehearsal of Samuel Barber's *Antony and Cleopatra* in the new Metropolitan Opera

House they had built, ran all the way across the top of the front page of the first *WJT*. My column—"What Happened in Fun City?"—ran across the bottom of the page, recounting the adventures of John Lindsay during the newspaper's hiatus. "The mayor did not have a bad summer," I reported, "compared to, say, Sukarno or Verwoerd. He kept the subways running. He kept the cross-streets free of snow."

Inside the first issue of the *World Journal Tribune,* the columnists and critics included Joseph Alsop, Bert Bacharach, Phyllis Battelle, Jim Bishop, Art Buchwald, Jimmy Cannon, Bennett Cerf, Bob Considine, Judith Crist, Heloise Cruse, Dear Abby, Joseph X. Dever, Evans and Novak, Emily Genauer, Leslie Gould, John Gruen, Joseph Kaselow, Allan Keller, Suzy Knickerbocker, Dorothy Manners, Norton Mockridge, Dr. Molner, Norman Nadel, Jack O'Brien, Clementine Paddleford, Inez Robb, Carl T. Rowan, Eugenia Sheppard, Sam Shulsky, Red Smith, Louis Sobel, Harriett Van Horne, and William S. White. A large percentage of them were gossip columnists. We had celebrity couples meeting, mating, splitting, and reconciling all in the same edition. The Widget—as we came to call it—was not a great newspaper. The first night, Breslin gave the paper six months. He was wrong. It lasted more than seven.

Still, during its brief life—even briefer for me, because I took a leave of absence in 1967 to write a book about Robert F. Kennedy—the *World Journal Tribune* provided me with several compelling assignments, starting with the murder, never solved, of future senator Charles Percy's daughter in Kenilworth, Illinois. Once more, worlds collided: The victim had gone to Cornell with my sister Nancy; one of the early suspects, quickly cleared, was a man who had worked with me at *Newsweek*.

Two months later, I covered the Sam Sheppard retrial in Cleveland, and the day of the verdict was one of the most fascinating of my life. The Sheppard case dated back to July 1954, when his wife, Marilyn, was bludgeoned to death in her own home in the suburbs of Cleveland. In a sensational Trial of the Century—one of several Trials of the Twentieth Century—Sheppard, a neurosurgeon, was found guilty of murder in the second degree and sentenced to life in prison. He protested his innocence and appealed the verdict, but for a decade, his motions for a retrial were rejected.

F. Lee Bailey, the Defense Attorney of the Decade, who in his early thirties oozed charm and cockiness, met Sheppard in prison in 1961 and by 1966 had taken the doctor's appeal to the Supreme Court of the United States and secured a retrial. The Supreme Court ruled that the carnival of publicity that had attended the original trial had deprived Sheppard of his rights to a free and unprejudiced trial. Of course, the retrial attracted almost as much coverage, and hyperbole, as the original. Bailey, who conducted a meticulous and shrewd defense, and I both were represented by Sterling Lord, the literary agent who had been my teacher at Columbia, and because of this bond, Lee invited me into the defense's inner circle.

On the day of the verdict, I accompanied the defense team to the courtroom in Cleveland, and after the judge charged the jury, I left with Sheppard, who was free on bail, and with Bailey, his associate Russ Sherman, and one of his research assistants, to await the verdict. Sheppard drove the short distance from the Cuyahoga County courthouse to our base, the Hollenden House hotel. It was mid-November 1966, and it was not a cold day, but Sheppard was wearing gloves. (His gloves seemed to fit, unlike the ones that popped up in a later Trial of the Century.) The gloves made me nervous. So did the fact that Sheppard drove with only one hand on the steering wheel, his right hand. During the trial, Bailey had elicited testimony that the killer of Marilyn Sheppard must have been left-handed, and that, therefore, Sheppard, who was right-handed, could not have committed the crime. "Lee," Sheppard said, as he drove toward the hotel, "I can't wait till we get this over with so that I can use my left hand again."

"Sam," Bailey said, "I didn't want to bring this up in court, because I didn't think it would help our case, but I've never met a surgeon who wasn't ambidextrous."

We had lunch at the hotel, and during the meal, Sheppard asked a question—I forget exactly what—that was clearly rhetorical. "Oh, Sam," Russ Sherman said, "that's like saying when did you stop beating your wife."

Silence.

Then Sheppard brightened and said, "After twenty blows."

Bailey interrupted. "No, Sam," he said, "it was only fourteen."

The gallows humor helped pass the time while the jury deliberated. We were joined by Ariane Tebbenjo-hanns, a German woman who, obsessed by the Sheppard case, had begun writing to Sam in prison and was now engaged to him. At the newsstand in the lobby of the Hollenden House, copies of a national sleaze sheet were selling briskly. The newspaper featured a story about Ariane, pointing out that her older half-sister, Magda, had been married to Joseph Goebbels, Hitler's infamous minister of propaganda, the man who had nurtured and perfected the Big Lie. In his book *Endure and Conquer,* Sheppard played down the familial connection. He pointed out that Magda and Ariane had different mothers, that Ariane's father intensely disliked his arrogant Aryan son-in-law, and that, while Ariane was too young to have been a Nazi, she was not too young to "detest the Nazis with a passion." Ariane bought a copy of the tabloid.

Late in the evening, just as the judge was getting ready to sequester the jurors for the night, Bailey got word that the jury had reached a verdict. We all rushed back to the courthouse. When the foreman of the jury announced that the defendant was not guilty, Sheppard jumped up and celebrated by slamming his fist against the tabletop. I am almost positive that he slammed it with his left fist.

Then we went back to the Hollenden House for a victory party, to toast Sheppard's innocence and Bailey's brilliance deep into the night. Several days later, Sheppard, on one of the late-night talk shows, revealed that he had had a pistol in his pocket and that he had intended to kill himself if the verdict had gone against him.

Two months later, I was back in Bailey's company, sitting with him in Cambridge, Massachusetts, bars as he outlined his plans to defend Albert DeSalvo, the self-confessed Boston Strangler. I started a column:

Some lunatic telephoned the Middlesex County courthouse yesterday and threatened to murder F. Lee Bailey, which upset Bailey very much, presumably because, if he is the victim, he may not be able to conduct the defense.

Lee Bailey does not like to see anyone else handle a major murder case. Right now, he has almost a monopoly in the Northern Hemisphere. He has Sam Sheppard safely out of prison, he has Carl Coppolino coming up for trial in Florida next month, and he has, among other clients, an accused murderer on Cape Cod, an accused murderer in Tucson, an accused murderer in Minneapolis and an accused murderer in Mexico.

His reputation is so strong and his record of acquittals so impressive that last year . . . he received a phone call from a woman out west who said she wanted to retain him *before* she murdered her husband. . . .

Bailey devised a most unusual strategy for the De-Salvo case. His client was not charged with murder, *only* with burglary, assault and battery, and "unnatural and lascivious acts." Bailey intended to prove that his client committed not only those crimes, but also the murders of thirteen women ranging in age from nineteen to eighty-five. Bailey's idea was to demonstrate that any man who committed so many heinous acts must be insane and must be found not guilty by reason of insanity, and then must be put away for life, to be studied, and perhaps even helped, by psychiatrists and criminologists.

The preliminary hearing produced testimony that one morning DeSalvo, posing as a talent scout for a modeling agency, had raped half a dozen women in their homes and then had masturbated as he drove to his own home for lunch. Theo Wilson, a feisty female reporter for the *New York Daily News,* who had covered the original Sheppard trial and the retrial, commented in a stage whisper that this case was going to be decided on penis envy.

I invited two guests to the trial of the Strangler—
the woman who was going to be my second wife and
the producer David Merrick, who was an attorney before he became an impresario and wanted to observe
Lee Bailey in action. Bailey was kind enough to leave
them house seats. My wife-to-be arrived while DeSalvo
was on the witness stand. She was wearing a very tight
sweater, and his eyes stalked her as she strutted across
the courtroom. For years afterward, she half expected
DeSalvo to escape from prison and track her down. I
suppose I am glad he didn't, even though it might have
saved me hundreds of thousands of dollars in alimony.

During the first recess after the sizable press corps
recognized him in the courtroom, Merrick held a
pseudo–news conference in the hallway. Why was he
at the trial? At first, Merrick said he was in attendance
because he was thinking of producing a musical about
the Boston Strangler. When he tired of that fiction,
Merrick explained that he was thinking of killing Clare
Booth Luce, the playwright and wife of *Time* magazine
founder Henry Luce, and that he wanted to see if Bailey would be the right person to conduct his defense.

Merrick thoroughly enjoyed his visit and that night
invited me and my future wife to join him for cocktails
at his suite in the Ritz Towers. He poured Dom
Perignon for us and persuaded me, for the first time in
my life, to taste beluga caviar. He got me hooked on
the pleasure of champagne and caviar, an addiction
that became quite expensive over the years, though not
nearly so expensive as alimony.

Bailey and I remained friends for a year or so until
he came to New York and invited my wife-to-be to go
out with him. The invitation did not include me.

Years later, I wrote a flattering profile of Merrick for *Life* magazine, and the morning after it appeared, Merrick called me. He was not happy. "You said I was born in St. Louis," he complained. "You were," I said. "You didn't have to say so," he said. We did talk about collaborating on his autobiography, but the project collapsed when he insisted the book begin, "Born on a junk in Shanghai harbor of missionary parents . . ."

Between the death of the *Herald Tribune* and the birth of the *World Journal Tribune,* Lenny Bruce died. Earlier, when he was convicted of talking dirty and sentenced to the workhouse, I had written, "So long as Bruce is not around . . . rapists will disappear from hallways . . ." When he died of an overdose of heroin, I wrote, "Lenny Bruce is dead, and the land is safe again."

I noted that he had talked about heroin the final time we spoke. "There are no legit junkies left in L.A.," he told me. "All of them are working for the federal cops or the local cops or for a magazine. You see a guy on the street, and he's got a needle in his arm, and you ask him what he's doing, and he says, 'What do you think I'm doing? I'm doing an exposé.' "

I wrote Lenny's obituary for *Playboy:*

Lenny Bruce fell off a toilet seat with a needle in his arm, and he crashed to a tiled floor and died. And the police came and harassed him in death as in life. Two at a time, they let photographers from newspapers and magazines and television stations step right up and take their pictures of Lenny Bruce lying dead on the tiled floor. It was a terrible thing for the cops to do. Lenny hated to pose for pictures.

I was proud of the lead. I was prouder of the ending:

One last four-letter word for Lenny.
Dead.
At 40.
That's obscene.

The obituary became the final chapter of a paper-back edition of Lenny's autobiography, *How to Talk Dirty and Influence People.*

When the *WJT* was mercifully dying, Bob Gutwillig, the editor in chief of New American Library, which was publishing *Turned On,* asked me if I would be interested in writing a book about the junior senator from the state of New York, Robert F. Kennedy. I said of course.

Senator Kennedy neither authorized nor approved the biography, but he was cooperative. The first time we met after I had begun the research, I mentioned that I had read considerable background material and that, so far, I had only one pressing question: Was his wife, Ethel, really as good a touch-football player as some accounts claimed?

"Would you do me one favor?" Bobby Kennedy replied. "Would you point out that my wife can do other things besides play sports?"

I repeated Kennedy's request to Breslin. "See," Jimmy said, "he wants you to lie already."

The book was magnificently illustrated, crammed with intimate and historical photographs of the photogenic Kennedys. I contributed forty thousand words of text. I estimated that my words were 50 percent favorable to Bobby, 20 percent critical, and 30 percent noncommittal. In other words, I liked him immensely. I still believe that if he had been elected president in 1968, he would have made a difference; he would have, in a meaningful way, changed the course of history. Traveling with the senator, on his chartered plane, I often had the sense of being completely safe, a strange assumption considering his family history. One time, on the plane, Bobby asked me if I missed covering sports. "No," I said. "It's the same thing as covering politics, except the athletes weren't smart enough to lie."

Once again, I couldn't resist the wisecrack. Kennedy didn't flinch. "Well," he said, smiling, "everybody in your business lies, too."

One chapter of my book was entitled "A Day with R.F.K.," and, as an earlier chapter had focused on November 22, 1963, it focused on a day that altered the shape of Bobby's political life. I spent most of that day at Hickory Hill, the senator's sprawling estate in McLean, Virginia:

> He came to the long dining room table wrapped in a monogrammed blue robe, and his wife greeted him, "Hail, Caesar." His blue eyes bleary from lack of sleep, his face unshaven, his hair even more unruly than usual, he seated himself to a breakfast of poached eggs and bacon, lifting the bacon with his fingers, and his hands began to quiver, slightly but noticeably. It may have been only fatigue, or it may have been the one overt sign of nervousness Robert F. Kennedy permitted himself on March 2, 1967, the day he delivered to the United States Senate his proposals to bring peace to Vietnam.
>
> Nervousness was logical. More than three years had

elapsed since the death of his brother, since he had been forced to set off on his own course, and now he was a senator. He was only the junior senator from New York, yet when he spoke his voice carried weight far beyond his title, beyond his experience, beyond the words themselves. His voice carried the weight of his name, the weight of his brother's memory.

His speech on Vietnam had been trumpeted and anticipated for weeks, a speech that would be interpreted by many as a decisive break with Lyndon Johnson, that would be cited by many as further proof of Bobby Kennedy's political impatience and imprudence, that would displease all the hawks, all who urged an expansion of American war efforts in Vietnam, and some of the doves, those who viewed with distrust any speech tempered by political discretion, those who sought little short of an immediate American withdrawal from Vietnam.

Bobby Kennedy knew his speech was certain to provoke strong political emotions, certain to inspire official retaliation, perhaps massive, perhaps Machiavellian. He turned to his wife, Ethel, who sat at his side, smiling, incorrigibly cheerful, dressed in her customary fashion, a purple maternity dress; she was expecting her tenth child in a few weeks. "I spoke to Teddy last night," the senator told his wife. "He said to make sure that they announce it's the Kennedy from New York."

After breakfast, as Bobby closeted himself with his aide Richard Goodwin to polish his speech one more time, his wife conducted a tour of Hickory Hill for Jack Newfield of the *Village Voice* and me. She led us to the basement to show us a few of the pets collected by Robert F. Kennedy Jr. Ethel Kennedy gingerly opened the door to the room housing young Bobby's animal kingdom. "His newest," she told us, "is a coatimundi. You should see him jump. He leaped over a couch chasing Bobby."

The coatimundi, a long, low, raccoonlike animal with a protruding, flexible snout, sharp claws, and prominent teeth, greeted our safari. At first, he was friendly, leaning on me, pawing gently at my pants leg. Ethel Kennedy turned to move toward Bobby's reptile cage, the home of assorted iguanas and snakes. Suddenly, Ethel screamed. Then she screamed again. "Get him off me," she cried. "Get him off me. He's biting me. Oh, God, he's biting me."

The coatimundi had attacked from the side, digging his claws and his teeth into her unprotected legs, and even though Ethel Kennedy, heavy with pregnancy, shook herself violently, the animal clung to her, biting her, scratching her.

I lifted Mrs. Kennedy off the floor—no easy feat, with a woman who was eight months pregnant and whom I did not know that well—and sat her atop a wooden cabinet, and when the coatimundi loosened its grip, I kicked it across the room. Newfield, who had been swiping at the pet with a broom, opened a door, let the animal into the hall, slammed the door, then rushed out a back door and ran to the front of the house to warn everyone that a mean-spirited coatimundi was dashing around loose.

Ethel Kennedy composed herself and accepted a ride to a nearby doctor who examined and treated her wounds. She came back with her legs bandaged and stained by antiseptics. She did not tell her husband; she did not want to distract him. At noon, Bobby Kennedy kissed his wife good-bye and, without noticing her wounds, drove off to deliver his Rubicon-crossing speech. "If these are all the scars the Kennedys end up with by five o'clock," Ethel said, "it'll be all right."

A month later, I received a letter from Ethel Kennedy. "Dear Dick," she began, "I guess I can call you Dick, if not Sweetheart or Saviour. After all, it's not every day that one is rescued from a mad coatimundi by a knight in a gray flannel suit—or was it blue serge? My grateful and happy thanks to you for removing my right thigh from the savage creature's fangs. . . .

"We have a small Chinese dragon here I'd like to show you. On second thought, if you'd care to inspect a small Chinese dragon, I'll be glad to give you directions to our basement. Looking forward to seeing you—on the first floor. With warm wishes and scars—Ethel."

Bobby Kennedy was not a spender. He often traveled without money, and at least once I had to give him change to buy a newspaper. On the Eastern Air Lines shuttle from New York to Washington, while all the other passengers paid with cash or credit card, I saw Bobby ask that the bill be sent to his office; not surprisingly, it was. When my book *R.F.K.* came out in the fall of 1967, he asked for free copies, which the publisher gave him.

Of all the politicians I have met, from Ford to Clinton, from Stassen to Stevenson, from Javits to Bradley, from Lindsay to Giuliani, Bobby Kennedy was the most impressive. He not only answered questions. He asked. He not only spoke. He listened. His concern for people less advantaged than he—which meant almost everyone in the world—seemed genuine.

The night Bobby was killed, in the spring of 1968, I was watching the California primary returns on television. I went to sleep shortly after 2 A.M., confident that he had won. Two hours later, my phone rang. Jerry Kramer, with whom I had just collaborated on a book, was calling to tell me that the senator had been fatally shot. That was neither the first time, nor the last, that the news of a death I did not expect made me feel as if I had been kicked in the stomach. The assassination drove me away from politics for a while, drove me out of New York City for a day. The day of the funeral service at St. Patrick's Cathedral, Kramer and I played golf at the far end of Long Island, as far as we could get from Manhattan.

Coincidentally, the last time I saw Robert Kennedy was at a football game in which Jerry Kramer played, in Baltimore, in November 1967, the Colts against Vince Lombardi's final Green Bay team, the champions of Super Bowl II. The senator told me that he had seen my book and that it was very handsome. "But who's going to buy it?" Bobby said. "It's expensive, and you know rich people don't like me."

After the *World Journal Tribune* folded, *New York* survived on its own, run by Clay Felker, its innovative editor. I never thought Felker was quite the communications genius he was considered to be, but I always liked him personally and respected his work ethic and his commitment. Once, when I accompanied him to one of those Manhattan celebrity cocktail parties everyone who isn't there dreams of attending, I said to Clay, "How can you take it? Nobody's here to have fun. They're all working."

"What do you think I'm doing?" Felker replied.

Felker quickly attracted investors to his publication, but when he chose to run a nude photo of a smiling Andy Warhol film star named Viva in the fourth issue of *New York,* a more shocking editorial decision then than now, the investors rebelled. One of them, Alan Patricof, invited Breslin and me to meet with him at Gallagher's, the site of our abortive union uprising. Patricof said the investors had decided that Felker would not continue as editor. Would I take his place?

I said I would.

This was a Friday night. I was told I would take over on Monday. I would hear more details the next day.

I never heard from Patricof again.

Felker ran the magazine, capably, for almost two more decades.

The Freeport Barons won state championships at Ebbets Field and the Polo Grounds, but I (front row, far right) was a power broker, not a power hitter.

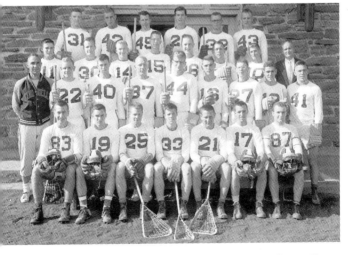

I stopped Jimmy Brown—three of his seven shots—when I (front row, no. 21) played goalie for Cornell and he played midfield for Syracuse.

Macho men: Jerry Kramer entertains Norman Mailer. I observe.
(Jill Krementz)

Best man: Bobby Kennedy bids for the presidency. I observe.
(Jill Krementz)

tried to explain football to Joe Namath, Johnny Unitas, and Jerry ramer, but coach Bear Bryant (with glass) knew more than all of s put together.

tried to explain women to George Mikan and Bob Cousy, but Wilt hamberlain insisted he knew more than all of us put together. No he disputed him. *(George Kalinsky)*

The Bobby Fischer show: Mayor John Lindsay and I applaud t[he] world chess champion as he stands on the steps of New York's Ci[ty] Hall. *(Dick De Marsico)*

The Joe Namath show: Muhammad Ali and George Segal join J[oe] and me and our sideburns on the set of our unconventional 19[ ] TV series.

They look mahvelous: Billy Crystal is probably funnier than my wife, but Trish is certainly prettier. I am not a contender in either category.

They look muscular: Does Bo know how much guts it takes to pose for a photograph between him and Jerry Kramer, my bestselling coauthors?

After Jerry Kramer, every football player wanted to work with me. . . . *(Mort Gerberg, New York Times Book Review)*

"HE HASN'T BEEN WORTH A DAMN SINCE DICK SCHAAP REJECTED HIS LIFE." *For Dick from Cousin Mort*

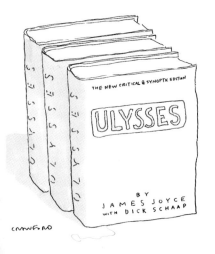

After Jimmy Breslin, every Irish author wanted to work with me. . . . *(Michael Crawford, Spy magazine)*

Mr. and Mrs. Greatest—
Muhammad and Lonnie
Ali—with Mr. and Mrs.
Schaap, and son David.

Schaap talk: Son Jeremy
hosts *Classic Sports Reporters*
on ESPN Classic . . .
(ESPN)

. . . while I host the regular *Sports Reporters* on ESPN. Mike Lupica
(right) thought Tony Kornheiser (left), Leonard Koppett, and I
would never stop listening. *(Cynthia Greer/ESPN)*

Who's that guy with Dick Schaap? On the golf course, the president of the United States solicited my advice. "You're away," I told
him. *(White House photograph)*

19

Of Broadway Joe and Tricky Dick

Jerry Kramer is among my most treasured friends, and even though we have little in common—he is strong and brave and gentile—he is, in many ways, the one I know best. We have worked together, traveled together, played golf together, caroused together. We have known each other's wives and girlfriends, sometimes both at the same time. We have watched each other's children grow up, his six and my six. Jerry has had three children with each of his two wives; I have had two with each of my three. We are equal opportunity husbands.

We have also written four books together. We have put our names on more than a quarter of a million words. We have listened to each other endlessly, and we know how the other thinks. "When you first meet your collaborator," Al Hirschberg, who wrote *Fear Strikes Out* with baseball player Jimmy Piersall, once told me, "it doesn't matter if you like each other or not, because by the end of the collaboration, you're going to hate each other." My experience, with Kramer and more than half a dozen other muscular collaborators, has been exactly the opposite. Partnership has, invariably, led to friendship.

I met Jerry in the early sixties, when I went to Green Bay to write an article for the *Saturday Evening Post* about Jerry's roommate, Jimmy Taylor. ("Jimmy Taylor, the great fullback of the Green Bay Packers, spent four years in college and emerged unscarred by education," the article began. The line was intended to be funny, but came out unkind. Vince Lombardi, the Packer coach, hated it and didn't talk to me for a few years.)

One night, when I entered the dormitory room Kramer and Taylor shared in training camp, Taylor was lying in his bed, and Kramer was sitting on his, reading poetry aloud. I would like to say that the poet was the intellectual Wallace Stevens—and I often have, according to a handful of old newspaper clippings—but upon further review, knowing Kramer's passion for the outdoors, I am fairly certain the versifier was really Robert Service, who limned the Yukon and mourned Dangerous Dan McGrew. In either case, it was the first time I had heard a professional athlete recite a poem that did not begin, "There was a young lady from . . ." Naturally, Taylor fell asleep.

In the spring of 1967, my editor at New American Library, Bob Gutwillig, impressed by a pair of baseball diaries written by pitcher Jim Brosnan, asked me if I knew a football player who could keep a diary. "Sure," I said. "Jerry Kramer." My nomination was based entirely on Kramer's private poetry slam. "Would you get in touch with him and see if he'd want to keep a diary?" Gutwillig said.

I did, and he did, and after six months of exchanging thoughts and tapes, after half a dozen visits to Green Bay and several road trips with the Packers—my newspaper had gone out of business, leaving me free time, and so had my first marriage, leaving me a bachelor for approximately one month—I knew that we had the material for a special book. Jerry was the perfect collaborator, open, intelligent, articulate, funny, reflective, a natural storyteller, closer in style, of course, to Service than to Stevens.

The book had everything going for it. The central character was the most intriguing man in football, Vince Lombardi. His supporting cast included such gifted and diverse players as Jimmy Taylor, Bart Starr, Ray Nitschke, Willie Davis, Willie Wood, Herb Adderley, and Henry Jordan, all of whom were elected to the Pro Football Hall of Fame. The most colorful personality was the Packers' veteran wide receiver, Max McGee, Paul Hornung's former roommate and nighttime running mate. Hornung himself, retired from football, made a cameo appearance.

The plot was as strong as the cast. The Packers, trying to become the first team in history to win three straight National Football League championships, struggled during the regular season. They won nine games, lost four and tied one, their second-worst record in seven years. Still, they won the Western Conference championship, and on December 31, 1967, in Green Bay, met the Eastern champions, the Dallas Cowboys, for the NFL championship.

That morning I drove from my motel to downtown Green Bay and passed a sign outside a bank blinking the time and the temperature: shortly before ten, and twelve below. The time looked right. The temperature

looked ridiculous. I had never heard of twelve below. I
assumed, incorrectly, that the thermometer was broken. By game time, the temperature slipped to thirteen
below, and the windchill factor—a northwest wind
scudded through the stands at fifteen miles an hour—
drove the temperature down to forty-five below. Even
in the press box, shielded from the worst of the cold, I
shivered.

The game, one of the most dramatic ever played,
was memorialized as the Ice Bowl. With less than five
minutes to play, the Packers, pinned deep in their own
territory, trailed, 17–14. I left the security of the press
box and started toward the locker rooms. Kramer had
told me Lombardi had convinced the Packers that they
never lost a game, but that sometimes the clock ran out
while the other team had more points. I looked at the
frozen field and the Packers' almost hopeless position,
and I decided that the title of our book was going to be
The Year the Clock Ran Out.

As I moved through the stands, the Packers moved
downfield. With thirteen seconds to go, they were one
yard from the goal line. Bart Starr elected to carry the
ball himself, and following a block by Kramer, dove
into the end zone. The Packers won the NFL championship for the third year in a row. In the locker room
after the game, Kramer, enjoying his unfamiliar role as
hero, stood before the television cameras while CBS
ran and reran and reran the slow-motion pictures of
Starr's touchdown, and Kramer's block. Millions of
Americans came to know Jerry Kramer's name for the
first time from one crisp, timely block. "Thank God for
instant replay," Kramer said, and we had our title: *Instant Replay: The Green Bay Diary of Jerry Kramer.*

If Jerry had not thrown the block, if Starr had not

scored the touchdown, if the Packers had not won the game, the quality of the book would not have suffered. ("It is one of the rarest of things," Jimmy Breslin said. "A sports book written in English by an adult.") But it would not have been nearly so commercially successful.

As soon as the first copies came from the printer in August 1968, I hand-delivered a couple of boxes to the press box at Soldier Field in Chicago the night the NFL champions, the Packers, played the College All-Stars, an annual contest. I did something that night I always wanted to do. When the cab taking me from my hotel got to Soldier Field, I reached into my wallet, took out a twenty-dollar bill, ripped Andrew Jackson in half, handed half to the driver, and said, "Come back and pick me up at halftime, take me to the airport and I'll give you the other half." He showed up, right on time. It was worth the trip to Chicago just to pull that stunt. It was also worth it because many of the sportswriters who received copies in the press box wrote glowingly of the book and sent it off to a strong start.

Instant Replay became at the time the bestselling sports book ever published, rising as high as number two on the *New York Times* best-seller list. It sold more than two hundred thousand copies in hardcover, more than two million in paperback. Kramer and I ended up splitting close to one million dollars in royalties. Our shares—more than Kramer earned from the Packers in eleven seasons in the NFL, more than I earned in eleven seasons at *Newsweek* and the *Tribune*—paid for our first divorces.

Frank Sullivan's annual Christmas poem in *The New Yorker* offered the greetings of the 1968 season to presidents, journalists—and one football player:

> Hail from the undersigned acclaimer
> To the Packers' rugged Jerry Kramer.

Never before had an offensive lineman earned such attention.

And more than thirty years later, an Internet company called Alibris ("Books you thought you'd never find") ran a full-page ad in *The New Yorker* featuring the cover of *Instant Replay*. The line above the cover read: "Jan. 19, 1970. Mom accidentally donates to church book drive." The line underneath read: "Nov. 30, 1999. Mom redeems herself on Alibris for son's 40th birthday."

No wonder when my third child, and first son, was born in 1969, we named him Jeremy and anointed Kramer his godfather.

The huge success of *Instant Replay* signaled the potential of sports books and led to offers from half a dozen publishers. Early in 1969, I found myself writing and researching three books simultaneously, which I do not recommend to authors of sound mind. I was living temporarily in a residential hotel called the Jockey Club in Miami, working with Jerry Kramer to put the finishing touches on *Farewell to Football*, in which Jerry announced his retirement from the NFL; collaborating with Joe Namath on his autobiography; and getting pro golfer Frank Beard started on his diary of the 1969 PGA tour. I was very lucky that I did not get mixed up and have Beard playing in the Super Bowl, Namath in the Masters, and Kramer on Broadway.

While I juggled those three, I also worked on my version of a golf game. Kramer moved into the Jockey Club for a few weeks and we played almost every day.

We usually played a "slacks" Nassau, betting a pair of trousers on the front nine, a pair on the back, and a pair on the full eighteen. The loser paid off in the pro shop. Kramer, after more than twenty operations, most of them major, still killed me on the course. I lost my pants, several pairs, and Kramer was smartly dressed, if you consider gaudy golf slacks smart, by the time he headed home to Green Bay.

Namath almost killed me, too, not in golf, but in trying to keep pace with his lifestyle. I didn't attend Super Bowl III, the game in which he and his New York Jets shocked the Baltimore Colts and the oddsmakers, but a week later an editor at Random House named Tony Wimpfheimer brought Joe and me together in Miami to discuss the possibility of a book. When our stone-crab dinner was over, the editor asked for the check. Namath had already taken care of it, quietly. I knew right then that he was different from most athletes (and all journalists). I liked him immediately, and we agreed to collaborate.

The only problem was finding time alone with Namath to concentrate on the book. His social schedule kept interfering. When Joe had to fly to New York on a business trip, I decided to go with him, just to have three uninterrupted hours together on the plane. We sat in the front row of first-class, and I took out my tape recorder. As soon as we reached our cruising altitude, a flight attendant brought us each two miniature bottles of Scotch. Soon, other passengers began sending their bottles to Joe, who shared them with me. I'm not certain how coherent my questions were, but I was alert enough to overhear a conversation between a flight attendant and a passenger several rows behind us. "What's he like?" the passenger asked.

"He's nice," the stewardess said, "but I like the intellectual one next to him better." Being called an intellectual next to Namath is not the most extravagant compliment I have ever received.

Life with Namath was never dull. A few months into our collaboration, I was a member of the entourage—friends, teammates, and a couple of journalists—who accompanied Joe to his hometown, Beaver Falls, Pennsylvania, to celebrate "Joe Namath Day." He also brought along two young women, a tall one and a short one, as gifts for his high-school buddies. I shared a limousine from the Pittsburgh airport to Beaver Falls with the tall one and Joe's father; she was very attentive, not to me, to Joe's father. During the parade through Beaver Falls, the short one seemed irked that Namath was getting more attention than she was. She decided to take off the see-through blouse she was wearing. She began getting more attention. Columnist Dave Anderson of the *Times* and I rode in the convertible that was carrying Namath. Joe waved, and we took notes.

At a dinner that night on a local college campus, Namath got up and spoke about his college days at the University of Alabama. He didn't have much money, he said, and he applied for a job working as a chauffeur for an attractive woman who lived by herself in a big house. "There were a lot of candidates for the job," Joe said, "but for some reason, I was picked. I was the lucky one. I drove the lady around, did chores for her, and one day, when I was putting away some groceries, she called to me from upstairs, 'Joseph, come up to my room.'

"I was very polite. I always did what I was told. I went up to her room. I walked in and she said, 'Joseph, take off my dress.' I was very obedient. I took off her dress."

The audience in Beaver Falls, including Joe's mother, began to stir nervously.

"Then she said, 'Joseph, take off my slip.' "

Joe noticed his mother's discomfort. "Don't worry, Mom," he said, then resumed the story. "Then the lady said, 'Joseph, take off my bra.' I obeyed. Then she said, 'Joseph, take off my panties.' "

By this time, Namath's mother was sliding under her table.

"Finally," Namath said, "the lady looked at me and said, 'Now, Joseph, don't let me ever catch you again wearing my clothes.' "

Even Joe's mother laughed.

After the dinner, the two young women returned to the Holiday Inn, and I noticed, as a reporter should, a queue forming outside the suite they shared. Joe was distributing his gifts, and they were distributing theirs. I went back to my room, wrote up my notes, and fell asleep. In the middle of the night, I heard a knock on my door and answered it. The tall one was standing outside my room, in tears, because one of Joe's teammates had crudely insulted her. I consoled her as best I could.

A couple of weeks later, Pete Rozelle, the commissioner of the NFL, ordered Joe to sell his interest in a New York saloon called Bachelors III. Rozelle said that "undesirables" frequented the establishment. I saw Johnny Carson in there once, but I don't think that's who Rozelle meant. He meant gamblers and gangsters, the kind of people who give a bar a bad name and good business.

Joe was one of the III Bachelors; the others were a former teammate named Ray Abruzzese and a restaurateur named Bobby Van. Joe decided he wasn't going to abandon his buddies. He decided, instead of selling, he was going to retire from professional football. He called a press conference. At Bachelors III at nine-thirty in the morning.

A small group of us rendezvoused in Joe's apartment shortly before nine, his lawyers, a few friends, and a pair of overnight guests, two unclothed young women I had never seen before. Joe would have introduced me to them, I'm sure, if he had known their names. Just as we were about to leave for the news conference, the phone rang. Bear Bryant, his coach at Alabama, was calling to try to persuade Joe to reconsider his retirement. Joe listened respectfully, then said, "I got to do it, Coach. It's the right thing."

We went to Bachelors III, and in front of a small army of newspapermen and broadcast journalists, Joe announced he was giving up the game. Tears welled up in his eyes. Frank Gifford and Kyle Rote, former New York Giant teammates and rival broadcasters, looked as if they were going to cry, too. So did Howard Cosell.

A quick word about Cosell: Once, while I was working with Joe, Howard came to Joe's apartment and the three of us sat in the living room, talking. Ray Abruzzese, Joe's roommate, woke up, heard Cosell's voice, shuffled into the living room naked, walked up to the TV set, and pushed the on-off button. When he still heard Cosell's voice, Ray turned, saw Howard, and said, "Oh, you're *here*. I was just coming out to turn you off." Cosell was speechless, for a few seconds.

During Namath's brief retirement, I accompanied him to a meeting at the New York City apartment of Commissioner Rozelle. It was an amiable meeting. Rozelle set the tone when he pulled two photos of Namath out of an envelope and asked Joe to sign them. "One's for my daughter, Ann," Rozelle said. "She's a real fan of yours."

I met another of Joe's real fans a few nights later at a Manhattan nightclub where Tom Jones was performing. After the show, we went to Jones's dressing room. A couple of minutes later, Sonny Franzese walked in. Sonny was to the mob what Namath was to the Jets. By any definition, except his own, Sonny was an "undesirable." "Hey, Joe," Franzese said, "when you gonna come out the house for some spaghetti?" Joe *and* Sonny laughed. Both knew the timing was not perfect.

After several weeks of discussions and compromises, Namath agreed to sell his interest in Bachelors III, to come out of retirement, at the age of twenty-six, and rejoin the Jets. He was ready to focus on football and I was ready to focus on writing. One day Joe said to me, "I can't wait until tomorrow," and I dropped my guard and said, "Why?" " 'Cause I get better-looking every day," he said. Joe had his laugh, and I had a title for our book. When I completed the manuscript, Joe came to my office, sat down next to my desk, and read the entire book. He didn't suggest a single change. "I think this is the first book I've ever read to the end," Joe said. He was probably kidding.

Our book came out in the fall of 1969, roughly two months after the publication of *Farewell to Football*. In a sense, I was competing with myself for book sales. The Namath book outsold the second Kramer book, but came nowhere close to *Instant Replay*. They were very different volumes. *Instant Replay* was a serious and successful attempt to bring the reader inside pro football. *I Can't Wait Until Tomorrow*, part put-on and part put-down, was a look at Namath's persona more than his world.

As a result of our collaboration, Joe invited me to be the cohost of *The Joe Namath Show,* to play sort of a poor man's Ed McMahon to his poor man's Johnny Carson. The show went on the air late in September and was syndicated, immediately, to more than forty stations. Joe and I didn't have the slightest idea what we were doing. We had been only guests on talk shows, responding to the host, not worrying about camera positions or commercial breaks, not *being* the host. Joe fumbled on the commercials more than he fumbled on the field. We had long sideburns and wore checked Pierre Cardin suits. I smoked cigarettes on the air, and we may have been the first talk show to serve alcoholic beverages to its guests, and its hosts, before they went on.

One of our weekly routines was to take questions from the audience for Joe to answer. Once, Ann-Margret, who had costarred with Namath in a forgetable movie called *C. C. Ryder,* stood up and said she had a question. "Tell me, Joe," she purred, "to what do you owe your quick release?"

Namath blushed and recovered quickly. "Half excitement," he said, "and half fear."

It was my responsibility to book the guests for our show. Each week, I booked a "sports" guest and a "show-biz" guest. One week, I invited the author Truman Capote to appear with the former middleweight boxing champion of the world, Rocky Graziano. The day we taped the show, I had to wait outside the studio for Capote's limousine because no one else connected with the show had even the vaguest idea of what Capote looked like. Or who he was, for that matter. When his car pulled up, I opened the door, and Truman looked at me and said, "Dick, what have you done with your hair? It looks marvelous."

On the show, Namath asked Capote if he had ever been an athlete, and Truman replied, "Oh, yes, I used to play center field on my boarding-school football team." He went on to boast that he beat Humphrey Bogart regularly at arm wrestling. Whereupon, Graziano looked at him and said, "Didn't I fight you a six-rounder in Cleveland once?"

Rocky/Truman was my finest booking. I tried one week to team Vince Lombardi with Tiny Tim, the falsetto, but Lombardi was busy.

Jerry Kramer, Tom Seaver, Woody Allen, Mickey Mantle, Jimmy Breslin, Willie Mays, Sally Kirkland, Dick Cavett, Muhammad Ali, and Claire Bloom, among others, found time to appear on our show. Woody told Joe what it was like to be a sex symbol and offered to share his secrets. Ali threatened to walk off the set when his fellow guest George Segal began discussing a nude scene he had filmed with Streisand. As a devout Muslim, Ali said, he couldn't listen to such talk. At the end of the show, I apologized to Ali, who was at the time suspended from boxing, and he said, "Aw, man, I got to do that. The CIA is listening, the FBI is listening, everybody's listening."

Claire Bloom mentioned that her favorite role was Juliet. Namath had recently seen the Franco Zefferelli version of *Romeo and Juliet*. "Were you in the movie?" Joe asked.

"No," Bloom said. "I did it on the stage in London."

I jabbed at Joe, "When you saw the film, did you know how it was going to come out?"

Namath said he didn't.

"What's the matter?" I said. "Didn't you see *West Side Story*?"

Actually, I was jealous. Imagine how wonderful it is

to see *Romeo and Juliet*—or *Hamlet* or *Macbeth*—not knowing the ending.

Not surprisingly, when my fourth child and third daughter was born, in January 1971, we named her Joanna.

I chose Frank Beard to keep a diary of the golf tour on the basis of our first meeting, in Oklahoma City, in 1968. We met at the national pro-am championship, a tournament I'll never forget because the winning score was 56, and the pro contributed only one stroke to the team score. His amateur partner shot a net 57, a gross 75 with an 18-handicap. People have been lynched for less. What made the story perfect was that the amateur's name was Cheatwood. Doyle Cheatwood.

I met Beard in the locker room. He was articulate and argumentative, which made him perfect for my purposes. He was also unusually candid. Frank said he was the second-cheapest man on the golf tour and his best friend, Charlie Coody, was the cheapest. When *Pro: Frank Beard on the Golf Tour* came out in 1970, Coody's banker walked up to him in Abilene, Texas, and said, "Charlie, I thought Frank Beard was your friend."

"He is," Coody said.

"But he said you're the cheapest man on the golf tour," the banker said.

"Well, I am," Coody said, with more than a hint of pride.

Beard also said, of the army of fans who followed Arnold Palmer, "They would cheer if he peed in the fairway." Unlike Coody, Arnie did not corroborate Frank's assertion.

*   *   *

During 1969, the Kramer, Namath, and Beard books were not sufficient to keep me busy. I created my own publishing company, Maddick Manuscripts, combining my wife's first name and mine, and assembled a staff comprised of myself and three others: Don Forst, the former assistant city editor at the *Herald Tribune,* who left the *Times* to join me; Pamela Susskind, daughter of the television impresario David Susskind; and Mel Ziegler, fresh out of Columbia Journalism School, where he had been my student. (Later, after a few years in the newspaper business, Ziegler and his wife-to-be, Patricia, launched a mail-order clothing business out of their San Francisco garage. They called it the Banana Republic, and when they sold the company a decade later, they collected a small fortune. Mel, who seemed to mellow with money, never returned to the newspaper business.)

Time magazine referred to our four-person operation as "the Schaap Shop"; one writer called us "a factory." If we were, we were the world's smallest.

Maddick Manuscripts published *The Year the Mets Lost Last Place,* a minute-by-minute account of the first critical week in the history of the team; *The Perfect Game,* Met pitcher Tom Seaver's autobiography; *Behind the Mask,* a baseball diary maintained by Bill Freehan of the Detroit Tigers; *The Open Man,* a basketball diary kept by Dave DeBusschere of the New York Knicks; *Cleon,* an autobiography of the Mets' Cleon Jones; *Amen: The Diary of Rabbi Martin Siegel; The Masters;* and *Pro. The Year the Mets Lost Last Place* came out in 1969, the others in 1970. I was definitely competing with myself.

My contribution to each of the books varied as greatly as the style of the books themselves. *The Year the Mets Lost Last Place* and *The Masters* were group efforts. I employed a dozen people on each project, many of them newspapermen, roaming the field and the course, interviewing, observing, feeding quotes and anecdotes to me. Paul D. Zimmerman worked on the Mets book and *The Open Man;* in both cases, he wrote the first draft, and I wrote the final, true collaborative efforts. Paul, the movie critic of *Newsweek* and author of the screenplay *The King of Comedy,* was a Princeton graduate, uncommonly intelligent, with two noticeable flaws in his education. He thought the word "pennant," as in "pennant race," was spelled "pennat," and the word "forward," as in the basketball position, was spelled "foward," logical mistakes if you grow up in New York and keep your ears open.

One of my reporters on the Mets book, fittingly, was the former Cincinnati and Chicago White Sox pitcher, Jim Brosnan, whose two baseball diaries had inspired *Instant Replay.*

I had met Tom Seaver before, but I got to know him during the 1969 season. One night in Chicago, in the final week of the season, I arranged for Tom and me to have dinner with Muhammad Ali at a restaurant called the Red Carpet in Chicago. Seaver and I showed up on time and were led to our table. Ali arrived late and was whisked into the kitchen. Someone thought he had come to apply for a dishwashing job.

My friend Jerry Kovler, who owned the restaurant, walked into the kitchen and said, "Champ, what are you doing here?"

"That's what I'd like to know," Ali said.

Kovler brought Ali to our table, I introduced Seaver and Ali to each other, and Ali launched into a lengthy monologue. After twenty minutes or so, he turned to

Seaver and said, "You a nice fella. What paper you write for?"

I explained that Tom was, at that moment, the best pitcher in baseball.

After dinner, Ali offered to drive us back to our hotel in his Cadillac coupe, equipped with two mobile phones, which were not yet ubiquitous. "What's your home phone number?" Ali asked Seaver.

Tom told him.

Ali dialed, and when Tom's wife, Nancy, answered, Muhammad said, "This is the baddest nigger in the world, and I'm out with your husband and five black hookers."

Nancy laughed. Tom had told her with whom he was having dinner.

As we pulled up in front of the hotel, a cab pulled up in front of us, and Ron Taylor, a relief pitcher for the Mets, stepped out. Taylor had been out for the evening celebrating the Mets' first-place finish. "C'mon," he said to Ali, "wanna fight?"

Ali and Seaver and I went up to my room, and while Seaver and I watched, Ali stripped off his jacket and his shirt and began shadowboxing. He was, at the time, banned from boxing for his refusal to join the armed forces, but he was in fighting trim. He talked and shadowboxed for half an hour, *whoosh, whoosh, whoosh,* never slowing down physically or verbally. It was a stunning performance, better than watching any other boxer fight.

The Perfect Game, the book I wrote with Seaver, was not a perfect book, not even close. Tom was twenty-five at the time, too young and circumspect to write an insightful autobiography. It was probably the weakest book I ever wrote, and I ran out of words several thousand short of the number the publisher desired. I felt so guilty I gave back part of the advance. I have resisted such heretical impulses ever since.

One of the dividends of working with Dave DeBusschere on his diary was the opportunity to get to know his roommate, Bill Bradley, who drove a used Volkswagen with no radio and wore clothes so outmoded his more fashion-conscious teammates laughed at him. They laughed at his wardrobe, not at his intellect. Even then, thirty years before he formally sought the office, his teammates called him Mr. President. Once, I went to dinner at a Greek restaurant with DeBusschere and Bradley, and the future presidential candidate drank so much ouzo he danced on a tabletop. Another time, DeBusschere gave a Christmas party at his home, and Bradley showed up wearing the white collar of a priest, even though it was not a costume party. Bradley went around offering to hear confession from his fellow Knicks.

None of the diaries after *Instant Replay* sold spectacularly, but they did well enough for me to be crowned king of the ghostwriters. A cartoon in the *New York Times Book Review* showed a football player sitting at the end of the bench, sadly sucking his thumb. Nearby, one of his teammates said to another, "He hasn't been worth a damn since Dick Schaap rejected his life." (Another cartoon, in *Spy* magazine some twenty years later, showed the jacket of a book: "*Ulysses* by James Joyce with Dick Schaap.")

I offered each of my potential subjects Schaap's Michelin, a five-page guide to successful diary-keeping.

"The little detail, the minute fact, creates reality," I suggested. "The more little details the reader is provided with, the more he feels a total sense of reality.

"It can be helpful," I lectured, "to go on the assumption that most of life, or at least much of life, is absurd, and that each man's preoccupation with what he himself does is even more absurd. Don't be afraid to poke fun at yourself and to poke fun at your particular field." I also advised my diarists to judge themselves as harshly as they judged others—or more harshly; if you criticize yourself, I said, your criticisms of others are more acceptable. And, finally, at the end of the guide, I wrote: "BE SURE YOUR TAPE RECORDER IS WORKING PROPERLY."

I was remarkably lucky in my choice of collaborators. The year Kramer and I worked on his diary, his team won the Super Bowl; the year Beard and I worked on his diary, he was the leading money-winner on the professional golf tour, ahead of Palmer and Nicklaus, who were at their peak; the year DeBusschere kept his diary, his team won the National Basketball Association championship. Seaver was not a diarist, but the year I followed him and the Mets, they won the World Series. I stumbled upon winner after winner; as the athletes say, I was in a zone.

But I tired of the corporate paperwork, and Maddick Manuscripts (like the union it was named after) eventually dissolved. I plead incompetence in all matters financial: I am one of the few people in modern times who bought a house in Greenwich, Connecticut, and sold it at a sizable loss.

I managed to squeeze in a few magazine articles between books. In 1968, I covered Richard Nixon's pres-

idential campaign for *New York,* accompanying him for
a few days during the Oregon primaries. Before we left
for Oregon, I met Nixon's press secretary, Herb Klein,
who asked me if I had met the candidate yet. I said I
hadn't, and Klein, knowing my background, said to
me, "You'll like him. He reads the sports pages first." I
did not mention to Klein that I would prefer a president
who read the sports pages last.

On the DC-8 flying from New York to Portland,
each reporter obtained a brief audience with the candidate, no more than fifteen to twenty minutes. When it
was my turn to ask questions, Nixon, who knew that I
had written *Instant Replay* (evidently, he read the
sports *books* first, too), phrased most of his answers in
sports terms. He spoke of "getting to first base" and
"hitting a home run" and "scoring a touchdown," and I
wanted to say, "Mr. Vice President, it's all right to use
a multisyllabic word. I'll try to handle it." But, of
course, I simply nodded.

At each stop in Oregon, Nixon, like all presidential
aspirants, delivered approximately the same speech
with small variations based on the site and the news of
the day. Almost invariably, Nixon would spread his
arms and say, "I'm not talking just about the United
States," then cup his hands close together and say, "but
about the whole world."

In Pendleton one day, as our entourage emerged
from the candidate's chartered plane, we ran the gaunt-
let of a receiving line. Nixon moved swiftly down the
line, shaking hands, freezing a smile, making small
talk, until he noticed that one well-wisher was looking
not at him, but over his shoulder. The vice president
turned around and saw Candice Bergen, the actress,
who was writing an article about the campaign for *Mc-*

Call's magazine. Nixon turned back and said, "Do you know who that is?" The man shook his head, and Nixon said, earnestly, "That's Edgar Bergen's daughter." Nixon existed in his own time warp.

When Nixon was elected president, the American Booksellers Association presented him with 250 books to provide "a typical, useful library for the White House family." The authors ranged from Art Buchwald to Eldridge Cleaver to Norman Mailer to Dwight D. Eisenhower to Henry Kissinger to Philip Roth, but I was the only author represented by four books: *Instant Replay, Farewell to Football, The Year the Mets Lost Last Place,* and *I Can't Wait Until Tomorrow*.

Richard Nixon and I developed a cordial relationship over the years, based mostly on his sports interests, definitely not on our conflicting political views. David Eisenhower, the grandson of one president and son-in-law of another, shared Nixon's passion for baseball and once appeared on a show I hosted, matching his knowledge of baseball trivia with Democrat Frank Mankiewicz's. Mankiewicz could name the whole starting lineup for the St. Louis Cardinals in the early 1930s. Both knew far more than I did.

When Nixon was president, he once suggested a play for the Miami Dolphins' quarterback Bob Griese to use in the Super Bowl. Griese was wise enough to reject it. Not long afterward, President Nixon ordered the planting of mines in Haiphong harbor in Vietnam. He called the action Operation Linebacker. I went on the air at WNBC in New York and announced that Operation Linebacker had been suggested to the president by Bob Griese, and that Nixon should have been wise enough to reject the play.

(One of the advantages to covering sports, in print

and, especially, on televison, is that you can get away with political and sociological judgments that would not be tolerated in covering "news." For instance, in covering a golf story with racial overtones, I once compared a country club to a plantation and said, "Golf was the first sport to be integrated, if you consider a white golfer walking with a black caddy to be integration." Sports may be, as Red Smith suggested, the "toy department" of journalism, but it gives you the freedom to play serious games.)

Several years later, after Nixon's impeachment, I was lunching one day at Le Cirque, a fashionable and pricey Manhattan restaurant, with my friend John Weitz, the designer and author, when the former president walked in. I had not seen him since his impeachment, but my reaction was instinctive. "Hello, Mr. President," I said.

"Dick," he said, "you know Admiral Rickover, don't you?" He pointed to the man next to him.

"No," I said, meaning that I had never met the admiral, not that I had never heard of him.

"He's the father of the nuclear navy," Nixon said, still trying to educate the sports guy.

I wanted to say, "That's the part I know," but, instead, I said, "How do you do?"

The admiral asked me what I did for a living.

I told him I was a broadcaster, specializing in sports.

He looked at me with as much disdain as I've ever seen one human being bestow on another.

That was the last time I saw Richard Nixon, or, for that matter, the father of the nuclear navy.

20

"Hello, Fellow Nazis!"

My personal life obviously revolved around my work in the late 1960s and, I suppose, in every other decade since my teens. On our honeymoon late in the summer of 1967, as the Green Bay Packers closed up training camp and moved into the regular season, Madeleine and I went to England, Majorca, and Ibiza, in search of bliss and stories. We found the stories.

It was a working honeymoon, but hardly an arduous one. I was writing an article for *Life* on the filming in Majorca of John Fowles's novel *The Magus*, and a travel report for *Holiday* on the Balearic island of Ibiza. We landed first in London, then motored to Dorset, on the southern coast of England, to visit Fowles and his wife at their home in Lyme Regis, which was later a setting for *The French Lieutenant's Woman*. John and Elisabeth Fowles decided to spook the Americans.

After a visit to a nearby pub, as Elisabeth drove through wind and rain down a dark dirt road leading to the Fowleses' farmhouse, John told us about an un-filmed screenplay written by Dylan Thomas, the story of a Scottish professor of medicine who bought cadavers from grave robbers who, when the graves ran bare, occasionally improvised their own corpses. One morning, at the start of a lecture, Fowles related with relish, the professor pulled the sheet off his latest purchase and saw the lifeless face of his mistress staring up at him. "A wonderful story," Fowles said.

When we reached the Fowleses' isolated three-hundred-year-old farmhouse on the edge of the English Channel, John said, "We have a ghost here."

"A wonderful old lady," Elisabeth said. "She worked so hard all her life."

The ghost's name was Emma Bowditch, and she had lived in the farmhouse in the nineteenth century, cleaning, cooking, and sewing for a house full of sailors. "I've never seen her," the author of *The Collector* lamented. "I wish she would materialize for me. Just once. I'm fascinated by her, of course."

"She materialized for our last guests," Elisabeth said.

"She usually materializes for Americans," John added.

"She stays in the guest wing," Elisabeth said. "If you sit in the room underneath the bedroom, you can hear her walking about. The house creaks."

"Windows bang in the night," said John.

"The light switch in our room is most curious," Elisabeth said. "You can turn it off and get into bed and thirty seconds later the lights will go on. I don't know why."

The battle against the Spanish Armada had begun just off the coast of Lyme Regis. "When the wind is right," John Fowles said, "you can hear the sailors outside crying on the reef where they were wrecked. It's an acoustical phenomenon, of course, but it does sound exactly like sailors crying."

"What worries me most," Elisabeth said, "is the lunatic who lived here before the kind old lady. He was committed to an institution. I wouldn't want him to come back."

"It's in the deed to the house," John said. "It tells which institution he was committed to. Would you care to read it?"

"This used to be a house where all travelers stopped," Elisabeth said. "They were always welcome here for tea. I worry about that."

"We broke the tradition," John said.

"Jane Austen," said his wife, "took tea in this room."

"Would you like to take a walk in the garden before going to sleep?" John asked.

During the night, shutters slammed, and faint cries echoed, and once, when I got up to go to the loo, I passed a door that had earlier been padlocked. Now it was open, and I could see, within the room, a table set for two with silver and crystal, and a candle flickering shadows on the wall. I hurried back to my bedroom, woke my bride, and told her I knew she had to be frightened. I also told her to move over and make room for me in a narrow single bed. Emma Bowditch did not join us.

In the morning, John Fowles materialized, looking rested, and said he hoped we had slept equally well. He sipped coffee and read the British papers and chuckled at the headline above a story about a dadaistic painter. "Hans Arp," the headline said, "Or I Shoot." (It joined my list of favorite headlines. Once, a contemporary of mine, Jack Mann, the sports editor of *Newsday,* assigned one of his reporters to write a story about the men who hold the stopwatches at the finish line of track-and-field races, only so that he could compose the headline "These Are the Souls Who Time Men's Tries.")

After England, we flew to Majorca to observe the filming of *The Magus*. A friend who worked as a publicist for the film company had arranged for me to be an extra in the movie. The first day on the set, I reported to wardrobe and was outfitted in a German SS uniform. Apparently, I looked good in it, because I was promoted on the spot, from enlisted man to lieutenant, and awarded the Iron Cross. I put on a pair of jackboots and immediately understood why the SS were so mean; the boots pinched. Then I walked onto the set and found myself surrounded by similarly dressed extras. "Hello, fellow Nazis," I said, cheerily, and none of them laughed. I was told later that they were Germans on holiday, and that some were wearing their fathers' uniforms.

I met the producers of the film and asked casually why the movie was being shot on Majorca when the novel was set in Greece. "Oh, we couldn't film in Greece," one of the producers said. "They have a fascist government." That made perfect sense to me until I realized we were filming in Franco's Spain.

The filmmakers took liberties with the novel. They turned an Australian flight attendant into a French flight attendant. They took twins and consolidated them into Candy Bergen. Michael Caine, as a young English schoolteacher, and Anthony Quinn, as a wise old Greek, were so suited to their roles, they seemed out of place.

In one key scene in the novel, the young Englishman

was forced to watch a film of the woman he loved making love to someone else, who happened to be a black man. In the movie within the movie, the black man became an Englishman, and when the time came to film the critical scene, the cast retreated to the bowels of a castle, the set surrounded by a curtain, so that no one but the director and cameraman could observe the simulated act of love. The motivation was secrecy more than modesty. It was immoral and illegal to film a nude scene in fascist Spain. Probably in Greece, too.

Candy Bergen rebelled at filming the scene—as I recall, she argued that acting was a sellout, and acting naked even more of a sellout—but, eventually, the producers prevailed, and Candy disappeared behind the curtain. When she emerged, an hour or two later, the producers, with whom I was sitting, thanked her profusely and told her she would not be needed during the afternoon.

Soon after Candy departed, a statuesque blonde paraded past us, apparently wearing only a bathrobe. "Who's that?" I said.

"That's the body," I was told.

"What do you mean?"

"Now we're going to film the same scene from the neck down."

The coproducer shook his head. "It wasn't easy to get a body," he said. "The season's over, and most of the Swedish girls have gone home."

"Couldn't you have used Candy?" I asked.

The producer remained discreetly silent. The implication, however, was that Candy's figure was not quite so stunning as her face.

Each night during our week in Majorca, Michael Caine took a group of us, perhaps a dozen, out to dinner. We always went to the same restaurant, a French pizzeria in Spain, and we always ate the same meal on the same checkered tablecloths, pizza as an appetizer, beef fondue as a main course, and Caine always picked up the check. He was charming as well as generous. I asked him when he first realized he was a star, and he said, "When the bank president pushed the clerk out of the way to handle my account."

On the one evening Caine did not play host, we went to a restaurant owned by an expatriate American who had appeared in Busby Berkeley musicals in the 1930s. He offered Chinese food on one side of the menu and Mexican food on the other. It was the worst Chinese food I had ever tasted, and, defying the law of averages, the worst Mexican.

I played a German storm trooper in the film. I held a submachine gun on a group of Greek resistance fighters. My commanding officer was one of the Redgraves, the least famous, Corin. The scene was shot in daytime, but with a filter that transformed it into nighttime. When I saw the movie in New York, my scene lasted only seconds, and in the darkness, I did not see myself. Even if I had been visible, I would have hated the film; it had little to do with the novel. The critics hated it more. Not even Candy, Caine, and Quinn could save it.

I have not had good experiences with movies. Before he made *Lenny,* the director Bob Fosse and I sat down and talked about Lenny Bruce. I shared memories and anecdotes with Fosse, and when he finished the film, he asked me to host a private screening. I did, and was pained by it, to the point where I had a headache that persisted for days.

By the time I saw Fosse again, at a Christmas party

at Herb Gardner's apartment, he had undergone open heart surgery. He asked me what I thought of the film, and I should have lied and said I loved it. Instead, I said I hated it. "Why?" Fosse asked.

"It had nothing to do with the guy I knew," I said.

"I couldn't find him," said Fosse.

I have never written a film, a large gap in my résumé, but once, when I was writing my newspaper column, a movie producer approached me with an idea. "How would you like to write a movie," he said, "about a newspaper columnist who gets his items from his dog?"

He was serious. "Why not make it a cockroach?" I suggested.

My literary allusion sailed past the producer. "Movie-goers couldn't relate to a cockroach," he explained.

Our project never came to fruition. I elected not to send the producer a copy of *archy and mehitabel,* Don Marquis's novel about a literate cockroach who could type only lowercase letters. *wotthehell, wotthehell,* as mehitabel used to say.

While Madeleine and I were in Majorca, I still had to write a books-and-authors column for *Book Week.* I found a subject, an Australian expatriate named Mark McShane, who wrote the book that was the basis for a wonderful film called *Séance on a Wet Afternoon.* McShane had suggested *Séance on a Wet Afternoon* as the title for his book, but his publishers had rejected it as too wordy and changed it to *Séance.* The movie restored the original title.

McShane told me that one day, when he was drinking in a waterfront bar in Majorca, he overheard a group of American sailors mentioning that the film,

Séance on a Wet Afternoon, was going to be shown on
their ship that evening. McShane, who had never seen
the movie, interrupted, introduced himself as the author, and asked if there was any way he could view the
film. The sailors contacted the ship, and the skipper
sent a launch to take McShane to and from the screening. "It was one of the few films I've ever seen," Mc-
Shane recalled, sadly, "that was infinitely better than
the book on which it was based."

From Majorca, we traveled southwest to Ibiza, the
neighboring island in the Mediterranean, an island, in
those days, still relatively unspoiled by tourists. The
major local industry was fraud, and the scent in the air
was larceny. At the tables outside the smoky cafés lining the docks of the city of Ibiza, forgers sat and
bragged of their latest works.

"I did an early Picasso."

"I did two Utrillos."

"I did three Mirós."

Back in the hills, in the interior of the island, a man
named Fernand Legros lived in luxury, waiting for the
storm to subside, the storm over the paintings he had
sold to a Texas millionaire named Meadows, paintings
condemned by experts as one million dollars' worth of
forgeries. Legros insisted that the experts were wrong,
and the paintings authentic, but he was a hero to the
forgers who drank on the docks.

Our first day in Ibiza, my wife coaxed me into a tiny
boutique on one of the dark side streets off the docks.
"I know that girl," she said, nodding toward the lone
salesgirl.

My wife had never been out of the United States before. She was a Jewish girl from Brooklyn, and we

were on a Spanish island in the Mediterranean, an island few Americans had ever heard of. "You're full of shit," I suggested.

"But I know her," she said. "I'm positive I know her from somewhere."

My wife turned toward the salesgirl. "What's your name?" she said.

The young woman looked up quizzically. "Corinne," she said, in a noticeable French accent.

"Corinne!" my wife said. "Corinne! It's me. Madeleine!"

They embraced. They had seen each other only once in fifteen years, but as teenagers, they had been friends and neighbors on Fire Island. Corinne was the stepdaughter of Patachou, the French entertainer.

To celebrate their reunion, Corinne, Madeleine, and I marched off to La Tierra, a nearby bar that resembled a comfortably furnished cave. We settled in a corner, on low benches facing a low table, and when the woman who owned La Tierra came to take our orders, my wife turned to me and whispered, "I know her, too."

I think I said, "You're full of shit," again.

"What's your name?" my wife asked the saloonkeeper.

"Arlene," she said.

"Arlene!" my wife said. "Arlene Braverman. You sat behind me in English class at Erasmus Hall High School."

Of course it was Arlene Braverman from Brooklyn, from the high school of Gilbert Price and Barbra Streisand, now Arlene of La Tierra, friend and hostess to all the painters and novelists, smugglers and swindlers, illusioned and disillusioned, who had come to live in Ibiza. She was living with a painter, a Scottish Jew, who specialized in buxom nudes, many of them closely resembling Arlene Braverman. My wife wanted to buy one of the paintings, to give to Erasmus High, but the artist insisted upon his standard price of ten thousand dollars. I asked him how many he had sold at his standard price, and he said, candidly, "None."

I found an old schoolmate in Ibiza, too, a Cornellian, a novelist, a classmate of my friend and editor Bob Gutwillig. His name was Clifford Irving, and his home had one of the few working toilets in Ibiza. A few years later he was in headlines, and incarcerated, as the author of a bogus autobiography of Howard Hughes. If Cliff was innocent of fraud, as he protested, then he had not learned anything during his years in Ibiza.

In the early 1970s, Clay Felker asked me to write an article for *New York* magazine on the ten most overrated people in New York City. My list was partly tongue-in-cheek. I accused Arthur Ochs Sulzberger, the publisher of the *Times*, of being overrated because, I wrote, he "does not rigorously impose his own views, his own crusades, his own preferences upon his newspaper. He is such an unusual sort of publisher he does not even call his newspaper 'my newspaper.' He calls it *'The Times.'* "

Abe Rosenthal, the managing editor of the *Times*, my rival as metropolitan editor when I was city editor—the *Times* never used a four-letter word when a twelve-letter word would do—wrote me an unhappy letter complaining that I had unfairly maligned his boss. I wrote back to Abe, defined "irony" to him— "the use of words to convey a meaning that is the opposite of its literal meaning," a practice not encouraged by his paper—and pointed out that by damning Sulzberger I was actually praising him. Rosenthal wrote back and apologized, explaining that he had "too many balls in the air" at one time.

My list also included the U.S. ambassador to the United Nations, an unsuccessful senatorial candidate named George H. W. Bush. "The Ambassador to the United Nations holds one of the most sensitive and potentially influential posts in the world," I wrote, "but if the Indians and the Pakistanis had not come to blows, George Bush would not have been recognizable to one New Yorker in a thousand. Now he is. Among Ambassadors to the U.N., Bush suffers, as almost anyone would, in comparision with [his predecessor] Adlai Stevenson. . . . People who have encountered Bush say that he's a pretty likable fellow."

Bush proved that he was a pretty likable fellow by throwing a party in honor of himself and the other nine most overrated and by inviting me and Clay Felker to the gathering at his home in the Waldorf Towers as the "guests of dishonor." His suite was just as comfortable as the one I had shared with Muhammad Ali a decade earlier. Seven of the ten most overrated attended the party: Bush, Sulzberger, David Merrick, McGeorge Bundy (president of the Ford Foundation), Sandy Garelik (president of the City Council), Gabe Pressman of NBC, and a man whose name no one knew, the chairman of the board of governors of the New York Stock Exchange, Ralph D. DeNunzio. Jacob Javits, Terence Cardinal Cooke, and Steve Smith took my article seriously. They did not show up at the party.

More than a quarter of a century later, when George Bush was getting ready to publish a collection of his letters, his secretary wrote to me and asked if we had corresponded at all about the "ten most overrated" list. I wrote back, said that we hadn't, enclosed a copy of the original article, and mentioned that recently, when I was interviewing Arnold Palmer, he had said that of the half-dozen presidents he had golfed with, George Bush was the best player.

President Bush wrote back to me and said, "Either Arnold Palmer was lying, or you were just trying to flatter me. My golf game stinks!" A pretty likable fellow.

The following year, I wrote of "The Ten Most Indispensable People in Town," and divided them, five who really were indispensable and five who thought they were. Among the latter, I included a new young disc jockey named Don Imus. I suggested he lacked modesty and wit, yet during the next few years, he invited me several times to be a guest on his show.

As I got to know him—we lived near each other in Connecticut and later in Manhattan—I grew to like Imus more and more. I even complimented him in print.

Since then, he has unfailingly abused me on his show.

By 1970, Richard Wald, my former associate at the *Herald Tribune,* was vice president of NBC News. He called me and asked if I would like to audition for a television job, to be the sports anchor of the NBC station in Los Angeles. I was in my mid-thirties, without a steady job, and found the idea of television and the West Coast tempting. I went to the studios and, with little direction or preparation, recorded my version of a local sports report. Everyone said, "Thank you."

Nine months went by, and I did not hear a word

rom NBC. Finally, mildly curious, I phoned Wald. "I guess I didn't get the job," I said.

"Didn't anyone ever call you?" Wald said.

"No," I said.

"Welcome to television," said Wald.

A few weeks later, Wald called and offered me a job as the sports anchor on WNBC, the network's New York affiliate. Despite his warning, I said yes.

21

Me and My Stablemates

When I'm asked whether I prefer newspapers, magazines, books, radio, or television, I point out that each has its up side: Newspapers provide the rush of immediacy, the opportunity in my *Herald Tribune* days to get on the subway and see someone reading and reacting to my column only a couple of hours after I wrote it. Magazines provide the space to say what you want—perhaps fifteen hundred to four thousand words—and the time to craft each word. Books are more uneven—it is difficult to make each of eighty thousand words sing—but they provide enduring proof of effort and, if it's there, talent. Radio, particularly the one-minute commentaries I began writing and reciting in the 1990s, provides an attentive audience; the listener can drive a car, for instance, and still hear and absorb every word. And television provides—great tables in restaurants. All maître d's watch TV. There is a down side too, to each medium. The television business, for in stance, is generally not for adults, on either side of the screen, which probably explains why it pays so well.

The day I went to work for WNBC, in 1971, I went on the air, twice, on the six o'clock and eleven o'clock news. I didn't know which camera to look at. I didn't know that the little red lights signaled the active camera. I couldn't read the TelePrompTer without running my eyes back and forth across the screen. I had butterflies in my stomach and tightness in my throat, and I sounded even more gravelly than usual. The television critic for the *New York Daily News,* Kay Gardella, reviewed my debut. "He sounded like he wasn't going to get through it," she wrote. "Unfortunately, he did."

I thought it was a very funny line, especially if it had been written about someone else. (Over the years, critiques of my work have become more tolerant. Described as "raspy" at first, my voice later was labeled "distinctive." The voice hadn't changed, only the perception. Some people actually tell me, "You've got a great voice." They're great kidders.)

My cohorts on the local news on WNBC were the anchorman Sandor Vanocur, a former White House correspondent; Gabe Pressman, the best and hardest-working street reporter on New York television; Frank Field, at the peak of a marathon career as weatherman and science expert; and Norma Quarles, a lovely person who was our token woman and token black and handled both roles with grace and skill. They all tried to be helpful. Vanocur asked me to lunch at the "21" Club; Field invited me to Ho Ho, a Chinese restaurant. They had different styles. Sandy was a national television celebrity, Frank a local hero. "Hello, Doctorfrankfield," the waiters at Ho Ho greeted him. "Please sit down, Doctorfrankfield."

When I started on television, fresh from print journalism, I believed that in the beginning there were the words, and in the end there were the words, and from beginning to end, they were *my* words, and the *way* I delivered them was immaterial. Gradually, I found out I was wrong. The words meant nothing if the viewer didn't absorb them. I worked on pronunciation, modulation, pace. I went to a speech teacher named Dr. Mitchnik, who specialized in accents and had a thick Russian-Jewish one of his own. Somehow, he helped me speak more clearly. I went to a woman, Lilyan Wilder, who also worked with Oprah, Maria Shriver, and George Bush. She helped me, too, although not as much, obviously, as she helped the others.

I discovered that I could not *write* for television, not the way I wrote for newspapers, magazines, and books. Instead, I had to *type,* condense, simplify. The viewer could not go back over my words, could not review or replay them. "Tell them what you're going to say," Gene Shalit, my NBC colleague, advised me, "then say it, then tell them what you've said." Gene used to sit under the camera and make faces to relax me. Gene gave great face.

Occasionally, I would slip a relatively artful sentence or phrase into a television script, but not too often, and not too complex, or it would lose both meaning and effect. I began to recognize that television, with its dependence on pictures, tended to have great impact (one picture of a burning child in Vietnam moved more people than all the dispatches in the *Times*), but little depth. Early in my broadcasting days, asked to do a story about the horse racing business, I said, only half in jest, "Do you want me to do it briefly and superficially, or at length and superficially?"

Jimmy Breslin encouraged me to be different, to stand out on television. "Do something outrageous," he recommended. On the eleven o'clock news one night, I did. I talked about Secretariat and Riva Ridge, the back-to-back Kentucky Derby winners from Meadow Stable, and referred to them, innocently, as "the two most famous stablemates since Joseph and Mary."

When the program ended, Jim Hartz, the anchor, a gifted broadcaster who later hosted *Today,* turned to me and said, "That was very funny. I just wish you hadn't said it on a program I was anchoring." I laughed and went home to bed.

At two in the morning, my phone rang. A reporter from the *Daily News* was calling. "What do you think about this furor you've created?" he said.

"What furor?" I said.

The reporter explained to me that, since my offhand remark, NBC had received some fourteen hundred telephone calls, almost all from offended viewers. I broke the phone-call record set when the network cut away from the decisive closing minutes of a Joe Namath–New York Jets football game to show the movie *Heidi.*

"I meant no offense to any of the four," I said, still asleep and still a smart-ass. Fortunately, the *News*man did not quote me.

At three in the morning, as the magnitude of the reaction to my words set in, I called Breslin. "Remember what you said about me doing something outrageous?" I said. "Well, I think I have."

"What did you say?" Jimmy inquired.

"I said that Secretariat and Riva Ridge were the most famous stablemates since Joseph and Mary."

"You ought to have your mouth washed out," my friend and mentor said.

The Catholic establishment was not amused, either. Terence Cardinal Cooke attacked me from the pulpit, getting even with me for having listed him among the overrated. A conservative Catholic publication called me "the Jew writer." A priest wrote to me on Church stationery and said I wasn't fit to eat the dung of the stable that had sheltered Joseph and Mary. I was accused of blasphemy and sexual innuendo. I protested that my remark was not sacrilegious, was not suggesting any kind of improper relationship between Joseph and Mary, was not equating them with animals; I was merely taking an absurd historical accuracy—I *still* think Secretariat and Riva Ridge *were* the most famous stablemates since Joseph and Mary—and making fun of it.

The morning after, I went to NBC expecting to hear my producer's reaction. He had no reaction; he was waiting to hear the news director's reaction. I went to the news director, who also had no intention of reacting precipitously. I followed the chain of command to Dick Wald's office, and when the network's vice president laughed (but asked me to be more circumspect in the future), the laughter trickled down. Still, I had to go on the air and apologize for my comment. I sort of apologized. I said I was sorry if I had offended anyone.

Several weeks later, I went to visit a friend in Lenox Hill Hospital, and when the elevator stopped in front of me and the door opened, out stepped Cardinal Cooke and Frank Sinatra. The cardinal and I had made up, and as we exchanged greetings in the hospital lobby, he mentioned that he and Frank had been visiting Ed Sullivan. If I were Ed Sullivan, and woke up in a hospital bed and saw Cardinal Cooke and Frank Sinatra looking down on me, I would have thought I'd died and gone to heaven.

The first producer who was assigned to me at WNBC acted as if he knew everything about the television business. He spent six months teaching me everything he knew. Not until then did I realize that he—and I—knew nothing. I had to start over, learn how to help, and be helped by, cameramen, editors, and producers, which ones to trust, which to question. I learned how to make a story look and sound good.

At WNBC, I could experiment, I could be outrageous, as long as I stayed away from religion. I stood in a New Jersey swamp outside the Lincoln Tunnel, stood on the future site of Giants Stadium, and said the dismal Giants had finally found a home they deserved. I wished the owner of the Giants, Wellington Mara, a cerebrum for Christmas.

The Giants, understandably, did not think highly of me. When they traded for a quarterback named Norm Snead, they did not invite me to the news conference introducing him. I didn't care. I scanned the Manhattan phone book, found a Norman Snead, and went off to interview him. He was a middle-aged black man who worked in a factory in New Jersey. I walked in, cameras rolling, approached Snead, the factory worker, and asked him how his arm was. "Which arm?" he replied.

The people who work in television are a strange breed. A large percentage, drawn by the perceived glamour, are more concerned with being in the television *business* than with doing the *work*. They compete more strenuously for jobs than for stories. Many are afraid to try to do anything *differently*. They go with what works, just as the sit-coms and the sit-drams do, perhaps because they feel the stakes are too high to take a chance. I greatly prefer the work to the business. I love the opportunity to make millions of people laugh—or cry. The *business* makes *me* laugh—and cry.

Many television practices irritate me, the practice, for one, of a correspondent signing off: "Dick Schaap, ABC News, Philadelphia." In my writing, I've always tried to build toward a punch line. What could be more anticlimactic than name, network, and site? If the viewer doesn't know what network he's watching, he's not very bright. If the viewer doesn't know where the story is taking place, the correspondent and the producer are not very bright. And if it's so important to build the identity of the correspondent, just make certain that the anchorperson leads into the story by mentioning the correspondent's name. Once is enough. Did you ever see a byline at the beginning *and* end of a newspaper story?

I have a complaint, too, about television critics. When they criticize or praise a correspondent, they almost always have no idea of how much the correspondent did or did not contribute to the story. Did he write the script? Did he edit the script? Did he merely mouth the script? Did the producer conceive the story? Did the producer hand-feed the questions and then the script to the correspondent? If you weren't there, you can't possibly know. Some correspondents who think syntax is a Bill Clinton levy actually believe they write their own scripts.

*   *   *

Before I knew what I was doing on air, NBC Sports gave me a network baseball show preceding their Monday night games. I went to Geneva, New York, to cover the debut of the first woman umpire in organized baseball, a woman named Bernice Gera, and on her first day at work, between games of a doubleheader, she resigned. My cameraman captured a magnificent shot of a stunned male umpire silently mouthing the words, "She quit."

I parodied the baseball clinics that were popular in those days, tutorials on the arcane arts of hitting the cutoff man, covering first base, executing the double play. I did a story on the more accessible art of signing baseballs, and the New York Mets' Tug McGraw, my kind of guy—once, asked whether he preferred grass or artificial turf, he said he didn't know, he had never smoked artificial turf—demonstrated the art. Tug explained that most minor leagues were in Florida and California so that each night, after a game, you could take home an orange or a grapefruit, wrap a piece of stationery around it, and practice signing your signature. "Once you can write on a curved surface," said McGraw, with a straight face, "you get promoted to the big leagues."

The local station asked me to do a weekly football show during the fall. I had two guests on each show, one a football player, the other not, a modified version of *The Joe Namath Show*. One week, I teamed Fran Tarkenton, the Giants' quarterback, with Edward Vilella, the ballet dancer. I suggested that ballet dancers just might be the best athletes in the world, and Vilella, a former boxer, and Tarkenton both agreed with me. Vilella may not only have been the best athlete I ever met; he may have been the most fortunate. Imagine being a ballet dancer, and being straight. Imagine the odds. Even Wilt might have been envious.

Jeanne Moutoussamy worked with me at WNBC. She was an artist and photographer, a beautiful young woman, and I had no idea that she knew Arthur Ashe, the tennis star, until I encountered the two of them embracing in an NBC hallway one night. After they married, I enjoyed telling people that I knew both of them before they knew each other.

Arthur was the most thoughtful athlete I ever knew. His ideas were never preconceived; they were always the result of research and reflection. He was a great athlete, champion of Wimbledon and the U.S. Open, but his achievements off the court, as an advocate of education, understanding, and racial pride, were far greater.

When Arthur died of AIDS, I covered the memorial service, a mass outpouring of affection, and wrote a script that began, "The score of Arthur Ashe's final match was love, love, and love."

The anchorman on the broadcast, Peter Jennings, didn't get it. He insisted my lead be changed. He said that love, love, and love implied that Arthur Ashe was a loser.

Peter's strength is reading out loud.

In the early 1970s, I lived in Greenwich halfway between Tarkenton and Tom Seaver, a pair of Hall of Fame arms. Once, both of them and their wives came to dinner at my house with the writer Erich Segal, whose novel, *Love Story,* had soared to the top of the bestseller lists. Segal dominated the conversation, but when he paused for breath, Tarkenton said, "The other day, I stayed out late on the practice field, and when I came into the locker room, two huge defensive tackles were sitting in front of their lockers, reading *Love Story,* and tears were rolling down their cheeks." Segal was so moved by the story of the bawling linemen he often repeated it on television talk shows. Tarkenton, of course, had made the whole thing up.

Segal reciprocated by inviting the Schaaps and the Seavers to an Erich Segal festival at Yale, a showing of films he had worked on, from the Beatles' *Yellow Submarine* to outtakes from *Love Story.* In Segal's apartment, we met one of his fellow professors of English, who later wrote of his encounter with Seaver in *Harper's* magazine. "The talk was light, easy, and bright," he reported, "and was produced almost entirely by the Schaaps, Nancy Seaver, and Segal. Because I was about the only member of the gathering who was a household name only in my own household, I was content to listen." When he became commissioner of baseball in 1989, the modest professor, A. Bartlett Giamatti, was neither so anonymous nor so reticent.

During the years Fran Tarkenton played quarterback for the New York Giants, Joe Namath played quarterback for the New York Jets, and the media loved to contrast them as the sinner and the saint, Broadway Joe and the son of a preacher man. The truth was that Tarkenton and Namath had much more in common than sturdy arms. The main difference was that Namath was single, and Tarkenton was discreet.

When I started in local television, I was nervous every time I went on camera. After a couple of years, I hyperventilated only when I went on network television. Eventually, I stopped being nervous at all. Now, whether I'm on ESPN or delivering a speech to a thousand people, I feel perfectly relaxed. But I still remember how much I dreaded standing up in high-school speech classes.

22

"The Magnitude of Me"

In the fall of 1972, restless holding only one full-time job, I accepted an offer to be the editor of *SPORT*. I couldn't resist. I had been reading the magazine since its birth in 1946; I had been writing for it for fifteen years. I warned the publisher I would be an absentee editor in the afternoons, that I would spend only my mornings at the *SPORT* desk, the afternoons and evenings at NBC.

I was editor of *SPORT* for five years—a span I measure by the fact that I awarded Most Valuable Player automobiles to Reggie Jackson, Gene Tenace, Rollie Fingers, Pete Rose, and Johnny Bench for their performances in the World Series; to Jake Scott, Larry Csonka, Franco Harris, Lynn Swann, and Fred Biletnikoff for their play in Super Bowls; and to Wilt Chamberlain, Willis Reed, John Havlicek, Rick Barry, and Jo Jo White for their play in NBA championships. I chose Mark Spitz, Secretariat, Muhammad Ali, Fran Tarkenton, and Julius Erving as *SPORT*'s performers of the year from 1972 through 1976, and hosted dinners to celebrate the last three selections.

The most controversial of my selections was Jake Scott in the Super Bowl game that completed the Miami Dolphins' 1972 season, the only undefeated and untied season in NFL history. Scott made two interceptions in that game; his teammate, Manny Fernandez, made a hundred tackles. My friend Pete Gent, a football player turned writer, kept me up most of the night before the game, which started at noon in the Los Angeles Coliseum, with temperatures soaring into the eighties. I think I dozed off before the kickoff, but awoke in time to see Scott make his interceptions. I wasn't quite alert enough to see Fernandez make his tackles. When I awarded the MVP car to Scott, with an assenting vote from Gent, Manny Fernandez wanted to make one more tackle, preferably from my blind side.

Two years later, I created a stir at Super Bowl IX by hiring a pair of Los Angeles Rams to cover the game for *SPORT*—Fred Dryer and Lance Rentzel, talented but not typical football players. Dryer, a Pro Bowl defensive end, told me about the time he went into a defensive huddle, and one of his teammates, eyes blazing, shouted, "C'mon, c'mon, there's no tomorrow," and Fred turned and started to walk off the field. "Where you going?" his teammate demanded, and Fred said, "If there's no tomorrow, I sure as hell ain't going to waste today playing football." Dryer later became a television star in the title role of the series *Hunter*. Rentzel scored thirteen touchdowns one season as a wide receiver and *looked* like a television star.

They both took their assignment seriously. They went to a costume house in Los Angeles, rented vintage outfits and Speed Graphic cameras straight from *The Front*

Page, tucked press cards in their fedoras, and descended on New Orleans for Super Bowl week. At a press conference for Chuck Noll, the coach of the Pittsburgh Steelers, Dryer stood in the back of the room, raised his hand, and said, "Coach, you've said the zone defense is on the way out. If so, where is it going?" Noll gave a straight answer. The National Football League was not amused.

When Dryer interviewed Fran Tarkenton, his former teammate and buddy on the New York Giants, he asked, "Fran, is it true you choke up in the big games?"

"It's true, Fred," Fran said, "I've won two hundred games, all little ones."

At a luncheon later that year honoring Johnny Bench for his role in the 1975 World Series, I also gave an award to Red Smith, who was every sports columnist's role model, for his years of distinguished work. The award was an engraved typewriter, and to indulge both my political and comedic sensibilities, I invited Alger Hiss to present the typewriter. Hiss had spent several years in prison, convicted of perjury, of lying about giving secret information to the Soviet Union, and a major and questionable piece of evidence against him had been an old family typewriter. "One of the things that kept me sane in prison," Hiss told the luncheon, "was reading Red Smith's column every day."

I was disappointed that I never got Red Smith to write for *SPORT*—Red was a sprinter, best suited to one-thousand-word bursts—but pleased that I bought the first piece of fiction *SPORT* ever published, the opening chapter of Pete Gent's landmark football novel *North Dallas Forty,* a haunting account of football players on a hunting expedition. I wanted the magazine to be different. I helped conceive and select the covers designed by art director Al Braverman. One showed Dr. J, Julius Erving, wearing scrubs in an operating room; another the multitalented Dave DeBusschere with six arms, two for passing, two for defending, and two for shooting; another the first woman to grace *SPORT*'s cover, the golfer Jan Stephenson; and another Reggie Jackson, the "Blood and Guts of the Fighting A's," posing as General George S. Patton, wearing his baseball uniform, a holster with pearl-handled pistols, and a four-star battle helmet.

I couldn't get George S. Patton to write about Reggie, but I did get George C. Scott, who won an Academy Award for playing the title role in *Patton.* Scott had attended journalism school at the University of Missouri and had planned to become a sportswriter until he discovered he was one of the best actors in the world. He agreed to write an article for *SPORT* as readily as Reggie agreed to pose for the cover.

When I arrived at Scott's Los Angeles home, ready to accompany him on a trip to see the A's play in Oakland, he told me he had taken the liberty of leasing a Lear jet for the occasion. That would have taken care of *SPORT*'s travel budget for a decade, but Scott insisted upon paying for the charter himself, and for the limousine that was waiting on the Oakland runway to whisk us to the ball park, and for our luxury hotel suites in San Francisco.

When we went on the field for batting practice, Reggie came over and asked, "Did you really fly up in a Lear jet?" I said we did. "What'd that cost?" Reggie wanted to know. I said I didn't know, but that it wasn't cheap. Reggie was impressed, and Reggie was not easily impressed, except, of course, by Reggie.

Reggie had been in a slump, had gone more than two weeks without hitting a home run, but the night we showed up he hit two home runs, the A's built a huge lead, and Reggie left the game after seven innings. Scott and I went down to the locker room to visit with him.

"Look," Reggie greeted Scott, "I don't want to blow smoke up your ass, but I want to tell you I appreciate you coming up here tonight. It isn't easy for *me* to find someone to look up to."

Scott's ego, which was not small, did not come close to Reggie's. I finished a distant third. A few years later, Reggie was a New York Yankee, waging a running war with manager Billy Martin. Once, defying Martin's instructions to hit away, Reggie opted to bunt, an act of insubordination that prompted Martin to suspend Reggie for five days. When Reggie rejoined the team, in Chicago, I was among the army of newsmen attending the reunion.

Before the game, Reggie entertained the media in front of his locker, and I outlasted the rest of the reporters. Finally, when Reggie and I were alone with my camera crew, I asked him what thought was uppermost in his mind during his suspension.

He considered the question for several silent seconds, then looked straight into the lens, and said, "The magnitude of me."

I could have kissed him. You can't invent lines like that.

Once, when I was editor of *SPORT,* Al Braverman and I decided to use a photo of Oscar Robertson on the cover. When the issue came out, I received a letter that read:

Dear Editor:
My name is Joey Smith, and I am eight years old, and I want to thank you for putting my favorite player, Os-

car Robertson, on the cover of your magazine. I live in
northern Wisconsin and twice a year my mommy and
daddy take me to Milwaukee to see the Bucks play.
When the game is over, I stand near the runway that
goes to the locker room, and I try to get autographs
from the players. Most of them just push you out of
the way and say, "Get the hell out of here." But not
Oscar. Oscar told me to go fuck myself.

I do not know whether the letter was really written
by an eight-year-old, but I certainly hope so. I have
told the story to Oscar, who assures me that the incident never happened. I like the kid's version better.

SPORT, like *Newsweek,* was not conducive to mon-
ogamy, although I suppose the fault, once again, lay
more with me than with the corporation. I met my
third wife, Trish, when she was working down the hall
from me at a sister publication called *American Home.*
I discovered that if I bent over and drank from the water fountain outside her office, I got a terrific view of
her legs. I drank deeply from that fountain, and frequently, even though there was another fountain, considerably more convenient, right outside my own
office.

Trish and I lived together after my separation from
Madeleine, and we were married in 1981, shortly after
my divorce. At our wedding party, Trish and our
friend Dr. Theodore Rubin, the psychoanalyst who
wrote the book that became the film *David and Lisa,*
informed me I was "an emotional munchkin." They
vowed to do their best to see that I grew up, and suc-
ceeded, up to a point. Ted was one of three therapists
at the party, which probably says something. One of

the others was Skeeter McClure, the former Olympic boxing champion.

While I worked at *SPORT,* NBC allowed me to spread out from the local to the network news, affording me the opportunity to contribute to the *Nightly News* and *Today* programs. John Chancellor was then the anchorman for *Nightly News,* and we quickly became extremely mediocre tennis rivals. After one of our matches, I tried to open a resistant window in the locker room and brought the frame crashing down on John, bloodying his forehead. I took him to the hospital, fearing that, if he was scarred, NBC would fire me. We both were unscathed.

Not long after I left NBC in 1980, someone suggested that *Nightly News* run a story on George Brett. "Who's George Brett?" Chancellor asked.

John was told that George Brett was a baseball player for the Kansas City Royals who, in August of 1980, was batting over .400, threatening to become the first player to hit .400 for a season since Ted Williams thirty-nine years earlier.

Chancellor listened and agreed that Brett sounded like a good subject. A reporter from NBC's Chicago bureau was dispatched to Kansas City. "This is for the John Chancellor show," the reporter told Brett.

"Who's John Chancellor?" Brett asked.

I was reminded of that story, which John loved to tell on himself, several years later when I auditioned for the role of narrator for Ken Burns's monumental PBS series on the history of baseball. I didn't get the job. John Chancellor did.

23

"Mo, This Is Billy"

In 1974, while I was editor of *SPORT* and a correspondent for NBC, I still found time to work on two books: *Massacre at Winged Foot,* minute-by-minute through the 1974 U.S. Open golf championship, and *Quarterbacks Have All the Fun,* an anthology of profiles of quarterbacks—two by me, the rest by such accomplished writers as Breslin, W. C. Heinz, Joe McGinniss, Dan Jenkins, George Plimpton, Myron Cope, and Larry L. King (not the King of *Larry King Live,* but the King of *Best Little Whorehouse in Texas* fame).

I was also approached about another book. Jack Molinas talked to me about writing his life story. A former basketball star at Columbia University who played brilliantly but briefly in the NBA, Molinas later recruited college players to fix games, to shave points. As a result, he had been the best athlete in Attica prison before he came to see me. He told me a story that summed up his life. When he was ten, growing up in a wise-guy neighborhood, two of the locals began arguing about how good an athlete this kid Molinas was. "I'll bet you a hundred bucks he can throw a rock over that apartment house," one of them said. "I'll bet you a hundred he can't," said the other.

They handed Jack a rock, and he threw it over the apartment house. "The guy who won the bet gave me ten bucks," Molinas told me. "It wasn't until a few years later that I realized I could've gotten twenty for not throwing it over."

That was the story of his life, a life cut short, to use John Lardner's phrase, by ballistics. He was shot to death sitting by a swimming pool in Beverly Hills.

We never wrote the book.

My film career revived while I was at NBC. I appeared with James Caan in *The Gambler,* and this time I had lines. I said, "Harvard 53, Dartmouth 51; Duke 60, North Carolina 56," and several other basketball scores. My portrayal of a sportscaster must have been convincing. In my next film, *Semi-Tough,* I played the role again, this time promoted to dialogue, interviewing Burt Reynolds and Carl Weathers, the opposing captains, the night before the Super Bowl. I was encouraged to ad lib, and Reynolds, winging his own answers, relaxed me.

Burt told me that before the shooting of one of the big football scenes, he told Kris Kristofferson, "If any of the players ask you if you played football in college, tell 'em you were a drama major." Burt and Kris walked onto the field, and Ed "Too Tall" Jones of the Dallas Cowboys shouted, "Hey, Burt, you ever play football?" Reynolds, an all-state high-school player, was a running back at Florida State. "I was a drama major," Reynolds said. Then Too Tall asked Kristofferson if he had ever played. "Oh, yeah," Kristofferson said, "and I was good, too. In fact, if I hadn't become a Rhodes Scholar, I might've played professionally." Jones smiled. In the simulated scrimmage, Kristofferson took a beating, and Reynolds was spared.

Many years later, Reynolds wrote me a wistful note. "We both should have stayed single," he suggested, "and bought a pro team together." Even if I'd stayed single, I'm positive Burt would have been the majority owner.

Typecast as a reporter, I was offered a third film role in the 1970s, but when I was told I had to be on the docks in New York at six in the morning, I declined the invitation to appear in *The French Connection*. It was not a smart career move.

In 1974, I set out for "the Rumble in the Jungle," the heavyweight championship fight between George Foreman and Muhammad Ali in Kinshasa, Zaire. I flew with a group of journalists on an Icelandic Air Lines charter that took us as far as Luxembourg. We paused for a day in Germany, in nearby Trier, and while we were there, we learned that, because of an injury to Foreman, the fight was being postponed for a month. We were invited to go on to Zaire, but the promoters and their publicists had lied to us so many times I was convinced the fight would never take place.

I decided to go home, through Amsterdam, by heritage and taste one of my favorite cities. I thought I'd have a night on the town in Amsterdam. Instead, I had a night on the runway. Our Luxair flight was the last to land at Schipol Airport before the hijacking of an Air France 747 by Japanese terrorists closed down the airport. We sat on the plane for four hours while Dutch soldiers clutched submachine guns and Dutch officials negotiated. No one was hurt, and I flew back to New York the next morning.

I saw the fight on a large screen at Madison Square Garden in a sky box that belonged to Downe Communications, *SPORT*'s parent company. Most of us, including me, were worried about Ali's safety, afraid that Foreman would administer the kind of fearsome beating he had given Joe Frazier the previous year. There were more than a dozen of us in the box, and only one, Ed Downe's chauffeur, a black man, predicted that Ali would win. Then came the confounding rope-a-dope, and the stunning and decisive victory for Ali, the least expected, and therefore most rewarding, victory of his career, a career I wish had ended with that victory. Several years later, I wrote in *Parade* magazine:

It should have ended in Zaire. It should have ended in a burst of light in the middle of the night, with a stunning victory, with drums and hearts pounding, with thousands of voices rumbling, "Ali . . . Ali . . . Ali . . ." It should have ended then with Muhammad Ali at the pinnacle of the most charismatic career in the history of boxing, perhaps in the history of sports, with Ali the born-again champion of the whole world. He should have been carried forthwith from the ring in Kinshasa, the capital of Zaire, and transported due east, across the heart of Africa, to Tanzania, and taken to the peak of Mount Kilimanjaro. And there, like Hemingway's leopard, he should have been frozen in snow, preserved forever, absolutely perfect.

It should have ended then, not so much for his benefit as for ours, for those of us who have shared our adult lives with Ali, for those of you—the younger ones—who have shared your entire lives with Ali, for those who found in him a magic style and startling substance, for those who soared and suffered with him, for those who feared the years of exile and the broken jaw inflicted by Ken Norton's fists might have weakened Ali, weakened him to the point where George Foreman could have done him permanent damage. It should have ended then, before the snow began to melt, before his speech began to slur and give rise to rumors of brain damage, before his cheeks grew so puffy that they threatened, even when he had not been punched in months, to push shut the brown eyes that once had glowed so brightly.

The editor of *Parade* at the time, Walter Anderson, has always insisted that the Ali piece was the best of dozens I wrote for him and among the best he ever published. Walter, one of my few true rivals at name-dropping, is among those rare and cherished editors who care about words and writers. A few years later, when he asked if he could list me in the masthead as the sports editor of *Parade,* I readily agreed. I felt like Queen Elizabeth; I was a figurehead.

At the end of 1974, Muhammad Ali was *SPORT*'s Man of the Year by acclamation, and he accepted our invitation to be honored at a banquet at the Plaza Hotel in January 1975. I set about assembling a suitable dais.

I wanted a comedian. I wanted Robert Klein. His agent said he was busy. With time running out, and Klein unavailable, a woman at the William Morris Agency told me, "Take Billy."

"Billy who?" I said.

"Billy Crystal," she said.

"Billy who?" I said.

I had never heard of Billy Crystal, which put me in the majority.

"He's very funny," she said. "Trust me."

"You're an agent," I should have said. "How can I trust you?"

Instead, I said, "What does he do?"

"He does a terrific imitation of Ali," the woman said. "Ali and Howard Cosell. You'll love him."

Reluctantly, I took Crystal. I didn't have much choice. I met him for the first time two minutes before we sat down to eat. He seemed like a nice, gentle person. He said he had been working as a substitute teacher at a junior high school on Long Island. Sometimes he taught social studies, sometimes girls' gym. He sat on the dais with Neil Simon and George Plimpton, two great writers, and Melba Moore, a great singer, and Muhammad Ali, the greatest. I thought Billy was out of his league.

I was the master of ceremonies, and halfway through the program, after Simon and Plimpton spoke, and Moore sang, I said, "And now—one of Muhammad Ali's closest friends!"

Billy Crystal stood up and moved toward the microphone, and Ali looked at me as if I were crazy. He had never seen Billy before. He had no idea who he was.

Billy promptly launched into his Ali-and-Cosell routine.

"Muhammad—may I call you 'Mo'?"

"Sure, Howard, but don't call me Larry or Curly."

"How fast are you, Mo?"

"I'm so fast, Howard, I can turn off the lights and jump in bed and be under the covers before the room gets dark."

Ali fell out of his chair, he was laughing so hard.

Billy Crystal was the hit of the evening, the star, in his first television appearance, of a syndicated program "*SPORT*'s Man of the Year."

Two lasting friendships began that night, one between Ali and Crystal, the other between Billy and me. None of us dreamed that someday Billy would be as huge in his field as Ali was in his. (When they posed with me for the cover of this book, the thought that was uppermost in my mind was: *The magnitude of them.*)

When Billy and I collaborated on *Absolutely Mahvelous,* he inscribed a copy of the book to Trish and me. "I'm so glad Klein wasn't available," he wrote.

Later in 1975, between book assignments, I pulled off my own triple play: simultaneously correspondent for NBC News, editor of and contributor to *SPORT,* and guest writer-in-residence (succeeding Jimmy Breslin) for the *Washington Star,* whose editor was our former boss, Jim Bellows. In September, I went to the Philippines for "the Thrilla in Manila," Ali-Frazier III, and in October to Boston for the equally dramatic seven-game World Series between the Boston Red Sox and the Cincinnati Reds, covering both events for the newspaper, the magazine, and the network. Sleep, I've always figured, was for sissies.

In Manila, I stayed at the Bayview Plaza Hotel, occasionally eating meals at its rooftop Japanese restaurant. From a table on the roof, I could look across Manila Bay and see clearly in the distance, guarding the harbor, the island of Corregidor and, off to its right, the strip of history called the Bataan Peninsula, the scene of so much bloodshed early in World War II. I could eat teriyaki and, at the same time, recall General Wainwright surviving the Bataan Death March, American soldiers and nurses evacuating Corregidor, and MacArthur, as he had promised, returning to the Philippines.

The ten-day trip to Manila was fascinating, a dizzying blend of curfews, cockfights, and custom-rolled contraband joints served at formal receptions on silver platters. President Ferdinand Marcos had imposed martial law upon the city, but the international journalists covering the fight were granted dispensations to go out after midnight, to accompany Ali on his nocturnal runs. No one wanted to miss one of Ali's impromptu performances. When Joe Frazier accused him of firing a gun from the street toward Frazier's hotel balcony, Ali countered that the gun was only a toy and, besides, "I ain't gonna shoot him. I don't want anything to happen to him before I get him in the ring. I'm praying for his good health."

Ali interrupted one of his workouts to jab at reports that he had introduced a beautiful young woman named Veronica Porche to President Marcos as "my wife." Veronica had been observed at Ali's side everywhere he went in Manila. She did not look like a bodyguard.

"She ain't my wife," Ali said. "Belinda's my wife. I ain't got but one wife." He also said that his relationship with Veronica was nobody's business but his own. "You tell people not to worry about who I'm sleeping with," he said, "and I won't worry about who they're sleeping with." Several journalists took the punch.

Ali warmed to the subject. "They're always looking for something bad to say about me," he said. "Now it's lady friends. Somebody once wrote in London that five girls came into my hotel room"—his eyes opened wide—"and only three came out."

Two days later, at six in the morning, I was sitting in Ali's hotel suite, preparing to interview him for the *Today* show, when Belinda marched in, straight from the airport. She ignored the cameras, walked up to her husband, put her arms around him, and said, "Aren't you glad to see me?"

Ali lied like a husband.

The Alis disappeared into an adjacent bedroom for round two of their reunion, and the sounds of conflict wafted out to the living room. Ali's trainer, Angelo Dundee, one of boxing's royalty, was sitting with me and my camera crew and wisely suggested we adjourn to the hotel coffee shop.

After several cups, I returned to Ali's suite, saw neither blood nor scars, and conducted my interview. It took ten minutes of uneasy conversation before Ali again became his effusive self, twelve hours before Belinda boarded a plane back to the United States, and almost two years before Veronica Porche became the third Mrs. Ali.

On the day of the fight, which was scheduled to begin at 10:30 A.M. Manila time, I was again in Ali's suite at 6:00 A.M. But this time, the battles were on the television screen. A local station was showing the first two Ali-Frazier wars. Ali preferred the second, the one he won. "Look at the way I'm slapping him," Ali said. "I had the power then I got now, he goes down."

Angelo Dundee's voice came through clearly on the television. "Stay there, stay there, dammit, stay there," Dundee shouted every time Ali moved away from Frazier.

"He's right, he's right," Ali said. "I stay there, he doesn't have a chance."

At seven, Ali went back to bed, and at eight, his

brother Rahaman and Lloyd Wells, a former scout for the Kansas City Chiefs, woke up the champion. A few minutes later, Veronica Porche stopped by to pay her respects.

Shortly after nine, we left the hotel, and by nine-thirty, an hour before fight time, we entered Ali's dressing room in the Philippine Coliseum in nearby Quezon City. Ali stripped and lay down on a brown couch, a towel across his waist, an air conditioner firing cool air across his body. By his feet, a silent television screen showed a meaningless preliminary bout.

Don King, the promoter, came in to see the champ. So did the Temptations, the singing group. Rahaman Ali wore a handsome white barong, the ubiquitous Philippine shirt-jacket, decorated with butterflies and bees and his name in large bold script. Cassius Clay Sr., the father of the Alis, wore a white suit with a pink shirt, looking more like a plantation owner than the descendant of plantation hands.

Angelo Dundee was there, and Bundini Brown, and a dozen others fired up for the fight. Ali yawned and stared at the ceiling. "Just another day's work," he said. "Just gotta go beat on another man."

"Gonna knock him out," Rahaman Ali said.

"Ain't gonna last eight rounds," said someone else.

"Just another day's work," said Ali.

The fight lasted fourteen punishing rounds, each man battered and drained by the furious pace. Just before the start of the fifteenth round, Eddie Futch, Frazier's trainer, fearing for his fighter's health, threw a towel into the ring. The fight was over. Ali lay down in the ring, trying, he said later, to find a pocket of cool air, trying to escape the crush around him.

Not until Ali returned to his dressing room did he realize how exhausted he was. Again he stripped and lay down on the brown couch, a towel across his waist, again the air conditioner firing cool air across his inflamed body. I congratulated him, and Ali said, "I'm tired. I've very tired."

It had not been just another day's work, he said. It had been one of the great fights in boxing history, a fitting climax to a magnificent rivalry.

That night, Joe Frazier, his swollen face hidden behind dark glasses, went to the postfight party he had planned, sang a song called "Knock on Wood," and danced with his wife. Ali, spent, stayed in his room and rested.

A few weeks later, the Red Sox, who had not won a World Series in fifty-seven years, and the Reds, who had not won one in thirty-five, met in a showdown certain to end one drought. The Reds were the Big Red Machine then, with a powerful lineup led by Johnny Bench, Joe Morgan, Tony Perez, and Pete Rose. (Three of them are in the Baseball Hall of Fame, and the fourth belongs there, for 4,256 reasons.) But my favorite player was on the other team, a left-handed pitcher for the Red Sox, the Spaceman, Bill Lee. The last time the Red Sox had won a World Series, in 1918, they had been led by another left-handed pitcher—Babe Ruth.

The day before the Series began, Lee stood in front of his locker surrounded by a pack of reporters. During a five-minute monologue, he endorsed zero population growth, condemned muggings in Manhattan, described the difficulties of teaching golf to a young woman with a full chest, discussed busing and vegetarianism, and punned that "Dentistry is a tough science—you have to have a lot of patience." He expressed his religious belief in pyramids, miniature versions of the imposing constructions of the ancient Egyptians, constructions that, he said, "were probably built by people from other planets utilizing levitation."

Lee was as hard to hit as he was to fathom. In the second game of the Series, he led Cincinnati, 2–1, when he was replaced in the ninth inning, with a man on second and no one out. The Reds rallied to win the game, 3–2 ("I'll be alive tomorrow," Lee said cheerfully after the game, "barring a traffic accident"), and with three of the next four games also decided by a single run, the Series came down to a decisive seventh game. The Red Sox nominated Lee to pitch The Game. "*The* game?" Lee said. "I wouldn't say it's *the* game. *The* game is hockey right now. We're intruding on their season."

Earlier, when Lee had been scheduled to start game six, before three days of rain permitted the rotation to be revised, he was asked if it would be the biggest game he had ever pitched in his life. He said no. "The final game of the College World Series was bigger," said the former University of Southern California star, "because that was for fun."

I didn't sit in the press box for game seven. I sat in the stands to share The Game with a fan:

The white-haired fan had been coming to Fenway Park to watch the Boston Red Sox play baseball for more than fifty-five years, and for more than fifty-five years he had dreamed of seeing the Red Sox win a World Series. As a youngster he had sat out in right field with his father in a grandstand seat, but now, as the Red Sox threatened to break out of a scoreless tie in the bottom of the third inning of the seventh game of the 1975 World Series, he was sitting in a front-row box seat, just to the left of the Boston dugout. He was in a perfect spot to call out encouragement to his friend Carl Yastrzemski, who was coming to bat, and to all Yaz's teammates, to urge them to make the Red Sox world champions for the first time since 1918.

The white-haired fan had missed the 1918 World Series—he was not quite six years old at the time—and he had missed the first two innings of the seventh game of the 1975 World Series because he had been delayed at his office in the city of Washington, D.C.

The white-haired fan was the majority leader of the House of Representatives, Massachusetts congressman Thomas P. O'Neill Jr., the man who was the hero of Breslin's book about Watergate, *How the Good Guys Finally Won.* Tip O'Neill followed baseball as passionately as he practiced politics, and he wanted to see the Red Sox win in 1975 as much as he wanted to see Gerald Ford lose a year later.

Bill Lee almost brought O'Neill and the Red Sox the championship they had been thirsting for. After five innings, Lee, O'Neill, and the Red Sox held a 3–0 lead over Cincinnati. But in the sixth inning, Lee threw a slow and high-arching curve ball to Tony Perez, a "blooper" pitch that Lee had thrown effectively several times earlier in the game. But this time Perez hit the ball out of the park, and the lead was cut to a single run. Lee was still in front, 3–2, when he left in the seventh inning, but the Reds rallied and won the game and the Series, and O'Neill was devastated. Lee, on the other hand, knew he would still be alive the next day.

In the 1980s, after Lee was out of the big leagues, blackballed according to his calculations, I went to visit him in Montreal. He told me about "El Niño," and the effects of the warm ocean current, long before anyone else ever mentioned it; he even insisted that El Niño had caused the Montreal Expos, his final big-league club, to trade one of his favorite teammates. "Dick was a lot of fun," Lee wrote of me in *Spaceman,* his autobiography. "We went back to the hotel and had a few drinks and then we had a few more. By ten P.M., he was saying he would do everything he could to get me back in baseball. At eleven, he was calling for a Congressional investigation into my charges of collusion. By midnight, we were both seeing God." Can you imagine a more prudent way for Bill Lee to say we inhaled?

I changed wardrobes often during my early television years. I went through a flamboyant period—checked sports jackets as bold as Lindsay Nelson's—and a turtleneck period, and even wore *distinctive* ties for a while. I progressed from hair-styling to coloring. The night my gray hair reverted to brown, a former NBC colleague, a weatherman named Harry Wappler, who had moved to Seattle, wrote to me, complimented me on the quality of my work and the color of my hair, and said that he used to work with my father.

Eventually, I realized that I didn't really want my clothes or the color of my hair to define me. I wanted my words to be noted, not my outfits. I turned to conservative suits, dark ones preferably, especially as I got older, which is a euphemism for heavier. I dreamed of being gaunt, even for a day, and finally, deep into my television career, I went on a crash liquid diet and lost fifty pounds in fifty days, a span that included Christmas, New Year's, and a Super Bowl at which I hosted a party for sixty and fed them all stone crab while I feasted on protein drink. Rumors spread that I had cancer, or AIDS, or both. I hit gaunt for about a day and a half, then, as soon as I resumed solids, began gaining weight, not quite so rapidly as I had shed it, but fast enough. In time, I regained my prediet figure. Now I dream only of being venerable.

The television camera, I learned, makes one look shorter, heavier, older, and dumber—not necessarily in that order.

In the spring of 1976, I was approached with a get-rich-quick scheme I found irresistible. Naturally, I didn't understand the financial complexities, but I was told that for years people had been making money by producing movies that lost money. It had something to do with attracting investors who needed to show losses for tax purposes.

The logic eluded me, but I was told that the same thing could be done with a book. I know it sounds bizarre, but the idea, as I recall, was for me to write a book that would lose money, which I had done several times without even trying. The investors would put a lot of money in the book, and I would get a lot of money and they would get a write-off. I had been chosen, it was explained, because within the tax laws, the writer (or filmmaker) had to be someone with a track record, with a proven ability to come up with a winner. I qualified on the grounds of *Instant Replay* and *I Can't Wait Until Tomorrow* . . . I had to finish the book in less than two months, presumably before the tax laws could be reformed.

Anyone with any business sense probably would have seen huge holes in the plan. Not me. I agreed to

write a fast book that would lose money. All I needed
was a subject.

The plan did not require that I write a bad book, so I
sought a subject that would interest me and impel me
to write quickly. I had recently commissioned an article for *SPORT* about Bob Beamon, who shattered the
world record in the long jump at the 1968 Olympic
Games in Mexico City, but then never again came close
to his historic performance. Only eight years after his
monumental leap, Beamon was practically forgotten.

A book about Bob Beamon? Why not?

The book started with my belief that Beamon's
jump—twenty-nine feet, two and a half inches, breaking the world record by almost two feet—was one of
man's greatest athletic achievements, arguably *the*
greatest. Track-and-field records commonly fall by
inches, by fractions of a second. In 2,500 years, from
Chionis of Sparta until Beamon, the recorded world
record in the long jump had been stretched only from
twenty-three feet, one and a half inches to twenty-
seven feet, four and three-fourth inches, an average of
barely two inches a century. Beamon had ripped off
eleven centuries of improvement in one perfect jump.

I had my title for the book—*The Perfect Jump*. Next
I had to find Beamon. The United States Olympic
Committee did not know where he was. Eventually, I
tracked him to San Diego and arranged to visit him. On
the plane heading west, I opened an envelope Beamon
had sent me. He had enclosed a paper he had written
for a graduate course in psychology at San Diego State
University:

I have an old faded photo proof of my mother. They
say my mother was a beautiful woman, small, thin,

quiet, yet compassionate. She conceived me with a very tall, handsome black man standing up, while her husband was away in prison. They say she loved to dance and would dance till late hours of the night. Dancing killed her, along with the consumption. My mother always said she wanted me to be an entertainer when I grew up. My mother wasn't supposed to have children; she lost several in miscarriages. She was very ill with tuberculosis carrying me. Somehow I made it. They say my mother hardly ever came near me, and when she did, she covered her face with a handkerchief, stood a few feet from my bed, looked at me and said, "My son." She never touched me or held me. This is all I know of my mother.

Suddenly, I had more than a title. I had a book, the story of a young man who escaped poverty and the ghetto, beat drugs and delinquency, overcame unbelievable odds just to get to high school, then to college, then to the Olympics.

I spent more than a week with Beamon in San Diego, saw the dusty gold medal he had buried at the bottom of a drawer, learned about his struggles and triumphs, his marriages, romances, injuries, and frustrations. I wrote the book in a month, beating the deadline.

The tax deal, of course, turned out to be a mirage, a figment of my greed and imagination, and after I split the modest advance with Beamon, I calculated I'd earned about two dollars an hour. I'm good at simple math. The funny thing is that *The Perfect Jump* was, and is, a good book, one of the half dozen that I've written that I'm most proud of. It came out only in paperback, for speed, and only in a token printing, so that the number of people who can corroborate my judgment is small.

I made a friend, instead of a fortune, and more than twenty years later, when Beamon was hosting a golf tournament in Miami for the benefit of the United Way, I was one of his guests. Trish and I and Bob and his wife Milana went out to dinner one night at Joe's Stone Crab in Miami Beach, and in the course of our conversation, we calculated that among us we had had fourteen marriages, three each for Milana, Trish, and me, five for Bob. I stood up, looked out over the restaurant, and announced, "We can lick any table in the place."

We drank to no more marriages.

On the basis of my Beamon book and my illustrated history of the Games, I qualified as an Olympic expert, but it wasn't until the summer of 1976 that I attended my first Olympics, in Montreal. Despite the shadow of Munich, the Montreal Games were the last at which journalists were not shackled by extreme, excessive security. We were permitted reasonable access to the Olympic Village, which housed the athletes of the world. In the Village, I spent much of my time with the U.S. boxing team, striking up a friendship with a teenager named Ray Leonard, who assured me he was going to college after the Olympics and would never fight professionally ("My decision is final, my journey is ended, my dream is fulfilled, I promised my mother, I promised my girlfriend"), and a relationship with Leon Spinks, Michael Spinks, Leo Randolph, and Howard Davis. All five of those fighters went on to win Olympic gold medals and four, all except Davis, became professional world champions, including the college dropout, Sugar Ray Leonard.

The night of the boxing finals, I emerged from the Montreal Forum with Don King, who, in his promoter mode, was still salivating. We waded through the madding crowd, searching futilely for an unoccupied taxi. Then King walked up to a limousine driver who said he was waiting for someone. Don flashed the face of Ulysses S. Grant on a fifty-dollar bill. That must have been who the driver was waiting for. He took us a few blocks to the Ritz-Carlton Hotel where we made our way to an elaborate dining room with canals twisting among the tables and ducks paddling in the canals. King beckoned the French Canadian waiter and said he'd like to order *canard*. The waiter was horrified. "We do not serve *canard*," he explained to King and the *canards* in the canals.

The 1976 Games, like every Olympics, were a reporter's feast, serving up an irresistible variety of stories. I drank cognac and ate breadsticks at a breakfast celebrating the fourteen-year-old Romanian Nadia Comanici, the first gymnast in Olympic history to record a perfect ten. (I never suspected that Nadia would eventually marry a gymnast from Oklahoma, Bart Conner, and I would run across them occasionally almost a quarter of a century later, and I certainly couldn't have imagined that by then my daughter Kari, who wasn't born until 1981, would work as a coach and counselor at the Texas gymnastics ranch run by Nadia's coach, Bela Karolyi. Karolyi kept camels, llamas, and an ostrich on his ranch and carried on conversations with them. "Bela, you're confused," my teenage daughter told Karolyi. "You go around talking to animals and patting little girls on the head.")

I lived in a motel not far from the Olympic Village in Montreal and frequently saw Bruce Jenner, the American decathlon champion, mostly because his wife at the time, Chrystie, occupied the room next to mine. I put Bruce on the cover of *SPORT,* wrote columns about him for the *Washington Star,* which had temporarily reclaimed me for its staff, and fashioned three stories about him for NBC. "Chrystie and I want you to know how much you were appreciated in Montreal," Jenner wrote to me. "Your relaxed, personal manner helped us cope with everything. . . . We can't thank you enough."

Not many athletes take the time to write a thank-you note. My first, as I recall, came from Gussie Moran, the woman who shocked Wimbledon in the forties by wearing lace panties—and shocked me by sending a bottle of men's cologne with her note—and the most recent from John Stockton of the Utah Jazz, a tiger on the court and a gentleman off. John did not send cologne. Mickey Mantle didn't exactly say thanks, but once, unsolicited, he gave me a photograph of himself inscribed, "Fuck you, Mickey Mantle." I know Mickey meant it affectionately. I hung it on the wall in one of my offices, and somebody stole it. I also receive occasional letters from athletes unhappy with my reports. Their message, essentially, is the same as Mickey's.

Two weeks after the Olympic Games ended, I was in Kansas City covering the Republican National Convention for WNBC and the *Star.* My fellow journalists included Art Buchwald, the humorist; Elizabeth Ray, the political party girl; and John Dean, the former Nixon confidant who triggered Watergate. John Dean, I wrote, "did to the whole Republican party what Elizabeth Ray did to only a handful of Democrats."

For one television story, I asked a dozen journalists,

including Buchwald and Ben Bradlee of the *Washington Post,* what was the best rumor they had heard during the convention, and the most intriguing answer came from a young female reporter, Jane O'Reilly, who said, "Three twenty-one."

I said, "What?"

And she said again, "Three twenty-one."

"Is that a rumor?" I said.

"Oh," she said. "I thought you asked me for my room number."

The morning after the convention ended, I asked Harold Stassen, his bid for the presidency once more rejected, if he thought the world would have been any different if he had gotten the Republican nomination in 1948 instead of Thomas Dewey. "I never dwell on what might have been," he said. "I care only about now—and the future." Then he dwelled on what might have been. "But," he added, "all the polls showed that I was running way ahead of Truman."

Stassen didn't get to the White House in 1976, but I did. I attended a presidential prayer brunch for professional athletes and shared a table with, among others, Red Smith, the hockey player Phil Esposito, and the soccer star Kyle Rote Jr. Esposito and I were the token sinners. Rote was one of eight athletes who delivered brief inspirational messages, each emphasizing a deep commitment to Christ. "It's not a very good day to be Jewish," Smith advised me.

I tried hard to be cynical, but when you tour the Lincoln Bedroom, the Queen's Room, and the Treaty Room, and then are welcomed to the East Room, the site of the brunch, by the president of the United States and Mrs. Ford, it is almost impossible not to be im-

ressed. President Ford did offer me a moment of déjà
vu when he told the gathering that, like the predecessor
he had pardoned, he always read the sports pages first.

In the mid-1970s, my former student, Paul Friedman,
was my boss, and my future boss, Doug Warshaw, was
my student, and if that isn't symmetry, and a reminder
to be kind to people on the way up, *their* way up and
ours, I don't know what is. Paul, whom I taught at
Columbia, became producer of the local news at
WNBC and then producer of *Today.* Doug was sixteen
when he enrolled in a sportswriting course I was teaching at the New School, and at the end of the course he
asked if he could intern at *SPORT.* He said he would
work for nothing, which fit our budget precisely. In the
seventies, he interned for me; in the eighties, he
worked with me as the sports producer on ABC's
World News Tonight; and in the nineties, he hired me at
the Classic Sports Network, which he oversaw until it
was transformed into ESPN Classic.

Paul and I drifted apart—he got caught up in the
business instead of the *work*—but Doug and I remained close no matter which one of us was theoretically in command. We were bound by a weirdly
similar sense of humor and by respect and admiration.
Doug knew me so well that once, when he and his wife
were enduring a terrifying plane ride through a storm,
a flight they feared might end in disaster, he told his
wife that my life was flashing before his eyes.

24

The Son of Sam

On July 29, 1976, an hour after midnight, two teenage girls were sitting and talking in a parked car in the Bronx. A young man walked up next to the car reached into a paper bag and took out a Charter Arm .44 bulldog handgun, squatted, and fired five shots into the car. The shots killed one of the young women Donna Lauria, and injured the other. The killer fled leaving behind only the bullets as a hint to his identity

During the next nine months, the same gunman struck five more times, each incident separated by at least a month, each taking place in the Bronx or in Queens, boroughs of the city of New York linked by the Triborough, Bronx-Whitestone, and Throgs Neck Bridges. Three times, the assailant fired at couples sitting in parked cars, twice at women walking on the streets. Forty-four-caliber bullets ripped into two young men and five young women. Four women, including Donna Lauria—connected only by their youth, their attractiveness, their dark hair, and the bull

ts that destroyed them—were dead. So were two
en. London's Jack the Ripper had not claimed so
any victims.

At the scene of the sixth shooting, which left an
ighteen-year-old aspiring actress and her twenty-
ear-old boyfriend dead in a parked car, the gunman
ft a letter for the police. He taunted them by identify-
ig himself. He was, he said, the "Son of Sam."

The New York Police Department, convinced that all
x shootings were the work of the "Son of Sam," as-
embled a task force, based at the 109th Precinct in
ueens, to track down the serial killer. The Bronx and
ueens were the battlegrounds, but the entire city
etered on the brink of panic. Every attractive dark-
aired woman between the ages of sixteen and thirty
ared she might be the next target.

The next note from the killer did not go to the po-
ce. It went to the *New York Daily News,* addressed to
e paper's star columnist, Jimmy Breslin:

Dear Mister Breslin,
Hello from the cracks in the sidewalks of NYC and
from the ants that dwell in these cracks and feed on
the dried blood of the dead that has settled into the
cracks. Hello from the gutters of NYC, which is filled
with dog manure, vomit, stale wine, urine, and blood.
Hello from the sewers of NYC which swallow up
these delicacies when they are washed away by the
sweeper trucks.

I'm just dropping a line to let you know that I appreciate your interest in those recent and horrendous
forty-four-caliber killings. I also want to tell you that I
read your column daily and find it quite informative.

Tell me, Jim, what will you have for July 29? You

can forget about me if you like because I don't care for publicity. However, you must not forget Donna Lauria and you cannot let the people forget her, either. She was a very, very sweet girl, but Sam's a thirsty lad and he won't let me stop killing till he gets his fill of blood.

Mr. Breslin, sir, don't think that because you haven't heard from [me] for a while that I went to sleep. No, rather, I am still here. Like a spirit roaming the night. Thirsty, hungry, seldom stopping to rest, anxious to please Sam. I love my work. Now, the void has been filled.

Perhaps we shall meet face to face someday or perhaps I will be blown away by cops with smoking thirty-eights. Whatever, if I should be fortunate enough to meet you, I will tell you all about Sam if you like, and I will introduce you to him. His name is "Sam the Terrible."

Not knowing what the future holds, I shall say farewell and I will see you at the next job. Or should I say you will see my handiwork at the next job? Remember Ms. Lauria. Thank you.

In their blood and from the gutter—"Sam's creation"—.44.

Breslin was both flattered and frightened by th chillingly literate letter, flattered because a dozen othe envious columnists and commentators wished de voutly that the killer had singled them out, and fright ened because he and his family, including a teenag dark-haired daughter, lived in Queens in Forest Hill Gardens, not far from the sites of two of the attacks.

I phoned Jimmy as soon as I heard about the lette "This is personal now," he said.

"You've got to write a book about this," I said.

"Yeah," he said. "But I don't have the time. You want to do it with me?"

I said sure—another chance to indulge my journalistic schizophrenia—and within a few days, we had signed a contract with Viking Press, Jimmy's publishers for several previous books. We decided we would write the book as a novel, for a variety of reasons, the most compelling being that we did not know who the killer was, that we were going to have to invent him and his background, another important one being that we did not want to go to the families of the victims, to press them about their daughters and sons, reopen wounds, and inflict fresh pain. Instead, we would invent names and biographies for the victims.

Breslin and I took to the streets and the discotheques of the Bronx and Queens to research the story. We hung out with detectives from the 109th Precinct. Once, walking from Lum's Chinese restaurant on Northern Boulevard toward the 109's station house around the corner, we passed two young people necking in a parked car. Breslin rapped on the window. "What are you, fucking crazy?" he said. "Here's twenty bucks. Go get a motel room." We went to the bars frequented by the victims. At one, Elephus, in Bayside, Queens, we figured we brought up the average age by ten years. We were the only people in the joint not drinking seven-and-seven, 7UP and whiskey. Breslin lit up a cigar, and a young woman asked him what it was. I spent hours with a teenager from the Bronx, asking her to describe to me in infinite detail the way she chose each article of clothing she wore to the discotheques, each layer of makeup, each shade of lipstick she applied. I learned about brown-out and

Blush-on, about Milliskin leotards and gold pouches tied around the waist with rawhide strings because a purse might easily be stolen.

The killer did not strike on July 29, 1977. He waited two days to celebrate the anniversary of his first slaying. He erupted in Brooklyn this time, near the Belt Parkway in Bensonhurst, not far from the Verazzano Bridge, his targets once again a couple of kids kissing in a parked car. He put two shots into the face of the young man and one into the head of the young woman. The attack took place a couple of hours after midnight, but within fifteen or twenty minutes, someone called Breslin and told him about the shooting, and Jimmy called me, and we rushed first to the scene and then to Kings County Hospital, where they had taken the two victims.

I went to a coffee shop operated by Black Muslims across the street from the hospital, ordered coffee to take out for Breslin and me, and started talking to the one other white guy in the shop. He said his name was Bill Clark, and he was a detective attached to the task force at the 109. For most of the evening, he'd been hiding in a van outside an apartment house in Queens. The guy he considered the prime suspect in the case, a certifiable cuckoo with an uncommon interest in serial killers, lived in the apartment house. As soon as the police radio barked word of the shooting in Brooklyn, Detective Clark ran into the house, busted open the door of the suspect's apartment, and found his man in bed under the covers. Bill Clark cursed the guy for being innocent and raced to the scene of the shooting.

He was sent to wait at the hospital until doctors surgically retrieved a bullet from the victims. Clark's boss wanted to know if the bullet was a .44. Clark never doubted it was. He was in the Muslim coffee shop stocking up on doughnuts and muffins and cookies for the nurses who were working in and around the operating room. "That way, they let you hang around," he said.

Clark soon got what he was waiting for—a bullet that had come out of a .44 Charter Arms bulldog and killed a girl.

Clark was a Vietnam veteran with two daughters, a cop in his late thirties earning well under forty thousand dollars a year, working night jobs and morning jobs to meet the bills. He was smart and honest and tireless, and if he wasn't fearless, he was close. Breslin and I got lucky. We asked Bill to help us, to monitor our manuscript, to make certain that it was authentic and accurate, that it felt and smelled right. Clark agreed. All we had to do was write it right.

Jimmy and I had already started. We had outlined the book not by chapters, but by scenes, and decided that Jimmy would write the scenes that focused upon the killer and the police, and I would write the ones that concentrated on the victims and the media. I would be the seamstress, stitching the scenes together, running the pages through my typewriter for continuity.

A week after the "Son of Sam" claimed his seventh victim, Breslin and I got the word one night that the NYPD had made an arrest, that a suspect in the serial killings was being brought to police headquarters in lower Manhattan. We hustled downtown. So did Roone Arledge, by then the president of ABC News as well as ABC Sports, spotlighting the network's, and his own, commitment to a breaking story. The suspect's name was David Berkowitz, and Bill Clark was among the first group of detectives to interrogate him. For

months, Clark had been building up a hatred for the
killer and his actions, but when he finally came face-
to-face with David Berkowitz, his rage subsided.
"How the hell can you hate this guy?" Clark told us after the meeting. "He's a marshmallow. He's gone,
completely gone. He doesn't have a sane bone in his
body."

Clark explained that the cops had asked Berkowitz if
he had committed the killings, and he had said yes he
had to each one.

"Why did you do it?" one cop asked.

"Because Sam told me to," Berkowitz said, no in-
flection, no emotion, a half smile on his face.

"Who's Sam?"

"He's a six-thousand-year-old man."

"A six-thousand-year-old man told you to kill these
people?"

"Well . . ." Berkowitz hesitated. "He didn't tell me
himself."

"What do you mean, he didn't tell you himself?"

"His dog told me. That's the way he got his orders to
me. Through his dog."

"The dog told you when to kill?"

"Yes, sir."

Berkowitz couldn't have been more cooperative.

Clark, Breslin, and I got out of police headquarters
before dawn. Bill and I went back to my apartment to
wash up. Then we went to NBC and Bill appeared on
the *Today* show and was the center of attention, an instant TV celebrity. Just like the rest of us, he was
hooked.

Bill became a great and loyal friend, and through
Breslin, Bill met Michael Daly, who wrote for the *News,*
and through Daly, he met David Milch, who wrote for

elevision, and through Milch he met Steven Bochco,
vho had created *Hill Street Blues,* and before long,
Clark was advising Milch and Bochco on a new show
called *NYPD Blue.* Bill appeared on the show, initiated
tory ideas, polished scripts, showed Jimmy Smits and
Dennis Franz how to act like cops, and, almost
overnight, he was a mogul, a big television producer.

He and his wife Karen, a former vice cop, lived in a
ive-bedroom house in Pacific Palisades, bought a
ountry home in upstate New York, dined in the best
estaurants, enjoyed luxury and vintage cars, won Em-
nys, and attended Super Bowls. Best, Bill remained a
good guy. When the Detectives Endowment Associa-
ion of New York honored him as its Man of the Year,
Clark stood up in front of his friends and cried.

With Clark's help, Breslin and I finished *.44,* and
Cork Smith, the editor of the book, who had also
vorked on a few of Jimmy's earlier books, flattered me
y saying, "I couldn't see the seams." Breslin's scenes
vithin the killer's head, dogs and demons howling,
vere sensational. I should have known that he would
iave no trouble getting inside a twisted mind.

When the book came out, some critics reviewed the
vook, some reviewed the crime, and some reviewed
immy and me. The book came off all right. But Bres-
in and I were accused and convicted of making money
ff a horrendous crime. "Who the fuck do they think
ve are?" Breslin said. "The Lawn Tennis Association?
Ve ain't amateurs. This is what we do for a living."

25

All in the Family

On October 18, 1977, I took my son Jeremy, a blos-
soming baseball fanatic, to the sixth and final game o
the World Series, the game in which Reggie Jackson o
the Yankees hit three consecutive home runs off th
first pitch from three different pitchers. I saw the firs
home run. At the time of Jackson's second, I wa
standing in line behind Carmen Berra, Yogi's wife
buying popcorn for Jeremy. At the time of the third,
was buying him a Coke to wash down the popcorn. H
was in his seat watching Reggie. "Nobody's had
game like that in the World Series since the Babe i
1928," Jeremy informed me afterward, rubbing it in.

The following spring, when I covered the baseba
training camps for WNBC, Jeremy made his debut as
television sportscaster. I handed him a microphone an
he interviewed Pete Rose. Rose was more receptive t
Jeremy's line of questioning than he was years later t
inquiries into his gambling habits. "How many mor

years do you think you'll play?" eight-year-old Jeremy asked thirty-five-year-old Pete Rose.

"Seven hundred more hits," Rose said. "I measure it in hits, not years."

"Oh," Jeremy said. "How many hits do you think you'll get this year?"

"Two hundred," Rose said. "I try for two hundred every year."

"Then you'll probably pass Cap Anson and Napoleon Lajoie," Jeremy said.

Rose's eyes popped. "Ol' Cap," he said. "You know ol' Cap? You know who he was?"

"Sure," Jeremy said. "He was an old-time ballplayer who was born in 1852 and died in 1922."

(Jeremy also knew that Napoleon Lajoie was born in 1875 and died in 1959, but he didn't want to show off.)

"Well, if you know that much about ol' Cap," Rose said, "you probably know whether I'll pass him or not."

"Of course you will," Jeremy said. "He only has about thirty-one hundred hits. You only need thirty-five more for three thousand."

"Thirty-four," Rose said.

"Thirty-four!" Jeremy said, shocked at his error.

"Thirty-four," Rose repeated. "You're just like all those official scorers, trying to take a base hit away from me."

Jeremy apologized, and Rose forgave him. "Now let me ask you a question," Rose said. "Who's the best team in the National League?"

"The National League? Hmmm. The Dodgers." Jeremy hesitated. "Or the Reds," he said.

"What do you mean, the Dodgers or the Reds?" Rose demanded. "Why did you have to say them first?

Why didn't you say, 'The Reds or the Dodgers'?"

Jeremy was agreeable. "The Reds," he said, "or the Dodgers."

"Gimme five," said Rose. He did not talk down to Jeremy. He treated him as an equal. WNBC ran the interview in its entirety.

During the summer of 1978, I covered Rose's race past 3,000 hits, past Cap Anson, toward Napoleon Lajoie, and his forty-four-game hitting streak, and seven years later, I covered his race past 4,191 hits, the major-league record held by Ty Cobb. When Rose broke the record, in Cincinnati, I asked him, "What would you say to Cobb if you could meet him?"

"I'd take a batting lesson from him," Pete said.

I'm not sure Jeremy would have gotten a better answer.

Until his banishment from baseball for gambling, Rose was a reporter's delight, uninhibited, uncensored, saying whatever popped into his head. When I gave him the award as the Most Valuable Player in the 1976 World Series, he stood up and blurted out, "This is the fifth time I've been on the cover of *SPORT*. That ain't bad for a white guy."

Several years later, when he was managing the Cincinnati Reds, I was among a group of reporters clustered around his desk in a cramped office. Rose sat behind the desk, wearing nothing but a towel around his waist, a huge slice of watermelon in front of him. Cameras rolled, questions came, and Rose, between answers, picked up the watermelon in his hands and dug into it, not the least concerned about maintaining an image. "Pete," one visiting newspaperman said, "I just want to ask you one question. I'm from San Francisco . . ."

And as soon as the writer said, "San Francisco . . ." Rose leaped to his feet and tightened the towel around his waist.

"Yeah, I need that," said the reporter, joining in the laughter.

In the fall of 1978, I took Jeremy to Boston to see the Yankees face the Red Sox in a playoff for the American League championship. On the plane going to Boston, the president of the American League, Lee MacPhail, sat behind us. Jeremy bombarded MacPhail with baseball trivia questions. Jeremy won, and so did his team, the Yankees—on a home run by Bucky Dent, who had, fortuitously, given us his tickets for the game.

Jeremy is my only relative who chose a career in sports, but my brother Bill dabbled in the business. While he was in his teens, I helped him get a part-time job at the *Long Island Press,* the paper that had swallowed my first paper, the *Review-Star.* Bill knew little about sports and did not get major assignments. "I write stories that are one or two paragraphs long," he used to say, "and I also write some short ones."

My brother has sustained his indifference toward sports. He has spent most of his life as a professional revolutionary, committed more to rhetoric, on which he is an expert, than to violence. As law student and lawyer, he participated in the defense of the Chicago Eight, the Attica rebels, and the occasional Black Panther.

One of the leaders of the Attica rebellion, the prison uprising that bloodied New York State in September 1971, was an inmate named Richard Clark, aka

Richard X or Brother Richard. Brother Bill beamed
when he introduced us, "Brother Richard, this is my
brother Richard." Bill is one of the few revolutionaries
I've met who has a sense of humor. When he and I
made funeral arrangements for our father, whom we
both loved greatly, the funeral director was Mr.
Lazarus. Bill looked at me, and I at him, and we managed not to crack a smile or resurrect a joke.

In a 1986 article called "My Brother, My Self," for
Gloria Steinem's *Ms.* magazine, I wrote:

> I do not really know my brother. I do not see him often
> or speak to him regularly, even though we live in the
> same city, and we both make our livings with
> words. . . . We rarely turn to each other for advice or
> criticism. We are not close in any customary sense of
> the word, and yet I love him very much and admire
> him immensely. . . . I take pride in almost every thing
> he does.
>
> I work for ABC. My brother works against the CIA.
> I write, mostly, to entertain . . . my brother, mostly, to
> incite. . . . I cover the American League. He covers
> American imperialism.

Ms. illustrated the article with a full-page photo that
showed me holding a portrait of the New York Knicks'
Willis Reed, resting my hand on the shoulder of my
brother, who was clutching a poster of Karl Marx.

Six years later, during Renaissance Weekend, an annual end-of-the-year retreat on Hilton Head Island, I
was one of more than a dozen participants asked to
stand up in front of the president-elect of the United
States and Mrs. Clinton and deliver a brief New Year's
Eve toast to the country. I toasted the country by toast-

ing "my brother Bill, a revolutionary dedicated to the overthrow of the CIA and the *New York Times,* and my friend Bill, a New York City homicide detective with all the prejudices of that office."

I explained that my brother Bill and my friend Bill had once attended meetings of the same underground organization—"my brother Bill because he believed in it, my friend Bill because he infiltrated it"—and that a quarter of a century later they were able to laugh about it.

After the toast, a third Bill—Clinton—told me, "I could identify with your brother." I hurried away from the party, phoned my brother Bill, and told him what the president-elect had said. My brother was not flattered. He did not want the Establishment on his side. Then I called my friend Bill Clark and told him what Mr. Clinton had said. "The commie," Clark said.

My sister Nancy has led the most conventional life of the three of us. She got pregnant and married in college, in that order, and, unlike my brother and me, remained married to her original mate, even when he, an outwardly sane psychoanalyst who graduated from Harvard Medical School, went through his own mandatory analysis. He worked on a public-health project in Colombia, and she taught English to Spanish-speaking adults. Ever since, she has taught Spanish to English-speaking children in Maryland. They own a summer home on an island best known for the wild horses that inhabit it, and are devoted to a pet computer and a collection of duck decoys. They enjoy the simple pleasures that I too often fail to make time for.

* * *

Among my other relatives, my cousin, Phil Schaap, the son of my Uncle Walter, may be the most accomplished. He inherited a love and knowledge of jazz from his father, and brought to this passion a photographic memory and an unusual mind. Name any date since the birth of the calendar, and Phil will tell you what day of the week it was. Name any jazz record, and he will tell you who is playing each instrument. He writes liner notes, restores recordings, teaches jazz at Princeton, and hosts so many hours on the radio each day that, once, in a poll to pick the number one jazz disc jockey in New York, Phil came in first, and I, who am musically disadvantaged, came in third.

26

"Lips That Touch Cosell's . . ."

In the late 1970s, two horses, Seattle Slew and Affirmed, won back-to-back Triple Crowns—the Kentucky Derby, the Preakness, and the Belmont Stakes—and, with the considerable help of a teenage jockey named Steve Cauthen, who rode Affirmed, inspired a surge of interest in horse racing that has not been matched since. When Slew won the Belmont to clinch its Triple Crown in 1977, I joined the horse's co-owners, Karen and Mickey Taylor, for a celebration on the roof of the clubhouse. Karen joyfully kissed everyone in sight. She even kissed me. Then she kissed Howard Cosell. Then she turned to kiss Barney Nagler, a wise old racing writer, and as she leaned toward him, Nagler pushed her away. "Lips that touch Cosell's," he said, "shall never touch mine."

I did not find Howard lovable, either. I knew him for more than thirty years, and only once did I see him mock himself. I was coming out of a Chinese restaurant, not far from Howard's apartment, and mine, and I bumped into Howard and his wife Emmy. Our families were friendly, and Emmy asked me about my children. While we talked, a group of young black kids came strolling down the street, spotted Cosell, and pointed at him. "There's Cosell! There's Cosell!" Howard graciously chatted with the youngsters for a few minutes, and as they walked away, he turned to me and Emmy and said, "Tough little monkeys." He was making fun of himself; only a short time earlier, he had been harshly criticized for calling an African-American football player a "tough little monkey."

Howard was not a racist, but he did have other faults. In a sense, he brought journalism to sports on television, and then destroyed journalism in sports on television. When he started, first on radio, then on television, he was the only sportscaster asking intelligent questions, probing for significant stories. He had a keen and inquisitive mind, and a broad vocabulary marred occasionally by a multisyllabic malapropism.

But at some point during his career, Cosell decided that he was more important than the story, that the questions he asked were more meaningful than the answers he elicited. He stopped probing and began promoting—self-promoting. He brought the cult of the individual to sports journalism. He spawned a generation of sportscasters who fell in love with their own shrill voices. It may be apocryphal, but, supposedly, Howard once said to Red Smith, "You know, there are fewer great sportscasters than one might think," and Red replied, "Howard, I know there is one fewer than you think."

Howard also could be cruel, abusing and embarrassing technicians and production assistants who had no weapons with which to fight back. When he picked on people his own size, it was usually behind their backs. Fueled by paranoia and animosity, he grew unfathomably bitter.

My friend Doug Warshaw once attended a class Cosell addressed at Princeton and counted the number of people he knocked by name—close to three hundred people in a two-hour lecture. Howard had no right to be bitter. He lived, by any standard, an exciting, glamorous life, knew all the rewards (and drawbacks) of celebrity, earned incredible sums of money, dominated his profession, and spent half a century with a loving and attentive wife. Howard should have gotten up each morning and said "Thank you" to somebody, but he preferred to say, "Fuck you," to everybody.

After his death, Cosell was greatly missed, but not greatly mourned.

I worked on NBC's weekend editions of *The Nightly News* during the late 1970s. I anchored the sports news. Jessica Savitch anchored the national and international news. The first night I worked with her, I said to Jessica, "I suppose people have told you you look like Lauren Bacall."

"Yes," Jessica said.

"Are you as bitchy as she?" I asked.

"Bitchier," Jessica said.

I liked her immediately. I thought she was going to have a terrific career in television. Trish and I double-dated with her and her fiancé and went to their wedding. Their marriage did not last long, and I switched to ABC, and over the next few years, as she drifted through drugs and a second marriage that ended in her husband's suicide, we rarely saw Jessica.

Then we heard that Jessica had died when a car in which she was a passenger missed a turn coming out of a restaurant parking lot and slid into the Delaware Canal in New Hope, Pennsylvania, and she was trapped and drowned. She was thirty-six years old.

A woman named Alanna Nash wrote a book called *Golden Girl* about the life and death of Jessica Savitch. Alanna went to Columbia Journalism School, where she was taught by Paul Friedman, whom I had taught.

Six degrees of separation is an exaggeration.

Further proof:

In the summer of 1978, a guy I knew, Dennis Smith, a New York City fireman, came upon a burning crate in a lot in the Bronx. The crate contained the dead body of a man named John Tupper. A witness reported seeing a yellow Cadillac pulling away from the lot. In less than an hour, the police stopped the yellow Cadillac and questioned its driver, who turned out to be another guy I knew, Buddy Jacobson, a New York City landlord.

I knew Dennis because he was also a writer, the author of a fine book called *Report from Engine Company 82*. I knew Buddy because he was also a horse trainer; in 1963, he had saddled more winners than any other trainer in the country. In the 1970s, Buddy operated a ski lodge in Vermont and came to me at *SPORT* trying to promote a hot-dog skier who weighed close to three hundred pounds. Buddy always looked for an angle.

After the overweight skier, Buddy turned to underweight women, operating a modeling agency, My Fair Lady, and maintaining a couple of apartment buildings that catered to models. Buddy, who was in his late forties, employed beautiful young women and dated them. "It takes just as much effort to fuck an ugly girl from Brooklyn," he explained to me, "as a beautiful one from Manhattan."

Buddy usually told the women from Manhattan he was thirtysomething or younger. He carried false proof of age and introduced his two sons as his brothers. In the mid-seventies, he began dating his prize model, a teenage beauty named Melanie Cain. Melanie and Buddy lived together in one of his buildings. John Tupper lived across the hall. One day Melanie Cain moved out of Buddy's apartment and moved into Tupper's. Not long afterward, Tupper moved into the burning crate in the Bronx.

Jacobson was arrested and charged with killing Tupper. Sal Prainito, an immigrant laborer from Sicily, was charged with assisting Jacobson. The laborer looked like a choirboy. "If he did not do it," Jimmy Breslin announced, "he is a disgrace to centuries of breeding."

The trial lasted eleven weeks, the longest trial in the history of the Bronx, and I signed a contract to write a book about the case. On occasion, when I couldn't get to the Bronx, Trish went for me and took notes. She and I became friendly with Audrey Barrett, Buddy's girlfriend, and the four of us, Buddy and me and our *shiksa* girlfriends, celebrated the Passover seder together in 1980. Buddy insisted to us that he was innocent, that Tupper was killed because of drug dealings, that he transported the body to the Bronx only as a favor to Melanie Cain. We believed him.

The jury did not. When Buddy was found guilty (and his codefendant not guilty), Audrey was devastated and stayed with Trish and me for a few days. Buddy stayed at the Bronx House of Detention. When I visited him, he still maintained he was innocent. I still believed him. Then Buddy was transferred to a prison in Brooklyn, and one day, when a friend who owed him money came to visit, Buddy and the friend switched clothes, and Buddy said good-bye to his friend and walked out of the prison, wiping out the debt. Buddy picked up Audrey and fled the city, the state, and the authorities. A month and a half later, the police arrested him as he spoke on a pay phone in Manhattan Beach in southern California.

There were no more escapes, no more seders. Buddy Jacobson remained in prison for nine years until he died of cancer. Up till the end, he claimed that he was innocent. Not that it mattered—I never wrote the book—but there was a part of me that always believed him.

27

"Is Bambi Your Real Name?"

It takes enormous ego to be a writer, to believe that people would want to read your words (especially an autobiography). It takes more ego to be a television commentator, to believe that people would want to hear your words *and* see your face. It takes the most ego to be a public speaker. I love speaking in public, from a commencement speech at a college to a keynote address at a convention to an informal talk with my grandson's fourth-grade class.

If you listen, I will come.

Need a master of ceremonies? I'm available. I barely know how to say no. My first annual assignment as an emcee was the Cornell Athletic Hall of Fame dinner, which started in 1978. The first year, we took in only remarkable athletes, my friend Meredith Gourdine, the Olympic medalist, for instance, and Dick Savitt, the former Wimbledon champion, and Ed Marinaro, who came in second in the 1971 Heisman voting and in two Super Bowls.

But by the eighth year, the field was so depleted of legitimate candidates that I was inducted. I would like to think it was for my virtues as a lacrosse goalie, but I doubt it.

I presided over the Cornell banquet for fifteen years, and emceed the Women's Sports Foundation dinner for its first decade, sharing the podium most often with Jane Pauley, once with Maria Shriver. In the early years, we held a meeting one day at Jane Pauley's office at NBC, and Steve Friedman, the brash producer of *Today*, walked in to see me sitting with Jane, Billie Jean King, Carol Mann, and a few other outstanding women athletes. "Dick Schaap!" Friedman said. "What are you doing here with all these dykes?"

Friedman got away with it. The women laughed. If I'd said the same thing, I'd have been whipped, deservedly.

The WSF dropped me as an emcee when they found out I was not a woman. Among my replacements, my favorite was Diana Nyad, a long-distance swimmer, who, the first time I met her, was being smeared with grease for a swim around Manhattan. As I gawked, a voice behind me delivered play-by-play on the greasing process. The voice was unmistakably Cosell's. I turned and discovered Peter Boyle, the actor, doing a Cosell imitation almost as good as Billy Crystal's.

In the 1990s, I regularly emceed the dinners of the Hank Greenberg Memorial Golf and Tennis Classic, the Amyotrophic Lateral Sclerosis (ALS, or Lou Gehrig's disease) Foundation, and the Center for the Study of Sport in Society. At one time or another, I was master of ceremonies for affairs raising funds to combat AIDS, cancer, Crohn's and colitis, arthritis, mental illness, cerebral palsy, juvenile diabetes, illiteracy, and almost every other ill known to man. The first time I received an award honoring my work on television, it came, fittingly, I suppose, from the Lighthouse for the Blind.

I found it difficult to say no to a good cause, or to a live audience. I also found it difficult to say no to a good check, an effective lure to address meetings of companies such as IBM, Philip Morris, Lucent, and Cargill, and to address professional gatherings of attorneys and physicians. Physicians are my least favorite audience. For the most part, they have few interests and no sense of humor.

As much as I enjoy an audience, I prefer parties of four people, or six at the most, unless I'm giving the party. Then I like big parties, love mixing and matching guests, introducing people to people who share similar interests, or conflicting ones. I throw one big party each year, the night before the Super Bowl in the city in which the game is being played.

On January 20, 1979, the eve of Super Bowl XIII, I hosted my first Super Bowl party. It was a small one, fewer than twenty people, held at one of my special restaurants, Joe's Stone Crab in Miami Beach. I decided to throw the party because WNBC asked me to cohost a pre–Super Bowl special, and the amount they offered to pay was so small I told them to put it toward a party, which they did.

Red Smith came, and so did David Susskind, and half a dozen journalists, and the best part was that my parents, retired in nearby Hollywood, Florida, were able to join us. Trish was ill and couldn't leave New York and missed the party, but every year since then, she and I have been cohosts, in Los Angeles, San

Diego, San Francisco, Detroit, Phoenix, Minneapolis, Atlanta, Tampa Bay, and Miami, and, best of all, in New Orleans. We have gathered in Mexican and seafood restaurants, in the two best Cajun restaurants in the world, in hotel suites and rented houses, and in the homes of friends.

The first party was the smallest. Since then, there have usually been sixty to ninety guests, and often more than one hundred. George Mikan showed up in Minneapolis, at the original Chi-Chi's, the place where Max McGee started his chain of Mexican eateries; Fran Tarkenton showed up in Atlanta, at Bimbo's, a restaurant named not after its clientele but its owner, a man named Bimbo Chutich. Ethel Kennedy came to a rented beach house in San Diego, Maria Shriver to a borrowed one in Malibu. Hall of Fame football, baseball, and basketball players and Olympic gold medalists attended. So did dozens of sports columnists, television commentators, producers, and cameramen.

In *A Year in the Sun,* his diary of a sportswriter's life, George Vecsey of the *New York Times* wrote:

> There are two great parties at the Super Bowl every year, the one thrown by the National Football League and the one thrown by Dick and Trish Schaap.
>
> I'm glad I saved my appetite for the Schaap party.
>
> The Schaaps teamed up with two friends, Hamilton and Midge Richardson, to rent K-Paul's, the popular Cajun restaurant. . . . The Schaaps [are] so friendly with [Paul] Prudhomme that he closed his place to the public tonight and personally cooked blackened redfish for over one hundred guests.
>
> This intimate little party included two senators, Gary Hart of Colorado and Christopher Dodd of Con-

necticut, Representative Lindy Boggs of Louisiana . . .
Jimmy Buffet, the singer, Ed Bradley and Bryant
Gumbel from television, Bob Pettit, the former bas-
ketball star . . . three former Green Bay Packers,
Willie Davis, Marv Fleming, and Jerry Kramer, and
Nick Lowery, the placekicker for the Kansas City
Chiefs. . . .

I am always amazed at Dick's ability to remain
friendly with the people he has interviewed in his long
career as television correspondent and writer . . . You
never know who will show up at his parties . . .

The best sight of the night was Trish Schaap, with
her honey-blond hair and lovely Scottish accent,
working in the kitchen alongside Paul Prudhomme,
who is about three times her size.

My wife? In the kitchen? Cooking? And I always
thought Vecsey was a reliable reporter.

I was equally shocked when I received the bill for
the party from Paul Prudhomme.

"I think there's something wrong with the bill," I
told him.

"Too high?" Paul said.

"Too low," I said.

He said not to worry, he had covered his costs.

The year the Super Bowl was played at Stanford,
Helen and Dick Elkus cohosted the annual party with
us at their handsome home in nearby Atherton. Dick
and I had been in the Army together in the 1950s, and
we had stayed in touch as he flourished in Silicon Valley enterprises far too technical for me to comprehend.

The Elkuses invited half the guests, and we invited
half. You could tell theirs from ours at a distance. Their
friends were elegantly dressed and unfailingly proper.

Our guests included a gentleman from Lawrence, Kansas, named Wesley Kabler, proprietor of a topless bar called the Flamingo Club. My friend Mike Rebich, an ABC cameraman, brought Wes, whom I had never met before. The Elkuses invited a man who was head-master of the finest girls' finishing school in the Bay Area. We introduced Wesley to him, and told him that Wes was in the same line of work, sort of. The head-master was not amused.

Two years later, our party was held at a house in Malibu borrowed from Bob Gutwillig, my onetime ed-itor. We were planning a cookout on the beach, and I had heard that one of Wesley's friends owned the best rib joint in Kansas. I ordered a hundred pounds of ribs to be delivered by Federal Express the morning of the party. The ribs arrived on time, with gallons of barbe-cue sauce, and a few hours later a white stretch limou-sine rolled down our driveway. Wesley and the owner of Don's Steak House and their attorney had decided they didn't trust a New York Jew to heat and serve ribs, so they flew in to supervise, which they did magnifi-cently. The ribs were so good that Patti Lupone, the ac-tress and singer, who is not a large woman, put away four or five good-sized slabs.

I had met Patti only a few days earlier on the plane from New York to Los Angeles. She came over to me and said, "Excuse me, but could I have your auto-graph—for my boyfriend?"

I said, "You're putting me on," and she said no and nodded toward her boyfriend, Matt Johnston, who has since become her husband and my friend. Matt is a graduate of Indiana University, addicted to Hoosier basketball.

Once, in the 1990s, when Patti was playing Maria

Callas in *Master Class* on Broadway, I invited Bob Knight, the Indiana basketball coach, and his wife, Karen, to see the show and then have dinner with Patti, Matt, Trish, and me. The Knights loved the play. When the curtain came down, five of us went to Joe Allen's, the restaurant where Peter Falk had once abandoned me, and Knight went back to the hotel to talk briefly to his team, which was playing in a tournament at Madison Square Garden. When he joined us at Joe Allen's, Knight walked up to Patti, whom he had never met, and, before he said hello, said, "Was Maria Callas left-handed?"

"I don't know," Patti said. "Why?"

"You made all your gestures with your left hand," Knight said.

Patti paused and thought. "That was my downstage hand," she explained.

While the rest of us marveled at Knight's powers of observation, he looked at Patti and said, "If I had twelve players who worked as hard as you do, I wouldn't have to coach very hard," and he won a fan for life. Her husband, of course, was already committed.

The Lawrence trio cooked the ribs, served the drinks, and then one by one passed out. In the middle of the night, the restaurant owner got up to look for the bathroom, slipped, fell down a flight of stairs, swore, and then started laughing. He had broken his arm. In the morning, the three got back in the white limousine, returned to the Los Angeles airport, and caught a flight to Kansas City. At cruising altitude, Wesley told a flight attendant he would like to buy a round of drinks for everyone on the plane. They were home in time to watch the Super Bowl on television.

A few months later, I paid my first visit to Lawrence, to accompany the Kansas University basketball coach Larry Brown on a recruiting trip to Emporia. We flew in a small prop plane, and as we were returning to Lawrence, I mentioned to Larry that I had a friend named Wesley who owned a bar called the Flamingo and did he have any idea where it might be. Larry thought for a while and then vaguely remembered passing the Flamingo on one of his daily jogs. "Of course, I couldn't be seen in a place like that," Larry said. Of course.

Larry did agree, however, to show me the way, if he could recall it. When we approached the Flamingo, close to midnight, the parking lot was empty and only a small light visible. Larry parked, and so did I. "I guess it would be all right for me to go in," he said.

The club was closed for the night, theoretically. But Wesley, expecting me to be late by Lawrence standards, had kept a bartender, a waitress, and an exotic dancer on duty to make my first visit to the Flamingo memorable. As Larry and I walked in, the dancer ran up to him and said, "Coach! I went to high school with two of your players." Larry said something like, "Sit on my knee and tell me about it."

Brown built an NCAA championship team at Kansas, which gave me excuses to revisit Lawrence. Even my wife came to the Flamingo. Wesley built a small shrine to me in the club, displaying a collection of my credentials to various sporting events, the invitations to my Super Bowl parties, and a gallery of photographs. Through Wesley, I became friendly with Gary "U.S." Bartz, who owned Don's Steak House, and Larry Sinks, who made a small fortune in the T-shirt business. Sinks printed up one set of T-shirts that had, on the back, a list in the Letterman fashion, of the ten things most likely to be heard at the Flamingo late at night. My favorite was "Is Bambi your real name?" I also liked "What time does Dick Schaap's plane land?" Wesley and Larry said they hoped I wasn't offended. I said I was honored.

Brown, the world's most restless coach, left KU the year after winning the national championship, frustrating and angering Jayhawk fans, and the year after that, I organized a roast to raise money for United Cerebral Palsy in Kansas City. Larry agreed to be one of the roastees, which took guts, and George Brett, the local hero, agreed to be the other, which did not. The roasters included Billy Crystal, who went to Larry's high school, Long Beach High on Long Island. "Larry was my idol," Billy said. "He was short and he was Jewish. I walked like him. I talked like him. I even moved four times."

George Brett's roasters included Tim McClelland, the American League umpire who was working behind home plate during the famous "pine tar" game between Kansas City and the Yankees in 1983. Brett hit what appeared to be a game-winning home run, but after Yankee manager Billy Martin protested, the umpiring crew, anchored by McClelland, ruled that Brett had too much pine tar on his bat. When the umpires delivered their verdict, a stunned Brett catapulted out of the Kansas City dugout, arms waving wildly, heading straight for McClelland. Fortunately for Brett, he was intercepted and restrained; eventually he was vindicated.

"They want me to say nice things about George Brett," McClelland said at the roast, "and I will—but not tonight. George is not too smart. He wanted to fight an umpire who was six-foot-six, weighed two hundred and fifty pounds, and was wearing a mask and holding a bat in his hand."

Brett laughed louder than anyone.

I used to tell George he was my favorite five-year-old in the world, that Peter Pan had a better shot at growing up than he did. Once, after we lunched on sauteed spinach at Tre Scalini, a Manhattan restaurant, he went across the street to a wig shop and bought a Rod Stewart wig and wore it to Yankee Stadium so that he wouldn't be conspicuous.

To my amazement, George grew up, and now, a member of the Hall of Fame, no longer an active player, George plays husband and father as well as he used to play bachelor.

I introduced friends to Lawrence, to the Flamingo, and the golf tournament it sponsored, the Open-Fly Open, at which Wesley's dancers drove the golf carts and served the beer. Barry Bremen came with me to Lawrence. We had met when I honored him as "Sportsman of the Week" on the *Today* show. He was not a famous athlete. He was a master salesman from Detroit who billed himself as the Great Impostor, and, in appropriate uniform, infiltrated the playing fields of the baseball and basketball All-Star Games, the U.S. Open golf championship, and a Dallas Cowboys' football game, the latter disguised, after losing weight, shaving his legs, and padding his chest, as a Dallas cheerleader.

Once, on national television, Bremen stepped up from the audience and accepted an Emmy on behalf of actress Betty Thomas without her knowledge or consent. In appropriate uniform, a tuxedo, Barry looked into the camera and said, "I want to thank Dick Schaap for making this possible." Then he was arrested.

I took Chuck Freiburger to Lawrence, too. I met him when I was covering the national touch football championships in a town called Fenton, Missouri. Chuck was a gray-haired attorney from Columbus, Ohio, the star quarterback for the team that won the touch football title. "My wife doesn't know I'm here," he told me. "She thinks I went to the grocery." I asked him what was the secret to his team's success, and he said, "Drinking."

I also took Chuck's son Danny, who had played quarterback for SMU, to the Flamingo. Danny sat down in the club, and while a lap dancer danced on his lap, I took my cell phone and called Danny's mother. When I reached her, I handed the phone to Danny and said, "Someone wants to talk to you."

In February 1980, I wound my way through traffic jams and red tape to Lake Placid, New York, site of the Winter Olympics and of the grave of John Brown, the abolitionist. I concentrated on covering two U.S. teams, biathlon and hockey, one familiar to American sports fans, one a mystery. I found the biathlon fascinating, a sport blending two contradictory disciplines, cross-country skiing and rifle marksmanship, one demanding furious motion, the other absolute stillness. "Skiing and shooting is a marriage made in hell," Don Nielsen, an American biathlete who graduated from Dartmouth magna cum laude in classics, told me. "Biathlon is turning from a rabbit to a rock and then back again."

I've always admired athletes who have to demonstrate a variety of skills—decathletes, for instance, competing in ten track-and-field events, some emphasizing strength, some speed; and "modern" pentath-

letes, engaging in swimming, riding, shooting, fenc-
ing, and running, facing in principle the same challenges as a Napoleonic courier. The well-rounded
athlete on the field often seems to be well-rounded off
the field, too. "We sit down at the dinner table," Don
Nielsen said, "and talk about everything from Bud-
dhism to calculus. We don't talk about things like ski
wax that the regular cross-country skiers talk about.
Our world is not defined by ski wax."

(Later in the 1980s, I got friendly with an American
pentathlete named Rob Stull, and when he told me how
short the U.S. team was on funds, I persuaded Wesley
Kabler and friends at the Flamingo to make a generous
contribution. The athletes were delighted. The U.S.
Olympic Committee was furious. A USOC spokesman
called the Flamingo a sleazy strip joint, but the pen-
tathlon team took the money.)

Covering the biathlon team at Lake Placid was relatively easy. The athletes were accessible, grateful for
recognition, and ignored by most of the media and the
spectators. It was far more difficult to cover the hockey
team. I'd met Herb Brooks, the coach, and Mike
Eruzione, the captain, before the Games began, but
once their unlikely march to the gold medal gained
momentum, they were besieged by journalists, fans,
and security.

So I covered the hockey team without going to any
of their games. I spent much of my time at a large Lake
Placid house that was temporary home to the parents
of at least a dozen players. The mothers and fathers had
become a team, too, and, while they shared crowded
quarters and Mrs. Eruzione's pasta, they also shared
their pride and pleasure with me. Occasionally, their
sons stopped by, which gave me the opportunity to in-

terview them. I did at least half a dozen stories about the hockey team for NBC, and even though I was denied the access that the sponsoring network—ABC in this case—paid millions for, my reports measured up.

At every Olympics I've covered, given the choice of attending an event or mingling with the athletes, listening to them, watching them interact, I've always chosen to skip the action and focus on the stories. At Lake Placid, typically, I saw parts of the biathlon competition and one of Eric Heiden's five gold-medal races, and nothing more.

(A decade later, when Heiden was in medical school at Stanford, he and I went to a National Hockey League game in San Jose, and in a large arena filled with thousands of sports fans, not a single one showed any sign of recognition of the most successful American athlete in the history of the Winter Olympics. Heiden, a rarity, a genuinely humble athlete—many *affect* humility—loved the absence of attention.)

During the 1980 Winter Games, the NBC cameraman, soundman, producer, editor, and I shared a house on the edge of Lake Placid, a few hundred yards from the headquarters of the U.S. Olympic Committee. Early one icy morning, I conducted a live outdoor interview for *Today* with the president of the USOC, Bob Kane. At the end of the interview, I mentioned to Tom Brokaw, the show's anchor, that Bob Kane had been my athletic director when I played lacrosse at Cornell, and Brokaw replied, dryly, and accurately, "I doubt that was the highlight of his career."

Immediately after the Winter Games, Bob Mathias, the 1948 and 1952 Olympic decathlon champion, and I toured for IBM, entertaining company meetings with Olympic history and lore. Only a few days after scoring the goal that stunned the Russians, Mike Eruzione joined us, and, of course, Mathias and I were relegated to "Who are those guys with Mike Eruzione?"

The following year, I went to Boston, Eruzione's hometown, to interview a bright new star in the National Hockey League, Wayne Gretzky of the Edmonton Oilers. Gretzky, Eruzione, and I went to lunch at a landmark pizzeria called Santarpio's, and, as Gretzky entered, I heard someone say, "Who's that guy with Mike Eruzione?"

28

"Hail, Caesar!"

In 1980, between the Winter Olympics at Lake Placid and the Summer Games in Moscow, I extended my personal record of never having held a job for double-digit years. After nine years at NBC, I moved to ABC. At NBC News, sports coverage had been tolerated. At ABC News, it was encouraged, enthusiastically, by Roone Arledge, who was at the peak of his considerable power.

Roone was famous for, among other things, not responding to phone calls or written messages. This led me to send him notes that ended, "I will presume if I do not hear from you that this meets with your approval." At least I *thought* about sending Roone such notes.

My first week at ABC, I was sent to San Diego to prepare a profile of Daley Thompson, the great British athlete who was favored to win the decathlon in Moscow. Thompson, the son of a Scottish mother and a Nigerian father, was only twenty-two at the time, as sleek and handsome as a panther, brimming with confidence and good spirits, instantly likable, sort of Muhammad Ali with a cockney accent.

When I met him, Daley was sharing a San Diego home with, among others, Richard Slaney, a British weight thrower, and Clifford "Snowy" Brooks, a British decathlete. The house was decorated in dirty socks and jocks, a world-record mound rising in a hallway. Slaney, once the winner of a "strongest man in Britain" competition, had tried to play football at San Diego State, but had given up the game because he couldn't understand why he had to hit his mates from Monday to Friday.

Brooks had tried out for the British decathlon team for the 1972 Olympics in Munich and had just missed qualifying. He then wrote to the Barbados Olympic Committee and said, "My father, whom I never met, I'm told was from Barbados. May I represent Barbados in the Olympic Games?" The Olympic Committee wrote back, "What size uniform do you wear?" Snowy Brooks carried the flag for Barbados in the opening ceremony in Munich.

Ironically, a quarter of a century later, when the secrecy laws in Great Britain were relaxed, Snowy checked the records at the orphanage in which he was raised and discovered that his father was a Canadian.

Snowy and I played tennis against Daley and my wife Trish, and Daley joined the lengthening list of world-class athletes whom I had defeated in sports not their own (Daley and Bobby Fischer in tennis, Wilt Chamberlain and Floyd Patterson in tonk). I believe it was the first time Daley ever played tennis. A few years later, his game improved dramatically, the result of dedication and a fleeting romance with a top British player named Sue Barker.

Daley filled a void in my people collection. He was my first Scottish, or at least half-Scottish, athlete, which pleased my Scottish wife. Daley and I shared five Olympics—he competed in 1976 (before I met him), 1980, 1984, and 1988, and commentated in 1992—and also shared our homes. He stayed at mine in New York, and I at his on the Thames. Daley became unofficial godfather to my daughter Kari, who was so thrilled by the honor that when Daley gave her a pole-vaulting medal he had just won, she threw it on the ground. She was not yet a year old.

While I was in San Diego, the ABC assignment desk called and told me to go to Switzerland the next day to cover a meeting of the International Olympic Committee. The United States was considering a boycott of the Summer Games in Moscow to protest Soviet military actions in Afghanistan. I caught a morning flight to New York, connected to an all-night flight to Switzerland, and arrived in Lausanne in time to prepare a story for that night's edition of *World News Tonight*. I did get a few words from my old athletic director, Bob Kane, the president of the USOC, who, in diplomatic terms, indicated he opposed a boycott.

My first week at ABC, I flew more than 15,000 miles, a strong hint of what was to come. I loved every mile. I could choose any story I wanted. I flew first class. I stayed in the best hotels. More important, I was allowed three, four, sometimes even five minutes for my feature stories. Sports became a major part of the weekend news show.

I went to London for Wimbledon, to Nice for the

Tour de France, to Spain for the World Cup, to Moscow for the Olympic Games, the ones that were boycotted by the United States. Early one of my first mornings in Moscow, I heard a knock on the door of my hotel room. I opened the door, and a Russian visitor announced, "Pete Axthelm [an old friend and a fine writer] told me you are a good person. I would like to be your friend."

He said he was a journalist, but unless reporters in Moscow earn a lot more than reporters in New York, he had other sources of income, most likely the KGB, the Soviet secret police. He treated me to lunches and dinners, fed me as much caviar as I could eat, and ordered as much vodka as he could drink. We shared many bottles of excellent Georgian white wine. One night, I returned to my hotel so buoyant that I called Trish in Scotland and giggled for ten straight minutes, at several rubles a minute. Another night, I told my new Russian friend that I regretted I had no secrets to tell him, but if he liked, I would make some up.

I was sorry that the U.S. Olympic team did not go to Moscow, but glad that I did. With only a handful of Americans in attendance, and with all the drunks, a sizable percentage of the population, hustled out of town, Moscow was less crowded and more navigable than any other Olympic city I ever visited. The rules on access to events, and to the athletes' quarters, and to historic nearby cities, changed daily, subject to bureaucratic whims, but by Olympic standards, the restraints seemed reasonable. One of the best discoveries was the U.S. embassy. Not only could you get a fast-food fix there—hamburgers and french fries in the commissary—but you could buy a four-ounce tin of caviar for ten dollars from an Italian chef who worked in the embassy. My evening meal often consisted of black bread, caviar, and Georgian wine, a banquet costing far less than the daily dinner allowance from ABC.

For once, helped by the eight-hour time difference—New York did not go to work till almost 6 P.M. Moscow time—I was able to attend almost any event I wanted to. I followed the stars of the British team. I watched Sebastian Coe and Steve Ovett win the middle-distance races, and Daley the decathlon. Daley arrived at my hotel one night at ten minutes to ten. All nonresidents were supposed to leave the hotel by ten. Without speaking a word of Russian, Daley charmed the security guards, visited for hours beyond the curfew, and, as he left, taught one of the Soviet guards to say, "See you later, alligator."

My star was, for the moment, on the ascendancy, and, after my first year at ABC, Av Westin, the executive producer of *20/20*, asked me to contribute to his program. Av was bright, had good judgment, and knew how to make suggestions to improve stories. The producers who worked under Av were, for the most part, gifted, too, and, with fifteen minutes or more for each report, I had the luxury of sufficient time to tell a coherent story, sufficient time to craft sentences, not merely type them.

(A warning: Working on TV is hazardous to a journalist's professional health—to his writing style and his interviewing techniques. You get lazy. You don't have to write descriptively because you're backed up by pictures, and you don't have to compose complex questions because you can't use complex answers.)

My first *20/20* assignment was a profile of the most prolific playwright on Broadway, my friend Neil Simon, and to tell the story, I interviewed a galaxy of funny people. The report began with Neil typing, and saying, "What do I do for a living? I write. And write. And write. And write."

"He writes when he's on trains," George Burns told me, "when he's on planes, when he's riding a bicycle, when he's jogging. He's always writing. Marsha [Mason, then Mrs. Simon] told me that he even writes when they're having, when they're having, when they're having, breakfast."

I asked Burns how he and Simon met, and Burns, who was in his eighties at the time, said, "They were doing *The Sunshine Boys* on Broadway and Jack Benny was supposed to be in it, and, as you know, Jack passed away, and they wanted someone to take Jack's place. They wanted someone who is old, which I am, and someone who is from New York, which I am, and someone who is Jewish. How they ever found out I'm Jewish, I'll never know."

Almost everyone I interviewed alluded to Simon's astonishing productivity. "I don't know if he's written more plays than Shakespeare," George Burns said, "but if he hasn't, by next Tuesday he will have."

I talked to Danny Simon, Neil's comic mentor, a talented writer who had never enjoyed nearly so much success as his younger brother. Danny was the model for the Felix character in *The Odd Couple*. When I told him that several people had compared Neil's output to Shakespeare's, Danny said, "To tell you the truth, when I think of Neil, I don't think of Shakespeare, I think of Shakespeare's brother. Do you know that when Shakespeare wrote his twelfth hit, his brother threw himself into a moat?"

When I interviewed Neil, he sat between a tennis

court and the swimming pool at the Beverly Hills Tennis Club. I asked him if he was writing a scene about a writer being interviewed between a tennis court and a swimming pool, "How would you make it funny?" Neil said he couldn't, not in this case because there was no conflict, and without conflict, there is no humor. "But if we were having this interview," Simon said, "and I were having an affair with your wife, and the audience knew it and you didn't, then there's conflict."

When the story appeared on *20/20*, Neil wrote to tell me how much he enjoyed it. "Danny's joke about Shakespeare's brother really broke me up," Neil said, "and at the same time touched me very much. . . . One gets used to the 'slings and arrows' of critics, and you find it almost easier to deal with than such an affectionate portrait as you painted. I guess you can never really remove the 'Jewish guilt' from the boy."

Early in my career, I loved to write about people I could skewer: "Edward Vincent Sullivan personifies television, which is not necessarily a nice thing to say about either of them," I began one story. "The friends of James T. Aubrey gathered yesterday to complain about the way CBS had treated him, and both of them were very upset," I started another. In later years, I tired of attacking people, even those who deserved it; I didn't enjoy being exposed to ego, greed, selfishness, and hypocrisy. I preferred to do stories about people I liked. In 1981, however, I made an exception to write a book about the principal owner of the New York Yankees, George Steinbrenner.

I didn't have strong anti-Steinbrenner feelings when I started the project. I didn't have strong pro-Steinbrenner feelings, either. I knew he had funneled illegal contributions into Richard Nixon's 1972 presidential campaign fund. I knew he had bullied employees. I knew he liked to play god with other people's lives. But I also knew he was often generous to individuals and to charities, had rebuilt a fading baseball dynasty, and shared my passion for New York City.

I wrote to Steinbrenner, told him I was working on a book about him, and asked for the opportunity to talk with him. His public relations man called to tell me Mr. Steinbrenner did not approve of my project. Mr. Steinbrenner wrote to tell me he did not approve of my project. He suggested I was using our relationship for my own profit, trying "to make a killing off my life and career."

"As far as using the relationship that has developed between us, I plead guilty," I wrote back. "I'm afraid that's the nature of being a journalist—making the best possible use of your relationships with people; I don't think that's necessarily evil. . . . In reference to your fear that I might make 'a killing' off your life and career, I hope you're right. After all, I do write *professionally*." Breslin would have been proud of me.

George refused to cooperate. He told friends and associates not to cooperate, either; some he asked, some he ordered. One of his friends, Bill Fugazy, probably had George's permission to tell me how upset Roone Arledge, my boss at ABC, would be if I wrote anything uncomplimentary about Roone's good friend George Steinbrenner. Fugazy said, "Roone," several times. R-O-O-N-E.

I wasn't impressed or intimidated. I wrote a fair book. I detailed Steinbrenner's virtues and vices, and it was not my fault the vices outnumbered the virtues. I researched my subject carefully. I loved one line his lawyer, the eminent Edward Bennett Williams, used in defending Steinbrenner against the charge of illegal campaign contributions. Some of George's recollections of certain facts, Williams said in court, were "not in conformity with objective reality." William F. Buckley himself could not have defined a lie more eloquently.

Many of Steinbrenner's lies were harmless and amusing. For instance, he told one reporter that he stood behind Stephen Sondheim, the composer and lyricist, in the Williams glee club—and boasted, "I could sing better than he could." A few years earlier, I'd written a story about Sondheim's dazzling collection of antique games for a magazine called *Games*, and I called and asked him if Steinbrenner had stood behind him in the glee club and if George had sung better than he did. "He certainly sang better than I did," Sondheim said. "I can't sing. I wasn't in the glee club."

I think Steinbrenner lies just for practice.

He did relent and grant me an audience as I approached the final pages of the book. He entertained me graciously for a day in Tampa, talked expansively if self-servingly, and reminded me that he and Elton Rule, who was Roone Arledge's boss, were good friends. E-L-T-O-N.

Steinbrenner was published in 1982, and the subject reacted predictably. First, he offered to buy up all copies of the first edition if I would correct what he perceived to be my numerous errors of fact and interpretation in the next edition. He wanted the book to conform to his version of "objective reality."

When I replied that I didn't think I could ethically exchange revisions for sales, he changed tactics. He had his latest lawyer, the notorious Roy Cohn, ask me to lunch to talk about the book. Cohn took me to Le Cirque (his place, not mine), sat opposite me, and, like his old boss Senator Joseph McCarthy counting Communists in the State Department, waved a list at me of 183 factual changes that Steinbrenner demanded I make in the paperback edition.

Barbara Walters happened to be sitting at the table next to ours. She knew Steinbrenner and had said many nice things about him for my book. She overheard Cohn's demands, leaned over, and said, "Take out all the nice things I said about George."

Cohn and I were not unacquainted. He had for a while represented my second wife during the divorce proceedings. Once, he and she and I and my attorney had a meeting in Cohn's office. He deliberately sat under the familiar photograph of him whispering in Senator McCarthy's ear. He didn't want anyone to make the mistake of confusing him with a decent human being.

During the meeting, my second wife grew angrier and angrier with me. Finally, she turned to her attorney and said, "Roy, he hates you. He hates everything you represent. He says you're a fag cocksucker."

Cohn did not take umbrage. He turned to me and said, "Well, that doesn't mean we can't be civil."

I had to laugh. I also had to laugh when my second wife dismissed Cohn as her attorney. She thought he wasn't mean enough.

(Years later, when I was a guest on Larry King's radio show, my second wife was the first caller, and as she began to vilify me, Larry, with the benefit of tape delay, cut her off. I laughed then, too. Imagine how long she must have been on hold to be the first caller.)

I gave in to Cohn on the Steinbrenner book. I made changes in the paperback edition—three or four minor changes, to correct what I accepted as factual errors, unintentional conflicts with objective reality.

In 1983, I won my first Emmy, for cultural reporting, for a look at Sid Caesar after the publication of his autobiography, *Where Have I Been?* the story of his successful struggle to escape drugs and alcohol. I began the piece:

> He was, at his peak, in the nineteen fifties, a giant of television, a colossus of comedy. He was Caesar, figuratively and literally, *Sid* Caesar, and his show, *Your Show of Shows*, made Saturday night the loveliest night of the week for millions of Americans who appreciated a fine mix of parody and poignancy, invention and intelligence. He made everyone laugh, and he made many think, think about how they could write funny, think about how they could act funny. He influenced them, shaped them, inspired them, an emerging tidal wave of wit, all of whom worked for him, and wrote for him: Mel Brooks, who went on to create *Blazing Saddles;* Larry Gelbart, who went on to create *M*A*S*H* for television; Neil Simon, who went on to create a show every year for Broadway; and Woody Allen, who went on to create Woody Allen.

When I interviewed Caesar for the story, he told me that at the height of his success, "I never really believed in myself. Some power was making me funny. I wasn't the one that was doing it."

Later in our conversation, after he had dismissed therapists with a Caesarian burst of psychobabble—'You got a psychiatrist and he says, 'All right now, your mother was your sister and your father was your brother 'cause your father was your sister, dadumda-dumdadumdadum, and that's a hundred and fifty dollars, please"—he told me that his older brother used to baby-sit him. "It was kinda boring to take care of me," Caesar said, "so he played a little game. He used to tie a string on the end of my carriage and let the carriage run all the way down a hill."

The carriage would go faster and faster, heading toward danger until . . . "My brother would pull me back up with the string, and I wouldn't know who was pulling me back up because there were no hands on the carriage. So I thought there was this power watching over me. And I didn't even get hurt. And—"

Caesar stopped and sat silent for several seconds. "That, yes, that's the first time I ever said that, you know that? That's what it was. My God! Wow! What pulled me back up? There were no hands. It had to be something. It wasn't me. And, and I took that all the way through my life. My God! That was it."

Caesar breathed deeply.

"That'll be a hundred and fifty dollars, please," I said.

I made Sid Caesar laugh. Imagine how good *that* felt.

I was pleased with the way the report ended, Sid and his wife, Florence, who had suffered through his addictions, sitting side by side on a couch. "I never said this before," Caesar said, turning to his wife. "I'm gonna say it on camera: I love you."

"Well, I love you, too," Florence said. "You've said it before."

"Not on camera," Sid said.

"Not on camera," Florence agreed.

"That's for everybody to see."

I can't vouch for anyone else, but I had tears in my eyes.

* * *

My strength as an interviewer is a simple one: I try to allow people to be themselves, to reveal themselves. I don't want them to put on a show. I don't want them to say what they think they *should* say. I try to relax them. I try to be probing, but not confrontational. I don't want my subject to be on guard. I want him to say what he thinks. I also try to stay out of the interview. I believe the answers are more important than the questions. I try to keep the questions short. The best question is often "Huh?"—which is my version of Breslin's "Whaddaya doin'?" The idea is for the subject to speak, not me. And, given the choice, rather than sitting in front of my subject and asking him questions, I would prefer to walk behind him, to observe and eavesdrop.

29

"Who Says the World's Greatest Athlete Has to Be Gay?"

In 1984, I covered the Winter Olympics in Sarajevo and the Summer Games in Los Angeles, never suspecting that the charming Yugoslav city would one day become a battleground far more bloody than the one I had witnessed, in the 1960s, in the southern California metropolis. I loved the spirit of Sarajevo, a true melting pot, its varied people, its cobbled streets, its tarnished history—in 1914, in Sarajevo, a teenage patriot named Gavrilo Princip assassinated Archduke Franz Ferdinand, heir to the Austro-Hungarian throne, and set off World War I—even the evil-tasting slivovitz, the homemade brandy that served as the national drink, and the strange pizzas baked with an egg on top.

Sarajevo gave me the opportunity to indulge my affinity for losers, for athletes who had no chance to win a medal, gold, silver, or bronze, in other words the vast majority of Olympians. Before the Games began, I met and interviewed the one-man Egyptian team, an

ighteen-year-old downhill skier named Jamil El
Reedy. El Reedy grew up in New York State, near Lake
lacid, and his father prepared him mentally for the
Olympics by subjecting him to a traditional ordeal—
orty days living alone in a cave in the Sahara, to re-
ect on his own insignificance, to realize, "I was like a
snowflake in the universe."

I befriended an equally microscopic athlete named
George Tucker. He was a luger, a one-man team for
uerto Rico, where he had been born when his father
was a film distributor in South America. George was
wice Jamil El Reedy's age, a thirty-six-year-old candidate for a doctoral degree in physics at Wesleyan
University. He had encountered the luge at Lake
lacid, and in the year before the Olympics, had made
everal practice runs, although never quite completing
ne before crashing. Even driving to New York's John
. Kennedy Airport, to catch his flight to Sarajevo,
Tucker crashed, wrecking his girlfriend's car. "I break
ars, sleds, everything," he said.

Tucker and El Reedy, part Walter Mitty, part Don
Quixote, were my kind of athletes, and, in competition,
hey exceeded their own, and my, expectations. Tucker
completed all four runs in the luge without crashing.
He came in thirtieth among the thirty men who com-
leted all four runs. El Reedy completed his downhill
un without crashing and came in sixtieth among sixty
skiers. Each had every right to be as proud as the
hampions were.

So did the four members of the Lebanese ski team.
hey had scored the greatest victory. They had sur-
ived. They had flown out of ravaged Beirut with
ombs falling on the runway and had made their way,
with no hope of winning, to Sarajevo. "We are here to

be represented," one of them told me, "to have our flag flying among all the others, to show that we're still living, we're not only dying."

Bonnie Warner had no chance of winning, either. She, like Tucker, was a luger, and no American had ever won an Olympic medal of any metal in the luge. But, unlike Tucker, Warner, the best American female luger, took her chilling sport seriously. "Everyone who watches us thinks we're crazy," Bonnie said, "but you have to be a sane person, very much in control. The daredevils crash. A schizo wouldn't make it down the hill. Everyone thinks I'm crazy. But I know I'm not."

Bonnie was a delight, a bright and ebullient young woman who had graduated from Stanford. After she gave up the sport of luging, she turned to piloting faster vehicles. She was one of the first women to fly Boeing 727s for United Airlines.

Before the Summer Games began, I spent as much time as I could with my friend Bob Knight and his U.S. basketball team, a team led by Michael Jordan, Patrick Ewing, and Chris Mullin. Charles Barkley and John Stockton, two of the best players in NBA history, both tried out for the 1984 Olympic team and were cut, an indication that the team was unbelievably talented or that Bob Knight wasn't always right.

I have two vivid memories of the pre-Olympic training. One came during the tryouts, when the 165-pound Stockton bravely took a charge from the 300-pound Barkley, and the other during a scrimmage, when Knight stopped the action, took a marker, walked onto the court, kneeled down, and wrote on the floor, "This is where Waymon Tisdale moved without the ball for the first time." Several weeks later, I asked each of the members of the U.S. team what animal their coach re minded them of, and while most leaned toward lion, tiger, and bear, and one suggested a shark, Tisdale smiled and said, "A pussycat."

The Olympic basketball games were less entertaining, the Americans breezing to the gold medal, winning nine in a row by an average of thirty-two points, one by less than double digits.

During the Olympics, I spent as much time as I could with Daley Thompson, who was defending the decathlon championship he had earned in Moscow. He intended to join Bob Mathias as the only men to win the Olympic decathlon twice.

To match Mathias, Daley had to defeat a formidable rival, a six-foot-seven, 235-pound West German named Juergen Hingsen, the holder of the world record in the decathlon. But Hingsen had never beaten Daley head-to-head, and when the German predicted he would bring home a gold medal, Daley said, "There's only two ways he's going to do that. He's either going to steal mine—or do another event."

"Daley is the better talker," Hingsen responded. "I am the better athlete."

Daley had once told me that in every competition, there are several athletes who would *like* to win, a few who think they *might* win, but only one who knows he *will* win. "Are you always the one who knows he will win?" I asked.

Daley winked. "So far, so good," he said.

Another time, I asked Daley what effect it had had on him as an athlete and as a person, the fact that he was black, and he stared at me, his eyes widened, and he looked at his arm and he said, "Oh my God, I am! No one ever told me before."

How could you not root for him?

Thompson and Hingsen waged a fierce battle in the two-day decathlon, a battle decided, really, in the seventh event, the discus. Thompson's first two throws were dreadful, and he knew that if he didn't improve dramatically on the third, he would fall behind Hingsen and be in danger of losing the gold medal. Thompson responded to the pressure, threw the discus farther than he had ever thrown it in his life, remained in first place, then pulled away and won the gold medal.

I rushed up with a microphone and a dumb question. "How do you feel?" I asked.

Daley saved me with a bright reply. "I haven't had so much fun, Dick," he said, "since Granny got her tit caught in a wringer."

Then Daley took a victory lap wearing a T-shirt he had asked me to purchase for him. The lettering on the front of the shirt said: THANKS AMERICA FOR A GOOD GAMES AND A GREAT TIME. But the lettering on the back, in a pointed reference to the chauvinistic nature of ABC's broadcasts, said: BUT WHAT ABOUT THE TV COVERAGE?

I bought the shirt for Daley at a small shop on Sunset Boulevard. At his request, I also bought him another shirt, which he also wore in the Olympic Stadium. This one, even more pointed, said: WHO SAYS THE WORLD'S GREATEST ATHLETE HAS TO BE GAY?

(The comment was aimed at rumors that Carl Lewis, the winner of four gold medals in Los Angeles, was gay. I told Lewis a couple of years later that I had purchased the shirt for Daley, and then I asked Lewis if he was gay.

"No," Lewis said. "But my sister Carol and I grew up together, and we were very close, and as a result, I

ave some traits that might be considered feminine and
he has some that might be considered masculine.")

The night Daley won the decathlon in Los Angeles,
got a call from a card-playing college friend, Bert
chneider, who produced the films *Easy Rider* and
ive Easy Pieces, telling me that he and his best friend,
ack Nicholson, were going out for the evening and
ould love to have Daley and me join them. I relayed
he invitation to Daley, who said no, he would rather
pend the evening with his auntie and his mates.

ver a seven-year period, I reported, wrote, and nar-
ted sixteen stories for *20/20;* five were nominated for
mmys, and two won. I thrived, as always, on variety:
thirtieth anniversary look back at the Bobby Thom-
on home run, a study of a young man from Brooklyn
rongly convicted of murder, a profile of Kareem Ab-
ul-Jabbar during the light period of his life when he
as able to poke fun at himself in the film *Airplane*
nd in a television rendition of Randy Newman's
Short People," a report on an assistant United States
torney who became a cocaine addict and stole half a
illion dollars' worth of drugs from the evidence safe
his office, an assessment of the boom in baseball
rds, a profile of the pop artist Keith Haring, stories
out Carl Lewis and a comic juggler, about the mak-
g of the book *A Day in the Life of America,* and about
e making of a controversial film called *Brazil.*

For a story on the rebirth of old television series as
ade-for-television movies, I visited Andy Griffith,
on Knotts, and friends on the set of a two-hour
isode of *Mayberry R.F.D.* Howie Morris was repris-
g his old role as the village derelict. I had inter-
ewed Howie, who was once a regular on Sid Caesar's

Show of Shows, for my Caesar story. Now, for hi
Mayberry part, he was unshaven, teeth blacked ou
hair frazzled, back bent, not a pretty sight.

I introduced him to the woman who was my pro
ducer on the project.

Howie Morris squinted at her and said, "I suppose
fuck is out of the question?"

He was right.

For the same story, I asked a CBS executive, "Is ther
any show you wouldn't bring back?"

"Yes," he said.

"Which one?"

"Mister Ed," he said.

"Why not?"

"The horse is a drunk."

For the story on baseball cards, I asked Yogi Berra if h
had kept any old cards. Yogi said yes, quite a few.

"Do you have any cards of Mantle when he was
rookie?" I asked.

"Yeah," Yogi said. "I got 'em lying somewher
around the house."

"They're worth a lot of money now. You ought t
look for them."

"Nah," Yogi said. "I prefer to remember Mickey :
he is."

(One of my few regrets is that in my younger an
more cynical days, I sometimes poked unkind fun :
Berra's intellect and physiognomy. He never took m
jabs personally, never sulked or scowled, or hit m
back, even though I deserved it. Yogi is one of the mo
beautiful people I know, unfailingly open and friendl
and he ain't dumb, either.)

* * *

had nothing to do with what I thought was the best uch in my story on *A Day in the Life of America.* I re- orted that at the end of the twenty-four hours of shoot- g pictures, the people running the project collected ousands of rolls of film from dozens of photographers d sent the film to be processed. At which point, the oducer introduced music in the background—the song om *Snow White*—"Someday My Prince Will Come." Prints.

pair of my *20/20* stories eventually grew into books. 1984, more than thirty members of the 1966 Green ay Packers, the team that had won the first Super owl, held a reunion at Lambeau Field. I knew all of em during the glory years, the Lombardi years, but ost only casually, and it wasn't until the reunion, and til the *20/20* story—plus a one-hour TV special, a deo, articles in *Playboy* and *Parade* magazines, and a ook, *Distant Replay,* all spawned by the reunion— at I really bonded with them and became part of a di- rse and loving family. The heads of the family were art Starr, on offense, and Willie Davis, on defense, oth born in 1934, just like Brigitte and Sophia and me. Davis, the great-grandson of slaves and the son of a borer, was the first member of his family to go to col- ge. He earned a master's degree in business at the niversity of Chicago, became a millionaire selling er and liquor and buying radio stations, and ended o on the board of directors of MGM Grand and sev- al other major corporations. Willie, a giant of a man, ughs heartily and speaks slowly, but thoughtfully. Af- r his teammates Henry Jordan, Ron Kostelnik, and onel Aldridge passed away, Willie told me, "I am

acutely aware that I am the only member of the defe▮
sive line who is still alive."

Max McGee, who scored the first touchdown in th
first Super Bowl, eventually sold his interest in th
ChiChi's restaurants for more than ten million dolla▮
and, through wise investments and hard work, parlaye
those millions into many more. Long after his playir
career ended, McGee donated a million dollars to h
alma mater, Tulane University, another million to fig▮
juvenile diabetes. Once, Max, his wife, Denise, Tris▮
and I were standing at a bar in Manhattan. My wif▮
suffering from hypoglycemia at the time, fainted. A▮
she fell, McGee, whose sure hands had snared eig▮
passes in Super Bowl I, reached out for her—and Tris▮
slipped through his hands. She was not hurt. But Max▮
pride was wounded.

Fuzzy Thurston, the only man on the team born ar▮
raised in Wisconsin, settled near Green Bay, nev▮
stopped being a Packer fan, and refused to be d▮
pressed by financial setbacks or the cancer that co▮
him his larynx, but not his sense of humor. "You got ▮
give me three strokes aside for cancer," he said as ▮
teed off not long after his surgery. (He also said, wis▮
fully, watching a group of kids playing sandlot foo▮
ball, "No one wants to be Fuzzy anymore.")

I played golf with Fuzzy and Max, visited Willie▮
office in Los Angeles, understood how much they r▮
spected Vince Lombardi, how much they loved eac▮
other. The *20/20* story ended with Jerry Kramer ar▮
Fuzzy Thurston on the sidelines at the reunion, obser▮
ing the new Packers on the field while in their min▮
they saw themselves, young and frisky. Kramer ar▮
Thurston each had an arm around the other's shou▮
ders, left guard and right guard firmly linked.

I appreciated the way the Packers accepted me, and they seemed to appreciate what I wrote and said about them. I delivered one of the eulogies at Ron Kostelnik's funeral. I wrote a story about Ray Nitschke's. I mourned the loss of Jordan and Aldridge, Elijah Pitts and Lee Roy Caffey. I loved Lombardi's Packers the way I loved Lenny Bruce and Muhammad Ali, all of whom I met at the start of the 1960s, when they were young, and so was I.

30

"I'm Not Worried About Death"

In the fall of 1986, I saw an item in the *New York Times* about an American athlete who had finished sixth in the decathlon in the 1968 Olympic Games and who now, eighteen years later, was dying of AIDS. His name was Tom Waddell, and even though I had written two books about the Olympics, and another about Bob Beamon, who was Waddell's teammate in Mexico City, I had never heard of Tom Waddell.

Still, without knowing him, I found his story compelling, the kind of sports story I had always looked for, one that far transcended the games, that could spark powerful emotions, that might even be significant. AIDS was a devastating disease, homosexuality and homophobia enormous social issues. As soon as I read a few sentences about him, I knew I wanted to write a book with and about Tom Waddell. But first I had to find him.

All I knew was that he lived in San Francisco. I called a gay friend, David Rothenberg, a Broadway publicity man and sports addict, who, in earlier days, had introduced me to Dave Kopay, a former Green Bay Packer who wrote a book about his ordeal as a gay player in the National Football League. I asked David if he knew how I could reach a gay Olympic athlete named Tom Waddell.

"Do you think we *all* know each other?" Rothenberg replied.

Then, fortuitously, I called an old college friend, Stu Schwartz, a psychiatrist in the Bay Area who, even though he was straight, might have a lead to Waddell. He did. One of his clients was a gay woman who knew Tom well. She gave his address to her therapist who gave it to me.

I wrote to Tom immediately, told him of the books I had written, and the Olympics I had covered, of how drawn I was to his story and how much I wanted to collaborate with him on a book. Tom wrote back and told me he was flattered by my interest, but he had already committed himself to another author, Robert Scheer, the *Los Angeles Times* correspondent whose lengthy and moving report on Tom had prompted the *New York Times* to publish its briefer version.

I was disappointed, but still the story gripped me. I felt I had to do *something* about Waddell. Then I thought of *20/20*. I approached Av Westin, and, while some TV executives might have shied away from the subject in the 1980s, Av didn't hesitate. He assigned a talented producer named Rob Wallace to work with me. I called Waddell and asked him if we could visit and interview him for *20/20*, and Tom said yes, he would welcome us.

As we flew to San Francisco in December 1986, Rob Wallace said to me, "I'm nervous about this story."

"Why?" I said.

"Because stories about homosexuals make me nervous," Wallace said, "and I think they make viewers nervous, too."

Rob's comment made me nervous.

A few hours later, Rob and I met Tom Waddell for the first time and spent a few hours with him. Then Rob and I drove to our hotel. "This is going to be a great story," he said.

"Why?" I said.

"Because I love this guy," Rob Wallace said.

I had my own preconceptions, my own fears, when I started work on the Waddell story. I grew up with the prevailing prejudices of the 1930s and '40s, my teenage friends and I cruelly taunting boys and men who seemed to us to be effeminate. We called them "fairy" and "Mary," trying to wound them with words, and succeeding. Later, I became more tolerant, less stupid. In the theater and literary worlds, even in sports, I made a few friends who were gay. But only a few. I had no idea what the gay culture was like until I met Waddell in San Francisco.

Tom, who, even in his illness, still had the frame and musculature of an athlete, invited me to the Harvey Milk Gay and Lesbian Democratic Club dinner. As we entered the lobby of the Hyatt hotel, one of the Democrats recognized me and grabbed my arm. "When the fuck are we going to get a hockey team out here?" he said. That night, I met a "fairy" who was once the Marlboro man and another who was in the rodeo cowboys' Hall of Fame.

My preconceptions took a beating, and so did my fears. When Tom decided he no longer felt comfortable working with Bob Scheer, he asked me to coauthor his autobiography. We both knew he was dying, and how important it was to work closely and quickly. He invited me to stay at his home, a sprawling high-ceilinged Victorian structure on Albion Street in the Mission district of San Francisco.

The first few nights I spent at Albion, I was frightened. I was afraid of using the dishes, the glasses, the shower, terrified of getting AIDS. Intellectually, I knew that AIDS could not be transmitted so easily, only through intimate contact, or through contaminated blood, and yet I worried. Eventually, I overcame my fears. I drank from the glasses. I ate from the dishes. I even showered.

I fell in love with Tom, just as Rob Wallace had, just as I had earlier fallen in love with Muhammad Ali and Herb Gardner and Jerry Kramer. Tom's range of talents was astonishing. He was an artist—a painter, photographer, and dancer—and an athlete—a college football player, gymnast, and track-and-field star so gifted, versatile, and dedicated that he made the 1968 United States Olympic team at the age of thirty. Tom was also a paratrooper in the United States Army and a physician who specialized, ironically, in infectious diseases. He was once ship's doctor on a Scripps Institution of Oceanography expedition to the South Pacific, and once personal physician to the brother of the king of Saudi Arabia. He was also the founder of the Gay Games, an athletic competition dedicated but not restricted to homosexuals, and he was the father of a young girl, Jessica, whose mother, Sara Lewinstein, was a lesbian who shared Tom's desire for a child. Tom enjoyed being asked how he and Sara ever conceived a child. "The usual way," he said.

The *20/20* story on Tom Waddell was the best work

I ever did for television. (*We* did, especially Rob Wallace and the cameraman Terry Morrison, both of whom brought sensitivity and a perceptive eye to the project.) The first time I viewed the finished piece, which was seventeen minutes long, I cried. The twentieth time I saw the piece, I cried.

Several scenes still haunt and delight me. One reunited Tom and Bill Toomey, the man who had won the decathlon in the 1968 Olympics when Tom had finished sixth. Toomey had no idea Tom was gay when they toured the world together after the Olympics, but in the 1970s, when Tom wrote to more than one hundred friends telling them that he was coming out, conspicuously, in the "Couples" section of *People* magazine, the only one who did not write back was Bill Toomey. Bill was still burdened by the athletic and homosexual stereotypes that Tom Waddell contradicted.

I called Toomey and asked him to fly from Los Angeles to San Francisco so that we could tape Tom and him together. Toomey said he would. When I met him at the airport, he was jowly, clearly overweight, and even though it was morning, alcohol fueled his breath. Bill had fortified himself for the reunion.

I drove Toomey to a practice field where Tom was coaching a gay track-and-field team. I dropped Bill at one end of the track; Tom waited at the other. Our camera, discreetly shaded by trees and equipped with a telescopic lens, followed Toomey as he walked toward Tom. They met and reached out and hugged, and the wireless microphone Tom was wearing picked up every word of their conversation.

"You're looking good," Toomey said.

"I want to feel a lot better than I do," Tom said.

"You're going to make it," Toomey said. "I know that."

Tom shook his head. "Well, I don't know what that means anymore," he said.

"You'll take five, you'll take five years, won't you?" Toomey said.

"I'll take five months."

Toomey stopped as if punched flush on the jaw. "Really?" he said.

"Oh, absolutely," Tom said. He looked at Toomey and smiled. "My head is in good shape over this," Tom said. "I need a new body, but my head's fine."

"Mine's not as good as yours," Toomey said.

"I'm not worried about death or dying at all," Tom said.

The reunion had a profound impact on Bill Toomey. He stopped drinking that day and went on a strict diet. Within six months, he had shed thirty pounds and looked like an Olympic champion again.

Another scene in the *20/20* story showed Tom standing in his kitchen talking to his friend John Hall. "You've brought me food when I've asked you to," Tom said. "You've cleaned my house, you've done my dishes, you've given me lots of moral support."

"Well, I love you," John Hall said.

"I know you do," Tom said. "That's why I ask you to do those things, because there are times when I get down, and there's John—you know, there's John to provide me with the kind of moral support that I need."

John Hall was a former advertising executive who had come out in midlife, dramatically altering his lifestyle and his occupation. He was training to become a nurse. Minutes after "To an Athlete Dying Young" aired on *20/20*, Hall received a telephone call from his mother.

"John," she said. "I just watched *20/20*. Was that you saw?"

"Yes, Mother," Hall said.

"How did you ever get the part?" said his mother.

The piece won an Emmy, and the reaction was overwhelmingly favorable. A few coworkers at ABC came out to me, told me they were gay, and said that if I ever worked on another story about AIDS or homosexuality, they would love to work with me.

Joe Namath stood up to fearsome linemen, Muhammad Ali to brutal punchers, Bill Clark to men with guns. But of all the brave people I've known, none showed so much courage as Tom Waddell. He never whined, never cursed his fate, and regretted only that he would not see his daughter grow up.

Certainly, I was not a brave person. My fears ranged from heights and roller coasters to pain and dying. I could never identify with the athletes I knew, men and women, who loved living on the edge; I wanted to live and work right in the middle, at ground level. Still, a small fraction of Tom's courage rubbed off, calmed fears that seemed so inconsequential compared to what he faced. Tom had a rare gift: Many people spot your weaknesses and go for the jugular; Tom spotted your strengths and went to them, made you feel better about yourself.

On July 7, 1987, Tom took himself off all medication—off the painkillers that blurred his memory, off the drugs that were supposed to slow or soften the ravages of AIDS. The next morning, he went to the hospital and received a blood transfusion to give him a spurt of strength.

Then he returned home and for the rest of that day and deep into the following, he and I sat and talked. He struggled for the memory to fill in the gaps in his life, to complete the frame of his autobiography. When he was satisfied that he had shared his story as well as he could, when he felt he could endure the frustrations of his failing mind no longer, he called Sara and Jessica to his bedside, handed his daughter a farewell present, a magic crystal ball, and kissed her good-bye.

On the evening of July 9, Tom decided it was time to die. Like many with AIDS, and with more access than most, Tom had hoarded a supply of morphine pills. Eric Wilkinson, one of Tom's dearest friends, took a triangular dish of green tourmaline and filled it with small pills, vividly purple. He handed it to Tom, with a glass of water, and Tom looked at the purple pills and said, "How gay!"

Eric and Suellen Manning, his friends for years, sat on the bed on each side of Tom, and Trish and I sat at the foot. Eric helped Tom with the glass of water and the pills, which were difficult for him to swallow. After half an hour, he had managed to take thirty-six pills. "That should be enough," Tom calculated. He winked at Eric and warned him that he was an accomplice.

It began to get dark outside, and no one spoke much. Eric and Suellen, both of whom had put in long hours caring for Tom, told him once more how much they loved him. He grew drowsier. His eyes flickered. And then he folded his hands on his lap and said, "Well, this should be interesting," and closed his eyes for the last time.

My wife and I kissed Tom good-bye.

The week after Tom's death, I wrote an article about him for *Sports Illustrated*. The story was called "The Death of an Athlete," and it was published despite some internal opposition at the magazine. It was not heavily edited, but someone took out a sentence in which I said, "I kissed Tom good-bye."

The magazine wanted to protect my masculinity.

An editor offered to leave the sentence in if I added, "on the cheek," but even though the phrase was accurate, I found the offer offensive. I simply cut the sentence.

It wasn't until after the article was published that I realized I could have saved the sentence if I had written then, with equal accuracy, "My wife and I kissed Tom good-bye."

If you don't want to be labeled a homosexual, it is always good to invoke the image of a wife.

Which I suppose is why many closeted homosexual athletes begin interviews, "As I was saying to my girlfriend . . ."

The reaction to the article was enormous and divided. "The worst and most disgusting story ever published in *Sports Illustrated,*" one reader wrote. "Trash" and "nauseating" came to the minds of other readers. "Faggots and lesbians are the disease!" one subscriber wrote, and more than one said, "Cancel my subscription."

But Tom and the article had supporters, too. "I am not a homosexual, an athlete or a doctor, but Tom Waddell's courage and fortitude will always serve as an inspiration to me," one man wrote. "Never in my life have I been so moved by a magazine article," wrote another. And a third said, "I just read it minutes ago, and as I write, the tears keep re-forming."

A few days after Tom's death, in the Albion Street home he had so painstakingly decorated, a couple of hundred of his friends gathered to celebrate his life, to tell stories about the man they loved, about the man who was—in the words of one of his friends—"the

ole model for every homosexual in San Francisco."
They came in business suits, and in leather, and some,
he Sisters of Perpetual Indulgence, even in drag. I
chose a business suit.

A bearded, earnest man, also in conventional attire,
walked up to me and wondered if he could ask me a
personal question. "Of course," I said.

"Have you ever undergone psychoanalysis?" he inquired.

"No," I said.

"That's funny," he said. "You're the first straight
man I've met who seems at ease among homosexuals
without psychoanalysis."

I took it as a compliment.

I was not quite so at ease a few months later when
Sara, Tom's widow, took me to a male and female gay
bodybuilding competition in San Francisco. I am not
turned on by people whose sinews are showing
whether they are male or female, straight or gay. I
don't like to ogle popping veins. Sara arranged for me
to be introduced at the competition, and I received a
standing ovation. The *20/20* and *SI* stories had made
me a minor hero in the gay community in San Francisco. I was also a minor hero in the football community in Wisconsin. I'm certain the two communities
overlap, but not by much.

I had not eaten dinner before the bodybuilding event,
so Sara, on her way home, dropped me at Artemis, a
restaurant she owned. I went in, sat down, studied the
menu, ordered a glass of wine, then looked around the
room and observed that, among more than a hundred
customers and employees, I was the only male.

The next morning, I called my wife in New York and
described the scene.

"Were they all gay?" she said.

"I don't know," I said. "I suppose so."

"That's the trouble with your fantasies," Trish said. "They always have a hitch in them."

It took me almost nine years to complete *Gay Olympian: The Life and Death of Dr. Tom Waddell.* I had never before taken more than a year to write a book. It was Tom's fault. If he hadn't been such a remarkable human being, if I hadn't felt such pressure to produce a manuscript that measured up to him, and if he hadn't died at forty-nine, if he hadn't left me without my most valuable source, I suspect I would have completed the book sooner.

While I was working on the book, the Gay Games, the quadrennial athletic competition Tom had worked so hard to create, were held in New York City. Naturally, I entered. I played tennis, doubles, in the over-fifty-five division. My partner was a friend of Tom's, Jim Hormel, the heir to the ham fortune who was later named by President Clinton to be ambassador to Luxembourg, stirring up a right-wing storm. Only eight teams entered our division, and when our quarter-final opponents failed to show up, presumably intimidated, Jim and I won by default and advanced to the semifinals, where we were soundly beaten, but consoled with bronze medals.

During the match that ended our bid for the gold, I demonstrated the one feature that distinguished my tennis game from similarly mediocre efforts: I hit forehands with either hand. The first time I stroked a left-handed forehand for a winner, one of our opponents did a double take and called to me, "Are you bi-?"

"I thought you'd never ask," I said.

When I finally finished the book, Greg Louganis, the Olympic diving champion, contributed an introduction. Greg had been closeted during his Olympic years, never confirming persistent rumors that he was gay, but he had come out as part of the opening ceremonies for the Gay Games in New York. I had known Greg for years. We'd always been polite to each other, even cordial. But every time I saw him *after* he came out, when he promoted his autobiography, when he starred in an off-Broadway play, when he said that he was HIV-positive, I hugged him. If I hadn't known Tom Waddell, I probably wouldn't have been able to go beyond a pat on Greg's back.

I expected *Gay Olympian* to be a bestseller. I had attended the Gay Games in Vancouver in 1990 and I had been the only male sitting at the hotel swimming pool who wasn't reading the bestselling memoir of Dave Pallone, a gay major-league umpire. Louganis's autobiography became an even greater commercial hit.

I thought I could write better than most umpires and many divers, which left me disappointed and surprised when *Gay Olympian*, despite favorable notices and ample exposure in the gay community, sold only a moderate number of copies, shattering two more of my preconceptions: that all gay men had money and that they spent much of it on books.

When Av Westin left *20/20* and was replaced by a less talented executive producer named Victor Neufeld, I was no longer invited to contribute to the show. Evidently, Neufeld's opinion of my work was no higher than mine of his.

31

"Boy, Have You Come to the Right Igloo!"

In 1986, when Billy Crystal and I coauthored *Absolutely Mahvelous*—Billy suggested we call it *The Bibble*, to see how carefully readers read—I also collaborated with two larger athletes, Phil Simms and Phil McConkey of the New York Giants, on their diary of a season that ended with them going to Los Angeles to play in the Super Bowl. Simms was a star, McConkey a member of his supporting cast. I teamed them up mostly because, at that time, Simms had little to say, or, more likely, little he was *willing* to say, and McConkey loved to talk. Simms threw passes; McConkey caught passes. I called the book *Simms to McConkey*.

Two nights before the Super Bowl, I took Simms and McConkey to dinner with Billy Crystal. Billy loved the Giants, almost as much as he loved the Yankees. He loved talking football with the two Giants. He asked Simms about the game plan, and Simms said they were going to pass more than usual. Billy asked Simms if he knew the opening series of plays, and

imms said he knew the opening play. Billy asked him
what the opening play was going to be, and Simms told
im it was going to be a fifteen-yard pass to Lionel
Manuel. Simms diagrammed the play with salt and
epper shakers. "Can I bet the guy next to me in the
Rose Bowl that that's going to be the first play?" Billy
sked.

"You can bet on it," Simms said.

Crystal bet on it. The first play of the Super Bowl
was, precisely, the salt-and-pepper-shakers play: Simms
rew to Manuel for seventeen yards. Crystal cheered as
oudly then as I cheered in the fourth quarter when one
f Simms's passes ricocheted off Mark Bavaro, the tight
nd, and McConkey dove and caught the ball just be-
ore it hit the ground in the end zone. Simms to Mc-
Conkey for a touchdown! The perfect omen. I hoped
imms to McConkey would score as well.

It didn't. The Giants started the 1987 season as
world champions, but a strike blighted the season,
orcing replacement players into NFL lineups, and by
he middle of October, when Simms and McConkey
were back in uniform, the Giants had lost five straight
ames and won none. Who wanted to read about them?

On one of my red-eye flights from the West Coast, I
appened to sit in front of Muhammad Ali, who, from
LAX to JFK, kept me awake by flicking my ear with
is finger. On one of my daytime flights to the West
Coast, I happened to sit behind Mel Brooks, whom I'd
net earlier when my wife and I wrote an article about
im for *Parade*. We chatted briefly and then the plane
ook off. After twenty or thirty minutes, I noticed that
he No Smoking sign had not yet been turned off. After
nother twenty or thirty minutes, I noticed that I could

look out the window and still see JFK Airport. After another minute or two, the captain announced that we had a problem with the landing gear, but, not to worry, we were going to make an emergency landing at JFK and hope that the landing gear held up.

Fire engines and ambulances lined the runway. A flight attendant told us that everyone in first class had to move to the back of the jumbo jet for the emergency landing. "I'm not moving," Mel Brooks told the flight attendant.

"But Mr. Brooks," she said, "you have to move."

"I'm not going to move," Mel said. "It would be bad for my image if my body were found in coach."

Mel moved. We all moved. And the plane landed without mishap, preserving Mel's reputation and my body.

Early in the 1980s, when Trish convinced me that we wanted to have a child, I agreed to undergo a reverse vasectomy. The doctor who had performed my vasectomy, which was swift, minor, and painless, told me that if he did the reversal, a considerably more complicated procedure, he would have a 20 percent chance of success, but that a doctor in St. Louis named Sherman Silber had a more than 90 percent record of success. I went to Dr. Silber.

Sherman is a microsurgeon; he is also a microperson, who towers over people only if they are under five feet tall. But Sherman makes up for his height with his ego. He is good, and knows it. He is also flexible. He wrote a book on fertility called *How to Get Pregnant*, and then, covering all bases, followed it with a book called *How Not to Get Pregnant*.

Sherman's interests are equally contradictory. He

rites poetry and hunts animals. He lives luxuriously
nd vacations primitively. One year, he took a holiday
mong Eskimos living in igloos on the frozen surface
f the Arctic Ocean. An Eskimo knocked on Sherman's igloo one night and asked if he was a physician.
Dr. Silber confessed that he was. "Several years ago,"
the Eskimo said, "I went to Alaska and had a vasec-
omy. Is there any place in the world where I can get it
eversed?"

"Boy, have you come to the right igloo!" Sherman
aid.

was one of Dr. Silber's few surgical failures, prompt-
ng Trish and me to adopt first Kari and then, almost
our years later, David, both of whom made us grateful
hat the reversal did not take. Kari and David came to
s when they were each three days old.

Because I was more experienced than Trish—I had
iapered and burped four biological children—I fed
Kari her first bottle away from the hospital. Because
rish and Kari were on vacation in Spain when David
rrived, ahead of schedule, he and I spent our first
ight alone. We shared my king-size bed. He slept
ke a baby, and I lay awake all night, afraid of rolling
nto him.

I remember clearly their first "solid" meals. Kari
ad chocolate ice cream, in Bermuda, smeared on her
ace and hands. David's was more exotic, cheese grits,
n New Orleans, prepared in his home by Frank Brigt-
en, one of the city's master chefs. Both ate as eagerly
s if they were my genetic heirs.

There is absolutely no difference between the pro-
ective and loving instincts inspired by a biological
hild and those inspired by an adoptive child. From the

start, Kari and David were ours to nurture and adore as much as if Trish had carried them from the moment of conception.

We did not hide the fact they were adopted from either of them or anyone else. We familiarized them with the term even before they could grasp its meaning. When Kari was barely two, Trish mentioned to her that she was adopted, and Kari looked up and said, "I'm a doctor?"

Between 1988 and 1994, I covered three Winter and two Summer Olympics, and the pleasure of covering the Games seemed to diminish with each one. In Calgary in 1988, the saving grace, or saving *lack* of grace, was the British ski jumper Eddie "The Eagle" Edwards, who had lived in a Scandinavian mental institution while preparing for the Olympics. Many people suggested he should have been confined longer, considering his lack of experience and aptitude and the sport's demanding and daunting nature.

I had heard about the struggles of Eddie the Eagle before the Games began, and when he arrived in Calgary, I was waiting at the airport, cameras rolling. He performed perfectly. With his skis on his shoulder, Edwards came off the plane and walked into a wall. I followed him, cautiously, for the next few days, through news conferences and practice sessions, and when he finally jumped in competition, I sat in the stands with his mother and father.

His father was a roofer; Eddie had been a roofer, too. "How good a roofer?" I asked his father.

"About as good as he is a ski jumper," Eddie's progenitor said.

His mother covered her eyes when Eddie jumped,
nd she did not open them until her husband and I and
ie roar of the crowd assured her that he had sur-
ived. He lived up to his billing and finished last in
ie competition.

Several months later, I was in Seoul for the Summer
ames. So was Daley Thompson, his bid for a third
raight decathlon title, at the age of thirty-two, frus-
ated by injury. But if Daley did not enjoy a victory, he
id enjoy the Olympic experience, living, as he always
id, among his fellow athletes in the Olympic Village,
lishing the camaraderie. Carl Lewis, on the other
and, enjoyed victory in Seoul—he won the long jump
nd, when the Canadian sprinter Ben Johnson was dis-
ualified for using banned drugs, the 100-meter
ash—but, as usual, segregated himself from his team-
ates, and lived outside the Olympic Village. Who
ays the world's greatest athlete has to be gregarious?

In 1992, I went to the Winter Games in the French
lps, and the Summer Games in Barcelona, enjoying
ie beauty and cuisine of both sites and the hospitality
f one, and then, in 1994, I had my worst Olympic ex-
erience, covering the Tonya Harding–Nancy Kerrigan
kirmish in Norway.

Lillehammer, the headquarters for the Games, was
orgeous, and so were the people, but the antagonism
etween the two American figure skaters was ugly, de-
ressing, and so appealing to television viewers and
etworks that I had to spend most of my time scram-
ling for tidbits from the young women who were la-
eled, by the people covering them, the Bitch and the
ore. I would much rather have concentrated on the
oss, the Norwegian speed skater Johann Olav Koss, a

Scandinavian Eric Heiden who also intended to become a doctor. A humanitarian, Koss donated much of his prize money to helping the people of the devastated Winter Olympic city of Sarajevo. He treated reporters kindly, too.

32

The Fat Guy, the Little Guy, and the Nice Guy

In the fall of 1988, Terry O'Neill, who contradicts the notion that a bright television executive is an oxymoron, came up with the idea of a weekly show featuring a panel of newspaper sportswriters discussing the week in sports, *Meet the Press* with muscles. He called the program *The Sports Reporters,* sold the idea to ESPN, and, considering my newspaper past and my television present, asked me if I would moderate the show. I thought it was a great idea; ABC News disagreed and refused to grant me permission to be the host. During the first six months of *The Sports Reporters,* I was allowed to appear only as an infrequent guest.

After six months, when the original moderator left New York, Terry asked me again, and I asked ABC again, and this time ABC gave its approval. Eventually, ABC swallowed ESPN, and Walt Disney swallowed ABC, and we all ended up in the belly of the same mouse. Right from the beginning, I loved hosting the

show. I loved alternating between traffic cop and ref
eree for a gaggle of sportswriters who were, in varying
degrees, intelligent, informed, articulate, and con
tentious, not necessarily in that order.

We had a terrific cadre of panelists: Mike Lupica—
who just interrupted my writing to remind me his name
had to come first—Bill Conlin, Ralph Wiley, Bo
Ryan, John Feinstein, Tony Kornheiser, Roy Johnson
Sally Jenkins, Bill Rhoden, Christine Brennan, Mitc
Albom, Skip Bayless, Mike Downey, Michael Wilbon
Ira Berkow, Pulitzer Prize winners Jim Murray an
Dave Anderson, Leonard Koppett, Jackie McMullen
and Jill Lieber, who once on the air referred to th
women's golf tour as "dykes in spikes," an appellatio
that might have cost a male panelist his life, or at leas
his masculinity.

We thrived on differences of opinion, but once
when we were taping, Bill Conlin and Ralph Wiley go
into an argument so acrimonious—Bill correcte
Ralph's pronunciation of the name Attila, as in Hur
less than diplomatically—Wiley, on the brink of tears
threatened to walk off the set. We stopped, they mad
up, sort of, and we retaped the segment. Not all of ou
disputes were quite so heartfelt. We used to do
weekly segment called "Face-Off," a head-to-head de
bate. One week we had Bob Ryan versus Mik
Lupica—I forget the subject—and when they finishec
just for practice, they did it again, switching view
points. The reverse debate was every bit as heated an
persuasive as the original. I suggested that we put bot
versions on the air, but Joe Valerio, the producer, pat
ted me on my head and rejected the idea.

Valerio, another ex-newspaperman, is the third an
most committed of the producers of *The Sports Re*

rters. Joe picks the panelists, chooses the topics, dis-
butes research, edits tapes, works full-time on the
ow. Terry O'Neill did it with one hand; Chet Forte,
s successor, did it with none. Forte was more con-
rned with point spreads than with repartee. Forte's
siness partner used to sit by the set and, as if he were
recting a commercial for a deodorant, bark at the
nelists, "Energy, energy, more energy." The Forte
gime mercifully did not last long, or the show might
ve died prematurely.

Instead, it has become a fixture, winning a dedicated
d diverse audience that includes just about everyone
the sports business: coaches, managers, players, all
tuned in to the show's format that Magic Johnson
ed to end interviews by saying, in our fashion, "And
w for my parting shot." Ann-Margret is a regular
ewer; so is Burt Reynolds. *"The Sports Reporters,*
ediated by the estimable Dick Schaap," critic Bruce
eber wrote in the *Times,* "does for hoops and horse
cing what *Crossfire* does for Whitewater and the
A." "Estimable" is almost as gratifying as gaunt.

In the show's second decade, Valerio, convinced that
miliarity breeds viewers, has elected to stick with a
aller pool of panelists, basically Lupica, Ryan, Con-
, Albom, Rhoden, Kornheiser, Feinstein, Wilbon,
d Rick Telander, juggled and served three at a time. I
n't envy Joe the job of picking the panelists—almost
ery sportswriter in America would kill to be on—but
l like to see more variety. I'd also like to see more
omen, but the one who used to appear most fre-
ently, and most effectively, Jackie McMullen, aban-
ned us, first for pregnancy and then for a job with a
al company.

Usually, when I miss a show, to enjoy a vacation or a

hip replacement, Lupica, who customarily sits on m
left, shifts comfortably into my seat. I hate to skip
show because I subscribe to the Wally Pipp theor
Don't ever take a day off. Pipp was the New York Ya
kee first baseman who once took a day off to clear
headache, and when he came back found that Lo
Gehrig had moved into his position permanently.
know that I am indispensable, but I worry that ne
everyone knows it.

The Sports Reporters provides all of us who partic
pate with remarkable exposure and frequent recogn
tion, which hasn't hurt anyone's career. Kornheiser, fo
instance, has his own national radio show, and h
Washington Post column, consistently witty and on
sometimes about sports, is required reading in the na
tion's capital. Lupica has had flings at his own radi
and television programs, pops up frequently on Do
Imus's syndicated radio show, and churns out bo
novels and nonfiction books. Albom, among many cre
dentials, is the author of *Tuesdays with Morrie,* th
bestselling nonfiction book in the country at the turn o
the century, and Feinstein has turned out a string o
bestsellers, the most successful on basketball and gol
All of them write uncommonly well, and all are mult
media stars, a dramatic change from my early years o
the sports beat, when hardly anyone crossed over fro
print to television, and sportswriters such as Dic
Young of the *New York Daily News* were openly antag
onistic to radio and, especially, television reporter
Young enjoyed shoving TV cameramen, particularly a
they were shooting. Young and Cosell feuded a
fiercely as Frazier and Ali.

I was a rarity when I first straddled the written wor
and the spoken word, but now the practice is commo

and most of my colleagues on *The Sports Reporters* are equally comfortable facing a microphone or a word processor. Bill Rhoden is more laid-back than most, but none of them, so far as I can tell, shies away from the spotlight.

And the spotlight is bright. Sports fans and athletes know us much more from our television appearances than from our writings. They may not know us by name—Lupica is often "the short one," Conlin "the fat one," and I, to Lupica's consternation, and my ex-wives' bewilderment, "the nice one"—but they spot us at sporting events and do not hesitate to tell us how astute, or stupid, we are. Each of us thinks of himself as exceptionally literate, yet we revel in the glory of our Sunday morning comments being reported on Monday mornings by *USA Today*'s Rudy Martzke, a borderline illiterate. Vanity, thy name is Conlin, Lupica, Kornheiser, Wilbon . . . and, of course, Schaap.

Which is why my favorite part of the show, and everyone else's, is the parting shot, a solo performance, a one-minute monologue uninterrupted except by bursts of laughter that are sometimes spontaneous. Lupica is our best, if not most sincere, laugher. He also is very good at having the last word, or phrase, before we go off the air. To be fair, Lupica is clever, bright, knowledgeable, and glib, and I like him, I honestly do, almost as much as I like picking on him. "Michael, you're an arrogant little bastard," I sometimes say, in jest, and he, depending on his mood, replies with either "Thank you" or "Bite me."

Michael's son, Christopher, at the age of twelve, came up to me after a show and said, "Why do you always pick on my father?" Then Christopher paused for a beat, and added, "I love it." (He has not made up his mind yet whether he wants to take over his father's seat someday, or mine.) I also love picking on Kornheiser, for his neuroses; Ryan, for his zeal; Feinstein, for his prolificacy; and Conlin, for the aforementioned reason. (Conlin's knowledge of subjects as diverse as jazz and the Internet is equally broad.)

Usually, we tape *The Sports Reporters* on Sunday mornings in New York City, late enough for us to analyze Saturday night events, early enough for us to finish taping by 9 A.M., to give Joe Valerio and the director Rob Cowen time to edit the program, making cuts if necessary, and the panelists time to get to Philadelphia or Washington or Boston or Detroit to cover an afternoon football, baseball, or basketball game. Each year, we do one show from the site of the Super Bowl, the day of the game, and one from the site of the Final Four, the day between the semifinals and the championship game. Once, we made the mistake of taping our Super Bowl show on Saturday, and that night, Eugene Robinson of the Atlanta Falcons was arrested and accused of soliciting sex from an undercover police officer. When we came on the next morning, without any mention of the arrest, we looked very foolish.

(Ironically, on Saturday night, walking through Miami's South Beach on the way to our Super Bowl party at Joe's Stone Crab, my wife and children and I happened to bump into Eugene Robinson, whom I knew from his Packer days. We greeted each other warmly and introduced our families, and then I went on to our party, and Eugene to his. He should have come to ours. Cameron Diaz was in Joe's, and my daughter, Kari, then seventeen, told the actress that her little brother David, who was thirteen, was in love with her and

wanted to meet her. Cameron Diaz graciously said
hello to my son, leaving him ecstatic and speechless.
Kari also met the Savage brothers, Fred and Ben, the
same night, and couldn't stop grinning.)

We have also done *The Sports Reporters* from the
sites of the World Series, the Tyson-Holyfield ear-bite
fight, and, once each, the Winter and Summer
Olympics. In 1992, during the Winter Games in
France, Joe Valerio, the producer, stayed in a small
Alpine village some twenty miles from our set in the
CBS broadcast center. The first Sunday, his driver
failed to show up, and Joe had to scurry around in the
predawn dark, trying in pidgin French to beg or buy a
ride to the studio; the second Sunday, an avalanche
buried the road between Valerio's residence and the
studio, and he had to scale the avalanche to reach a second driver on the far side. Joe got to the studio both
weeks, and both shows got on the air, but he has never
again taken us to a Winter Olympics. Four years later,
the day before *The Sports Reporters* was to be taped in
Atlanta's Olympic Park, a bomb exploded and the park
was shut down, cordoned off, sealed for more than
forty-eight hours. Valerio scrambled and found a
makeshift studio in time to get the show on the air. I
missed that show; I was busy learning to live with a
new hip. I doubt that we'll do *The Sports Reporters*
again from a Summer Olympics, either.

The acceptance and endurance of *The Sports Reporters* led ESPN to give me my own half-hour interview show, *Schaap Talk,* which, with little promotion
and less audience, survived for slightly more than a
year. Each week, in addition to a guest, I always
arranged a mystery caller, someone out of the guest's
past, to phone in anonymously with a question or com-

ment. Once I asked a woman who had dated Steve Young in high school to call in while I was interviewing the San Francisco quarterback.

"How come you're still not married?" she asked Young.

"You sound like my mother," said Young, who did not recognize the voice.

"I know your mother," the woman said.

"You do?" Young said with surprise.

The woman revealed her identity—she had become Miss America—and Young, then a bachelor, sounded disappointed to learn that she was now a happily married mother living in Texas.

I later became host of a more durable show, *Schaap One on One,* created by Doug Warshaw at Classic Sports Network, and continued when Classic Sports evolved into ESPN Classic. ESPN, and its parent company, believe fervently in synergy, which, in essence, means using every area of the company to promote and endorse every other area. We used to call it incest. My favorite example is that *The Sports Reporters,* at the start of its second decade, officially became *ESPN the Magazine's The Sports Reporters,* raising the fascinating question of how a months-old magazine could give birth to a show ten years its senior.

Schaap One on One has survived and flourished, a series of half-hour conversations with noncontemporary sports figures. Jim Brown, Henry Aaron, Bo Jackson, Bill Bradley, Paul Hornung, Richard Petty, Bill Walton, Joe Namath, Daley Thompson, Billie Jean King, Bob Gibson, Jerry Kramer, and Martina Navratilova are among the dozens of athletes with whom I've gone "one on one" after their playing careers had ended. The name of the show is appropriate.

It is "one on one," not *"mano à mano,"* a conversation, not a duel, not an interrogation, an opportunity for the subject to talk about the memorable moments in his or her life and career, the triumphs and the defeats. Martina spoke openly of her homosexuality, Don Newcombe of his alcoholism, the race driver Bobby Allison of the deaths of his two car-racing sons. *SportsCenter* highlights an athlete's talent; I try to highlight his nature.

Talking with vintage athletes, most of them members of my own generation, makes me young again, at least for thirty minutes, and, I hope, rejuvenates them, too. With many, of course, it is a reunion, with some an introduction. Sherman White came on one show, my basketball hero when I was in my early teens, a six-foot-nine forward with a jump shot at Long Island University, a certain pro star until he got caught shaving points and never played a minute in the NBA. Dolph Schayes appeared, too, another of my early basketball heroes, only sixteen when he started playing for New York University, only twenty when he began the first of his sixteen seasons in the NBA, selected almost half a century later as one of the fifty greatest players in the history of the league, the only Jewish player in that elite company. I went one on one with Tommy Henrich, "Old Reliable" of the New York Yankees, teammate of Joe DiMaggio and scourge of the Brooklyn Dodgers, and with Warren Spahn, who won more games than any other left-handed pitcher in baseball history, all of them unforgettable athletes who, to varying degrees, had been forgotten by younger fans. Once, I would have paid to talk to any of them; now, I was getting paid.

All I had seen and heard and learned during my half

century in sports and journalism came into play in my contributions to *SportsCentury*, the ambitious end-of-the-century project conceived by ESPN and coordinated by an indefatigable young producer named Mark Shapiro, who supervised sixty hours of programming and more than seventeen hundred interviews, most of them, it sometimes seemed, with me.

Actually, Mark and his staff interviewed me only half a dozen times, but each session was a lengthy one, and most were conducted by Mark himself, who had managed to cram into his thirty-year-old mind a hundred years of names, feats, statistics, anecdotes, and more. His questions were always informed and usually incisive, and if you didn't know better, you would swear he had witnessed the Long Count, the Black Sox, the Ice Bowl, and many more historic sports events that took place before he was born.

Shapiro used me as if I were half encyclopedia and half Bartlett's, digging for information and for quotes, preferably in anecdotal form, much of it about my experiences with athletes whom younger ESPN correspondents considered ancient. During my career, I had interviewed seventy-five of *SportsCentury*'s top one hundred athletes (Babe Ruth, Jim Thorpe, and Babe Didrikson were the most notable exceptions), knew more than forty of them socially as well as professionally, and had written books with or about six of them.

Mark enlisted me to host a couple of his shows, most importantly a simulated *SportsCenter* show for December 31, 1949, looking back on the first half of the century. I both moderated and participated on a panel of sports reporters so antediluvian that I was its youngest member. Jim McKay, Jack Whitaker, Curt Gowdy, and Dave Anderson had me by at least five years apiece. It was good to be the kid. We pretended we were in a newspaper city room. We dressed in authentic midcentury shirts and shoes and ties and suits and sports jackets. I could have worn my bar mitzvah suit. We sat among old Royals and Underwoods, and for verisimilitude, copy boys drifted through the background, including an old friend of mine named Joe Goldstein, the world's most persistent press agent, who actually had been a copy boy half a century earlier.

I contributed to *SportsCentury* and helped publicize it. Shapiro invited me to moderate news conferences featuring some of the top fifty athletes—we had Jim Brown, Carl Lewis, Bill Russell, Martina Navratilova, and Wayne Gretzky together one day, not a bad lineup—and others featuring some of the forty-eight voters. I, in turn, invited Mark to be a regular on my weekly ESPN radio show *The Sporting Life,* and each Saturday we discussed the next athlete in the countdown to the number one athlete of the century. It was a chance for me to show off my knowledge, and my friendships, and for Mark to promote his programs. It was quintessential Disney synergy, but it was also fun, for us and, I hope, the listeners.

John Walsh, a fellow reformed newspaperman who had risen, or fallen, to senior vice president and executive editor of ESPN, asked me to contribute to another phase of the *SportsCentury* project. He asked me to write one of the chapters for *SportsCentury* the book. The idea was to have a lengthy chapter devoted to each of the ten decades of the century, each focusing upon an athlete who, for some reason, personified that decade. I was awarded the 1950s, and the Baltimore Colts' quarterback John Unitas, largely because he was the central figure in the 1958 sudden-death overtime game between the Colts and the New York Giants for the National Football League championship. "That game, that day, a compelling drama orchestrated by Unitas and acted out before a vast and fascinated audience," I wrote, "has been called ever since 'the greatest game ever played.' It may also have been the most significant. It spawned America's obsession with pro football and nurtured America's obsession with television. It shaped the rest of the century."

Once again, as in so much of my career, I found myself in heady company. David Halberstam wrote the introduction to the book; Tony Kornheiser and Joyce Carol Oates contributed the chapters that followed mine. Michael MacCambridge, the book's editor, put together a striking and readable package, fleshed out with briefer profiles of less significant stars, with history, with trivia, and with magnificent photos and graphics. The book quickly moved onto the *Times* bestseller list, and I took part in several promotional book signings. Successfully promoting and selling a book from which you receive no royalties is a classic case of mixed feelings.

Several years earlier, I had enjoyed even headier company in the seventy-fifth anniversary edition of *Forbes* magazine. My essay on the state of sports in America appeared right in between essays by the creators of Herzog and Rabbit, Saul Bellow and John Updike, both winners of the National Book Award, one a Nobel laureate, the other merely a Pulitzer Prize winner. Updike's "Where Is the Space to Chase Rainbows?" preceded me and began with a simple question: "Why, when we have it so good, do we feel so bad?" Bellow's "There Is Simply Too Much to

Think About" followed me and began with a simple statement: "Asked for an opinion on some perplexing question of the day, I sometimes say that I am for all the good things and against all the bad ones." I was out of my literary league, but I was not embarrassed by my own simple opening:

Athletes are better than ever.

They are taller, heavier, faster, stronger, smarter.

In every sport in which achievement can be measured objectively, their progress is stunning.

A girl barely into her teens swims more swiftly than Johnny Weissmuller swam in the Olympics, or in his loincloth.

A high school boy jumps farther and sprints faster than Jesse Owens jumped and sprinted in front of Hitler.

A thirty-year-old married woman surpasses Jim Thorpe's best marks in a variety of track and field events.

Even a man over forty runs a mile faster than Paavo Nurmi ran in his prime.

The performances are so much better.

But so much of the joy is gone.

Then I lamented the greed and hypocrisy that permeated and stained sports near the end of the twentieth century.

33

Happy Birthday from the President

In my teens, I dreamed of meeting even one great athlete. In my dotage, half a century later, in the 1990s, I collaborated with three of America's greatest athletes on autobiographical works—Hank Aaron, Joe Montana, and Bo Jackson. For the Aaron book, *Home Run,* celebrating the twenty-fifth anniversary of his record-breaking 715th home run, Henry and I worked together on an autobiographical chapter called "I Just Hit Baseballs." It was only seven or eight thousand words long, and I felt slightly guilty when the heavily illustrated coffee-table book was published, and, on the cover, I received second billing, below Aaron but above Ted Williams, who contributed the foreword. Among the three of us, we had hit 1,276 major-league home runs.

For *Montana,* commemorating the end of his dazzling National Football League career, Joe and I collaborated on forty thousand autobiographical words to complement hundreds of magnificent photos of Joe and his family and his teammates. Montana was not the ideal writing partner: He was too unimpressed with himself. He was so unimpressed that he could barely remember the details of the defining performances of his career—he vaguely recalled once throwing a touchdown pass to Dwight Clark, a play, in the 1982 NFC championship game, generally considered one of the four or five most dramatic in NFL history—so unimpressed that, unlike most athletes, who speak of themselves in the first person, "I . . . I . . . I . . ." or in the third, "Bo . . . Bo . . . Bo . . ." Montana spoke of himself in the second person: "*You* do this, and *you* do that . . ."

You enjoy getting to know a Henry Aaron, a Joe Montana, one still not comfortable with the acclaim he didn't receive, the other still not comfortable with the acclaim he did receive, one a high-school dropout from Mobile, Alabama, a breeding ground for great baseball players, the other a Notre Dame graduate from western Pennsylvania, a breeding ground for great quarterbacks. You stay in touch with both; you count them not as intimates, but as friends.

But my relationship with Bo Jackson is special. Bo is special. In the *SportsCentury* poll for the athlete of the twentieth century, I voted Bo number one, just ahead of Jim Brown and Wilt Chamberlain, well ahead of Michael Jordan and Babe Ruth, an opinion shared by none of the other forty-seven voters. But for pure athleticism, which was supposed to be the *SportsCentury* gauge, for sheer speed, strength, and agility, Bo was the best I ever saw.

When he walked through a locker room, brimming with naked power, muscles rippling, every other athlete stopped and stared at him. Bo was the only man ever chosen for the baseball All-Star Game and the

football Pro Bowl the same year. Bo was named the
Most Valuable Player in the All-Star Game and he
might have been the Most Valuable Player in the Pro
Bowl if, a month earlier, he hadn't suffered a hip injury
so severe that his hip eventually had to be replaced,
and his athletic career had to end prematurely, but not
until after Bo, in his first major league at-bat after his
hip replacement, hit a home run.

In college, Bo was a 230-pound sprinter, and in high
school, a teenage decathlete. He is an accomplished
fisherman and hunter, a skilled diver and swimmer, a
creditable tennis player, and, since his baseball and
football days ended, an awesome golfer. In 1999, he
played in his own charity golf tournament in Florida
and won the long-drive competition with a 330-yard
effort. He played in my charity golf tournament in
New Jersey and, with four women as his teammates,
came in second. "I'm not coming back next year," he
warned me, "unless I can have those same four women
as partners."

During the *SportsCentury* countdown, I asked Bo
how many events he thought he would win if all the
world's greatest athletes competed in a dozen different
sports. "I'd lose in basketball," he said. "I'm terrible in
basketball." I asked Jim Brown the same question, and
Jim, as sure as Bo of his own ability, simply laughed.

The year our book, *Bo Knows Bo,* was published, in
1990, he was the dominant athlete in America, bigger
than Joe Montana, who won his fourth Super Bowl at
the start of the year, bigger than Michael Jordan, who
had not yet won his first National Basketball Association championship, bigger than anybody. Bo's fame
sprang from his versatility, real and imaginary, his
baseball and football performances, plus an inspired

ries of Nike commercials, the "Bo Knows . . ." se-
es—"Bo Knows Hockey," "Bo Knows Cricket," "Bo
nows Soccer," "Bo Knows Everything"—that made
m seem larger than life, a superman. And he was. He
as the greatest highlight film in the history of sports;
 hit home runs out of sight, ran past and over tack-
rs, made baseball throws and catches beyond belief.
e was the epitome of spectacular.

And when the hip injury cut short his athletic career,
 accepted it without complaint, without bitterness,
ithout "What if . . . ?" He missed his friends among
s teammates, the camaraderie of the locker room.
at he didn't miss the cheers at all.

Bo certainly didn't miss the reporters, either. "I have
ly two friends among the media," he once said.
)ick Schaap is one of them, and I can't remember the
ame of the other."

1992, for the first time, my wife and I went to Re-
aissance Weekend, the annual gathering on South
arolina's Hilton Head Island of political, economic,
altural, sociological, educational, and athletic figures,
ost of them hugely impressed to be in the company
 the others. The company, during the five years we
tended, included, just to name-drop a few, Indiana
overnor Evan Bayh, Supreme Court Justice Harry
lackmun, columnist Art Buchwald, Mahatma
andhi's grandson, Virginia senator Chuck Robb, his
other-in-law Lady Bird Johnson, Barbra Streisand,
mbassador to the Court of St. James's Philip Lader,
lympic champion Edwin Moses, South African–born
ithor Mark Mathabane, JFK confidant Ted Sorenson,
d Admiral Elmo Zumwalt, plus fistfuls of college
esidents, congressmen, and journalists, and, of

course, the main attractions, Hillary and Bill Clinton
Men, women, and our children, we all participated i
panel discussions on subjects ranging from love to pa
enting to public policy. Except maybe Barb
Streisand. I didn't see her on any of my panels.

On our way into the ballroom of the Hyatt Regenc
Hotel on New Year's Eve, December 31, 1993, the en
of President Clinton's first year in office, my wife mer
tioned to him that I played golf. She was exaggeratin;
of course, but a few minutes later, a gentleman whom
presumed to be a Secret Service agent approached m
and asked me if I'd like to play golf with the presiden
on New Year's morning.

"What time do we tee off?" I said.

"Eight o'clock," he said.

"I'll be there," I said.

"We can't stay up late," I told my wife. "I have to g
a good night's sleep. I'm playing golf with the pres
dent of the United States in the morning."

She wasn't impressed. "It's New Year's Eve," sh
said.

We stayed at the New Year's Eve party until well a
ter midnight, and when we left, the president was sti
surrounded by celebrants, sipping champagne an
singing songs. I got to the first tee fifteen minutes be
fore he did. A small pack of journalists followed him
Somehow, I managed to hit my drive in the air and o
the fairway—not far, but safe. At least no one laughee

During our round, the president shared a golf ca
with Michael Porter, a Harvard Business School pro
fessor, an author, and, most important, an excelle
golfer. I shared another with Rob Mortensen, a phys
cian from North Carolina whose specialty was spor
medicine, just in case. We drew a sizable gallery, cor

ering the hour and the day, and half a dozen Secret
vice agents accompanied us in golf carts. My con-
sations with the president were not profound, un-
s you consider "You're away, sir," or "Nice shot,
. President," to be particularly insightful. I did
esdrop on Mr. Clinton and Michael Porter. They
re discussing economic policy, and I didn't under-
nd a word.

Once, when I chanced to hit a decent drive, the pres-
nt gave me a high-five. Another time, when I hit an
ant shot that whistled past the president, I wondered
at the Secret Service would have done to me if my
ot had struck Mr. Clinton. Professor Porter led our
rsome with an 81, the president shot a 90, and I
ught up the rear at 105. At least I didn't slow any-
 down. I played poorly, but swiftly and honestly. At
 end, the president autographed the scorecard for
 and gave each of his playing companions three golf
ls bearing his signature and the presidential seal. I
s glad he didn't give us the balls before we teed off;
ould have lost them.

The next morning, the *New York Times,* in a story in
early edition, reported: "Mr. Clinton spent much of
 five-day weekend here on the golf course. Among
 partners [during the five days] were Governor Evan
yh of Indiana, Dick Schaap of ABC Sports and
chael Porter, the Harvard Business School profes-
"

In the late edition of the *Times,* the story read, "Mr.
nton spent much of his five-day weekend here on
 golf course. Among his partners were Governor
an Bayh of Indiana and Michael Porter, the Harvard
siness School professor."

'd been cut, deleted from the article, discarded like

a nonperson, and when a *New York Post* gossip colu[m]
nist asked why, "a spokeswoman for the *Times* sa[id]
only that the sportscaster's name was 'trimmed f[or]
space.' " I was wounded by the slight, and wondered[if]
the fact that my brother Bill edited and published *Li*[fe]
of Our Times, a periodical dedicated primarily to cri[ti]
cism of the *New York Times,* may have had some be[ar]
ing on the trim.

Over the next few years, my wife and I encounter[ed]
the Clintons at Renaissance, at a couple of dinner p[ar]
ties, and, once, at a White House reception. I have [a]
photo of my wife with the president, and you can s[ee]
the lust in the eyes. Not *his* eyes. *Hers.*

At the start of a weekend during the baseball str[ike]
of 1994–95, the White House called me and asked h[ow]
I could be reached during the next few days. I ga[ve]
them my itinerary. On Sunday afternoon, I went to [my]
grandson Noah's seventh birthday party in New Jers[ey.]
When I arrived, my son-in-law, Steve Levin, w[as]
standing outside his home, anxious to tell me that t[he]
White House had called and would be calling back [at]
three o'clock.

The phone rang promptly at three. The preside[nt]
wanted to talk about the strike. I sympathized with hi[m]
trying to deal with the baseball owners. I told him w[hat]
the attorney Edward Bennett Williams, who had be[en]
an owner of the Washington Redskins and the Bal[ti]
more Orioles, once told me: "The only thing dumb[er]
than a dumb football owner is a smart baseball owne[r."]
I also told him what the baseball player Ken Singlet[on]
had told me during an earlier player-owner confron[ta]
tion: "The owners screwed us for a hundred yea[rs.]
We've been screwing them for five. We still ha[ve]
ninety-five to go." The president quickly realized tha[t]

1't have a clue to ending the strike. He started to say d-bye, and I said, "Mr. President, could you do me vor? I'm at my grandson's seventh birthday party. uld you wish him a happy birthday?"

Mr. Clinton said he would be happy to, and Noah got he phone and talked to the president of the United es for about a minute. When he got off, I said to ah, "The next time you have show and tell in school, 't tell them about this. They won't believe you."

night in 1995, when I was a guest on ABC's *World s Now*, a show that airs in the middle of the night caters to insomniacs, I mentioned that many years ier I'd been approached about becoming a theater ic for a New York newspaper. I said that I had told er Falk of the offer, and he had looked at me and I, "Stick to the real world."

he day after I told this story, the producer of ld News Now* approached me about becoming a iter critic for the program. I thought for about five onds and said yes. As usual, I couldn't resist a nge of pace.

wasn't totally unprepared to review plays on adway and off. I had edited the theater department ing my days at *Newsweek* and, when I moved to the ald Tribune*, in the days before critics were admit- to previews, Walter Kerr had used my office to te eloquent and intelligent reviews in an hour or . I loved reading his reviews, even though I fre- ntly disagreed with him. For several years in the 0s, as senior editor and city editor, I had seen al- st every Broadway show, the good and the dreadful. he seventies and eighties, I had tried to see mainly d ones.

For the last five years of the twentieth century, a
into the next, I reviewed the theater for *World Ne*
Now. I did not pretend to be an authority on theatric
history or technique, but, in prose as entertaining a
could deliver, I tried to let viewers know what the sh
was about and whether it appealed to me and might a
peal to them.

"If Willie Loman had aged as gracefully as *Death*
a Salesman, the play he dominates, he might still
working that New England territory," I wrote.

"*Ashes to Ashes*, the new Harold Pinter play, la
exactly forty-five minutes, which is just long enou
for Pinter to confuse, confound, and capture you."

On the other hand:

"Irving Berlin lived till he was more than one hu
dred years old. Fortunately, he did not live lo
enough to see the current Broadway revival of l
once-wonderful musical *Annie Get Your Gun*."

"With the opening of a so-called thriller call
Voices in the Dark, the Broadway season got off to
frightening start. The fear was that *Voices in the Da*
might be an omen of the coming season."

"*Taller Than a Dwarf*, the new comedy by Elai
May, is being presented on Broadway without an int
mission. I suspect this is to avoid an early and ma
exodus."

I preferred to be generous in my reviews—when y
have written as many books as I have, you know h
deep a savage review can cut—but when I thoug
something was terrible, I said so. I was not always s
cure in my judgments, but as I measured mys
against the more erudite critics, a very sizable corps
found myself generally, but not always, among the m
jority. When I disagreed sharply, I reminded myse

at one of the fascinations of the theater is that every
erformance is a new one, some far better than others,
d the same play with the same players could, on dif-
rent nights, inspire appraisals equally honest and in-
ormed yet diametrically opposed. Still, I envied the
ritics for whom reviewing and studying the theater
as a full-time occupation. They knew their field as
ell as I knew baseball, or better. As a matter of fact, a
uple of them knew baseball better than I did, too.

The critics I'd known for decades, such as Clive
arnes of the *New York Post* and the late Jack Kroll of
ewsweek and Mel Gussow of the *New York Times*,
eemed less surprised to see me reviewing shows than
me of the theatergoers. At the opening of Tom Stop-
ard's play *Hapgood*, one woman saw me taking my
at on the aisle, did a double take, and said, "What are
u doing here?"

"Schizophrenic," I replied.

I might have told her that Stoppard was, too. The
ritish playwright once asked me, through an inter-
ediary, for the autograph of Marcus Allen of the Los
ngeles Raiders, and, though I could not imagine
hy Stoppard wanted it, I got it for him. I am positive
m the only man in the world who has voted for Mar-
s Allen for the Heisman Trophy and Tom Stoppard
r a Tony.

I received at least one rave review for my reviews. I
as standing outside the Union Square Theater one
ening, waiting to see the Pulitzer Prize–winning
it for the second time, when a Japanese gentleman
proached me and said, "Excuse me, do you work
r ABC?"

I said, "Yes."

"I thought so," he said. "You are very big in Tokyo."

I said, "Huh?"

He explained that he regularly watched *World New*
Now, which aired in Tokyo not in the middle of th
night, but the middle of the afternoon.

"I teach American drama at a Tokyo university," h
said. "I am here tonight to see this play because of you
review."

I said, "Thank you," and he said, "What else shoul
I see during my week in New York?"

Whenever I judged a play or performance by
friend—Herb Gardner, for instance, or Neil Simon (
Patti Lupone—I inserted a disclaimer into my reviev
confessing the relationship. Fortunately, I loved Herb'
Conversations with My Father, which I saw in thre
different cities, and I loved Patti in *Master Clas*
which I saw three times in one city. But I hated Neil'
last play of the century, and said so, and still we re
mained friendly.

Some of my contemporaries question the ethics (
writing about friends, in sports or in the theater, and
understand their concern, but I refuse to give up eithe
the relationships or the writing and, instead, try ver
hard to be honest. Once, when Bob Knight delivered
stupid courtside speech, saying that when he died, h
wanted to be buried upside down so that his critic
could kiss his ass—during a week when he had bee
accused of head-butting one of his players—I went o
the air and said I didn't know whether Knight was
head-butter or not, but I did know that he was a but
head for his comment. I didn't see Knight until sever
months later, and when I did, instead of yelling at m
as I expected, he said, to my astonishment, "I kno
that you did that for my own good. . . ." Wayman Ti
dale was right; Knight is a pussycat. Sometimes.

Knight's career as head coach at Indiana ended
dly. He was fired in 2000 after a series of incidents
at angered the administration of the university. His
itics cheered. When Knight agreed to appear on
SPN for his first television interview after the firing,
y son Jeremy was assigned to conduct the interview.
remy did a great job. He was neither rude to Knight
r intimidated by him. He was probing without being
tagonistic. He remembered that he was the inter-
ewer; he was not the story. He aimed the spotlight at
s subject, not at himself. I could not have been
ouder of Jeremy, and I could not have been more dis-
pointed when Knight, trying to deflect Jeremy's in-
stence that he stick to the subject, suggested that
remy had "a long way to go" to live up to his father.
r one thing, Knight was wrong: Jeremy handled the
terview better than I would have; for another, Knight
uld have been outraged if someone had used him
nilarly, to criticize his son Patrick, his assistant
ach.

conducted less confrontational interviews on *World
ws Now*. Patti Lupone came on with her actor-
other Robert Lupone and talked about their grand-
other who was a bootlegger. One of my favorite
ople, Gordon Parks, the photographer-composer-
et-author-director-and-more, came on, deep into his
ghties, and recalled his childhood in Kansas. Uta Ha-
n, the octogenarian actress and acting teacher, spoke
Paul Robeson, the ultimate athlete-achiever, All-
merican football player at Rutgers, pioneer in the
ational Football League, Phi Beta Kappa at Rutgers,
st in his class in law school at Columbia, an extraor-
nary singer whose "Ol' Man River" remains the clas-

sic rendition, an actor who did Shakespeare onsta
and O'Neill in films, and, always, an outspoken soci
activist. As a teenager, Hagen played Desdemona
Robeson's Othello.

"How good was he?" I asked.

"To tell you the truth," Uta Hagen said, "he wasn't
very good actor. But he made up for it with his voi
and his presence."

In the mid-1990s, I became a candidate for the positic
of dean of the Columbia School of Journalism, n
alma mater. A fellow CSJ and Cornell graduate name
Steve Conn proposed me for the job, and the peop
who endorsed my candidacy, in letters so glowing eve
I was almost embarrassed, ranged from Muhamma
Ali to Gloria Steinem to Bill Bradley to Vernon Jorda
and also included the president emeritus of Corne
the former mayor of New York City, a Minneso
Supreme Court justice, a couple of Pulitzer Prize wi
ners, plus a sampling of my former employers and fo
mer students.

From a financial standpoint, I had no right to app
for the post. I would have had to take a drastic cut
pay. But I persisted. I wanted the job badly. I wanted
have the opportunity to "give back," the prevailing e
phemism for justifying one's own career and principle
I love journalism—its excitement and its possibiliti
when it is practiced honestly and enthusiastically-
and more than anything else, I wanted to share and i
spire that love. I wanted journalism students to reali
what a special profession they had chosen, how fort
nate they were and how important they were. I wante
to attract to the school my friends who would expla
how satisfying it is to write and report well.

I was a finalist, but I didn't get the job. It went, in-
ad, to a former journalist who had become the press
cretary to a politician. Maybe that spoke more elo-
ently to the state of journalism than I could have.

I consoled myself, as usual, by writing books. I
ayed Boswell to Nick Bollettieri's Johnson. Nick is a
nnis coach who, at some stage of their careers, tu-
ed Andre Agassi, Monica Seles, Boris Becker,
nus and Serena Williams, Mary Pierce, and Jim
ourier, all of whom earned Grand Slam champi-
ships. He also taught Anna Kournikova, who earned
llions. He is one of those rare egomaniacs who can
ke criticism without flinching. He is also one of those
e people who has had more wives than I. Our mar-
ge thrived. We called our book *My Aces, My Faults*.
y game did not improve.

irty years after Starr, Nitschke, Davis, McGee, and
mpany won the first Super Bowl, the Green Bay
ckers put together another formidable team, and as
ey began to win regularly, and as I saw a bond de-
lop between the 1966 and 1996 teams, between Bart
arr and Brett Favre, the quarterbacks, and between
illie Davis and Reggie White, the anchors of the de-
nse, I decided once again I wanted to write a book
out the Packers. My literary agent negotiated a con-
ct with Avon Books with an unusual clause: My ad-
nce went up by $10,000 if the Packers played in the
per Bowl, by $25,000 if they won it. I rooted for
e Packers as passionately as I had once rooted for the
ew York Knicks and the Brooklyn Dodgers, and it
asn't only because of the bonus money. It was be-
use for the first time since the old Packers, I felt like
rt of a team.

Of course it wasn't the same, because of the diffe
ences in age (I was way ahead of them) and incom
(they were way ahead of me), but it was surprising
close. Just as the young Packers embraced the lega
of the old Packers, they embraced me. Favre and h
two closest friends, center Frank Winters and tight en
Mark Chmura, accepted me. So did Reggie White an
his friends on the defense, Santana Dotson and Euge
Robinson and Sean Jones.

I loved researching the book, exploring the histo
of the city and the team, examining the special rel
tionship between the Packers and their fans. I love
finding links between the old Packers and the new
Santana Dotson, who played for the new Packers, w
the son of Alphonse Dotson, who was drafted by t
old Packers. When Antonio Freeman of the new Pac
ers played high-school football in Baltimore, he use
to run a pass route called a "Carroll Dale," without th
slightest suspicion that Carroll Dale was one of the o
Packers. Just as the players were connected, so we
the fans, the sons of men who had seen Bart Starr sco
the winning touchdown in the Ice Bowl now watchin
Brett Favre pass the Packers into the Super Bowl.

The Packers won Super Bowl XXXI—as the gan
ended, I stood in New Orleans' Superdome next
Fuzzy Thurston, who had tears trickling down h
cheeks—and my book, *Green Bay Replay,* quickly b
came a bestseller, but unfortunately, for me and th
publisher, only in the state of Wisconsin.

Many people have watched me on television and to
me that I have a perfect face for radio, and while I'
sure they're only kidding, I tend to agree with then
I'm one of the few people on television who, to my d

appointment, has never been accused of being just another pretty face. But if I'm surprised that my face has lasted thirty years on TV, I'm astonished that I am now heard regularly on radio, on one-minute commentaries three times a week and on a two-hour show my son Jeremy and I cohost once a week on ESPN radio.

I suppose thirty years of hearing me has built up a tolerance for my timbre, and my radio show survives because of the quality of the guests—from Patti Lupone and Burt Reynolds and Kenny Rogers and Brian Dennehy to Joe Namath and Henry Aaron and Joe Montana and Jim Brown and Bo Jackson to Bill Bradley and Andrew Young and Chris Dodd—my preferred mix of sports and show biz and politics. One of my regular visitors is a man who combines almost all my interests—Mike Reid, former Penn State All-American tackle, former All-NFL tackle; composer of country and western hits, and of a ballet, an opera, and a musical that might be heading to Broadway. Once, I had Mike on with Wayman Tisdale, the former basketball star, who, at the end of his NBA career, formed a blues band; he played the saxophone, and wrote some of the music. They never mentioned sports.

I find the radio show most enjoyable when two guests interact—Bob Knight talking to Bill Parcells, Skeeter McClure to Lonnie Ali, Paul Hornung to Regis Philbin, Billy Crystal to Joe Torre. With the slightest prodding, they do the work, and I get paid to listen.

And, of course, between interviews, I get to tell stories:

Once, during college basketball's Final Four in Seattle, I invited Bob Knight and Vince Lombardi Jr. to join me for dinner. They had never met before, and when they arrived at the restaurant, I introduced them to each other by saying, "Vince Lombardi Jr., this is Vince Lombardi Jr." Neither of them laughed.

Once, during a baseball All-Star Game, also in Seattle, I enlisted George Brett and Tommy John, a pair of legitimate big leaguers, to help Barry Bremen, the Great Impostor, slip onto the field in a New York Yankee uniform. Barry wore a wireless microphone, and my camera followed him from a distance as he roamed around the outfield before the game, shagging flies. He introduced himself to real All-Stars by saying, "I'm Barry Bremen, I'm an impostor, but don't worry, I'm harmless."

At one point, Barry introduced himself to a journeyman pitcher, Sid Monge of the dismal Cleveland Indians, who was on the American League All-Star team only because every team had to have a representative. Barry got as far as, "I'm an impostor . . ." and Monge interrupted and said, "So am I." A few minutes later, I walked over to Danny Kaye, who owned a share of the Seattle Mariners, and said, "Mr. Kaye, what would you say if I told you there was an impostor on the field?" and the man who played Walter Mitty looked at me and said, "What would you say if I told you I wasn't Danny Kaye?"

Once, during a Super Bowl week in Los Angeles, I walked up to Russ Grimm of the Washington Redskins and asked him what he'd do to win the game. "I'd run over my mother," Russ said. Then I went to Matt Millen of the Los Angeles Raiders, Grimm's rival since college, when Matt played for Penn State and Russ for Pitt. I told Millen what Grimm had said. "What would *you* do to win this game?" I asked. "I'd run over *his* mother, too," Millen said.

* * *

Some people have a gift for remembering minutiae. I do not. Some have a gift for remembering events. I do not. But I do have a gift for remembering anecdotes.

I could go on and on. I think I already have.

Parting Shot

The question I keep asking myself is: What am I going to do for the *next* fifty years?

The same old thing, I hope.

Except I suppose I should marry less and sleep more. It's possible.

I interviewed George Abbott, the playwright and director, when he was 106 years old. He had already outlived, by many years, the theater that had been named after him. He had also outlived the pacemaker that had been implanted in his chest when he was 96. Mr. Abbott, frail and wrinkled, no longer sparkled, but, at least, he spoke. Everyone who knew him still called him "Mr. Abbott." My cameraman said, "How ya doing, George?"

I interviewed Arthur Reed, who was, at the time, purported to be the oldest man in the world, when he was 123. A black man bred in the days of slavery, he was born *before* Lincoln was assassinated and died *af-*

ter Kennedy was. "They made me out of good dirt,"
Mr. Reed told me.

Of course, I have also spent considerable time with
athletes, most of whom are convinced they will live
forever.

But they probably won't, and neither will I. I have
lost too many friends in recent years, delivered too
many eulogies, written too many obituaries:

> When Harold Rosenthal, a sports reporter for sixty
> years, was living in Boca Raton a couple of years ago,
> in semi-retirement, he used to put as the return address
> on his letters: Bottom of the Ninth, Florida. Even in
> his eighties, Harold had a wry sense of humor and a
> gift for a great line. When he worked on the *New York
> Herald Tribune,* covering the Dodgers, Yankees, Gi-
> ants, and Mets, he was a terrific sports correspondent,
> and when he switched from the newspaper business to
> the U.S. Mail, he was my favorite correspondent.
> Every time I got a letter from Bottom of the Ninth,
> Florida, I rushed to open it, to see what nugget of
> sports lore, profound or profane, Harold, my friend
> and mentor, was sharing with me. Harold died this
> week, but I can't imagine those letters stopping.
> Somehow, sometime, from somewhere, I look forward
> to getting a letter from Top of the Tenth.

At the end of the century, I lost one of my oldest
friends, a friend who predated Breslin, Gardner, Ali,
Kramer, and Crystal. *SPORT* died. I was sorry to see
the magazine go, but glad that I had contributed memories of my editorship to the fiftieth anniversary edition in September 1996. In that issue, one of our

former writers, Charley Rosen, an intellectual basketball coach, offered kind words—and cutting ones. "It
was a fairly literate magazine, with a hip and sarcastic
touch," Rosen said. "[But] he would edit everything so
it came out sounding like Dick Schaap."

I still love my work—still feel guilty when I call it
"work"—love burrowing into archives and dictionar-
ies, searching for a telling fact, a precise word, digging
for stories, conjuring up unusual approaches and intriguing twists, fine-tuning the rhythm of a phrase or a
sentence. I still love *affecting* a reader or a viewer or a
listener, making him or her laugh or cry, cheer or hoot.

And I still find that the only time I can figure out
what I truly feel and what I truly think is when I am
staring at a keyboard.

It is the final week of the first month of the year
2000—the beginning of the new millennium or, to us
purists, the end of the old—and I start the week by
writing the last pages of the first draft of my thirty-
fourth book. The next day, for ESPN Classic, I tape
One on One with Bob Feller, who struck out seventeen
batters in a big-league game when I was one year old;
with Joe Garagiola, whose enthusiastic *Today* show interview with Jerry Kramer helped make *Instant Replay*
a bestseller; and with Duke Snider, the Dodger who
dueled with Mickey Mantle and Willie Mays when the
three best center fielders in baseball all played in the
city of New York. "We're witcha, Duke," we Dodger
fans used to yell.

And that night, I go to the annual BAT dinner, the Baseball Assistance Team fund-raiser, and I see Sandy Koufax and tell him, kiddingly, of course, to stop bothering

me, to stop begging me to interview him on television, and Sandy, who shuns the spotlight and hoards his privacy, laughs easily.

The following day, I fly to Atlanta, site of the Super Bowl, and as I am leaving my hotel to go to dinner, a man stops me and introduces himself. "Ron Mix," he says, and all I can think is *What are the odds against running into the greatest living Jewish baseball player and the greatest living Jewish football player on consecutive nights—in cities a thousand miles apart?* Mix, who played tackle for the San Diego Chargers, is in the Pro Football Hall of Fame, Koufax in the Baseball Hall of Fame, both bright and articulate men. The next night, I am certain I will run into Dolph Schayes, the greatest living Jewish basketball player, but I come up empty.

The night before Super Bowl XXXIV, Trish's flight from New York is canceled because of the threat of snow in Atlanta—today's Atlantans fear snow the way earlier Atlantans feared Sherman—and I host our Super Bowl party. My friend Rich Bloch, lawyer, baseball arbitrator, musician, and magician, whom I met, fittingly, at Renaissance Weekend, performs magic at the party, and the guys from Kansas, Wesley and Bartz and Sinks and Lanny Reidl, bring the barbecue and the sauce and the T-shirts, and Fran Tarkenton, whom I haven't seen in a few years, doesn't make it to Bimbo's, frightened away by the snow that never materializes.

The morning after the party, Super Bowl Sunday, I host *The Sports Reporters,* and try to keep order among Mike Lupica, Mitch Albom, and Michael Wilbon, none of whom is shy about his opinions. Two days later, I'm in Orlando as master of ceremonies at a dinner honoring Muhammad Ali, and the following

week, after pausing in New York to review a revival of
George Bernard Shaw's *Arms and the Man* and moderate another edition of *The Sports Reporters,* I deliver a
speech in the Bahamas. I don't think I am in danger of
boredom.

It all sounds as surreal to me now as it would have
sounded fifty years ago when I covered my first game,
wrote my first story, typed my first byline.

How can I complain about anything? I am married to a
woman who is as beautiful and exciting as she was
when we met almost a quarter of a century ago, who
tolerates my flaws and acknowledges my virtues, who
encourages me to think and feel and prods me to
strengthen my bonds with all of my family. My daughters Renee and Michelle have challenging careers, as
psychologist and lawyer, respectively, and loving husbands and children. It is prosaic justice that Renee,
who survived thirty years without the slightest visible
interest in sports, has been transformed into a Yankee
fanatic by her three pin-striped sons; Michelle is a
partner in her law firm, perhaps partly because she is,
genetically, a workaholic. My son Jeremy is not only a
skilled and dedicated reporter, but, above all, a decent
young man, whose praises are constantly sung to me
by the people who work with him and know him; my
daughter Joanna Rose works at a publishing house and
writes poetry that sometimes puzzles me, but always
impresses me; my daughter Kari, artist and singer and
athlete and student, another workaholic clone, is starting college, following Michelle and Jeremy and me
and my father and my sister and my brother to Cornell;
and my son David, a gentle giant, six-foot-three by the
age of fifteen, a basketball player who runs and jumps

like someone who is white and Jewish, is as loving as a child can be.

It's been a quick trip, from boy wonder to old-timer, but it's been a great trip.

I can't wait for the next leg.

Acknowledgments

I would like to thank by name everyone who is mentioned by name in these pages—I couldn't have done it without you—but if I were to do that, it would take another book. So I will thank by name only people who are not mentioned by name in these pages. Which brings me, first of all, to my astute and persistent literary agent, David Black, who works remarkably hard, even though, thanks to his stewardship of *Tuesdays with Morrie*, he doesn't really have to. Of course, I am exceedingly grateful to the author of *Tuesdays with Morrie*, who certainly did not have to write the introduction, but did, with the kind of grace and wit and kindness that this book only aspires to. Two editors must be thanked, Lou Aronica, who commissioned the book, and David Hirshey, who took over the project when his company, HarperCollins, absorbed Lou's. Hirshey is a good writer turned good editor who, despite my stubborn resistance, persuaded me to improve my words. Stacey Pressman, a student at Columbia

Journalism School when this got started, provided research that sometimes corroborated, and sometimes corrected, my memory. And on all matters literary, allusions or interpretations, I turned to my personal English professor, Rita Jacobs, and was invariably enlightened. The friends and relatives who read all or part of the text found themselves in that text, with the exception of Beth Nissen and Karen Burns, who are both exceptional people. I am grateful, as always, to Jeanne Collins, who is both secretary and friend, and to Dan Cohen, the wizard who rescues me from computer hell. My buddy Neil Leifer took the jacket photo; he and I and Muhammad and Billy converged in Detroit in the summer of 2000. After our photo session, Crystal took us to dinner at a mansion converted into a restaurant. We sat in a private room, and Ali took one look at the lavish surroundings—oil paintings and paneled walls—and stage-whispered, "Separate checks." In return for his magnificent photo, Neil can have my table at Rao's whenever he wants. So can the two guys who posed for the cover. Thanks to everyone, and love to everyone's wives.